We All Have Souls and
I Think We Can Prove It

Tom Blaschko

Pine Winds Press

Pine Winds Press
An imprint of Idyll Arbor Incorporated
39129 264th Ave SE, Enumclaw, WA 98022
www.PineWindsPress.com

Cover Design: Curt Pliler
Pine Winds Press Editor: Sandra Swenby

paper ISBN 9780937663127
e-book ISBN 9780937663424

Library of Congress Cataloging-in-Publication Data

Names: Blaschko, Thomas M., author.
Title: We all have souls and I think we can prove it / Tom Blaschko.
Description: Enumclaw, Washington : Pine Winds Press, 2017. | Includes bibliographical references and index.
Identifiers: LCCN 2017019466 | ISBN 9780937663127 (alk. paper)
Subjects: LCSH: Soul--Miscellanea. | Parapsychology. | Occultism.
Classification: LCC BF1999 .B651456 2017 | DDC 128/.1--dc23
LC record available at https://lccn.loc.gov/2017019466

For the Sidhe and Nature Spirits, our co-creators.

For Pachamama and Inti Tayta who give us life to walk the earth.

For the Rider at the Crossroads that he may open the paths to Spirit.

For Daddy Death who welcomes us back to our other home.

For all the beings who keep us safe as we walk our paths.

For all of us who bring light and connection and understanding to this physical realm.

And for all these beings in all their other names and all the beings we don't know the names of.

We have a lot of allies to help us with our work, and they deserve our thanks.

Contents

ACKNOWLEDGEMENTS

So many people have helped my on this journey. If I have missed any, I hope they will forgive me.

My life has been much richer because of my karate practice. It has allowed me to live bravely and accomplish more than I ever could have without it. I especially want to thank Tsutomu Ohshima, Caylor Adkins, Ron Thom, Tom Muzila, and Randy McClure for their instruction and friendship. My Caltech and Boulder karate friends: Phil Morgan, Steve Bankes, Jeff Ross, and Manfred Chiu. Others on the path: Mike Panian, Burk Dowell, Pam Logan, Jerry Bentler, Carol Baker, Hugh Glaser, John Todderud, and Jesse Schulte. Some of them taught me and others of them forced me to really understand ki so I could explain it to them. There are many other people in Shotokan–Ohshima who shared wonderful practices with me. Thanks to all of you.

On the shamanic path I have walked with the humans Adolfo Ttito Condori, Rodolfo Ttito Condori, Betsy Bergstrom, Deborah Bryon, Ana Larramendi, Alida Birch, and Chenoa Dawson. I have also worked with Pachamama, Inti Tayta, Apu Rainier, Apu Sgorr Ruadh, Apu Ausangate, Apu San Jacinto, and my *khuyas*. The world we've walked in is sometimes strange, but it is a place of powerful healing.

Jeremy Berg and David and Julie Spangler teach Incarnational Spirituality and the Sidhe. Orion Foxwood teaches old-time conjure and witchery. Michael Dunning has learned from the Yew trees and passed that lore on. All of them understand soul reality deeply from the paths they follow.

Rupert Sheldrake has been a pioneer in bringing the structure of science to research on souls, even if he doesn't use the word "soul." Jamie Pennebaker, John Evans, and Gary Craig have made souls healthier through their work. They don't use the word soul either.

Thanks to those who read through drafts of the book and offered valuable suggestions and corrections: Mark Lawrence, Patrick Harpur, Joseph Drumheller, Michael Willingham, Lori Barnes, Elizabeth Pickard, Jeremy Berg, and Eric Newhouse. Special thanks to Julie Davey who found many ways to improve my writing. They made the book better.

For their personal support, in addition to all the other things we have explored together, I want to thank Doug Anderson, Mark Lawrence, Lori Barnes, Patrick Harpur, Julie Davey, Eric Newhouse, joan burlingame, Phyllis Rodin, and Dave Valberg.

A special thank you to Perry Edwards for being Perry. There is no other like him — a traveler to the distant frontiers of soul reality.

In the tradition of acknowledgments, the most important one is last. Sand Swenby carries with her the Light. I am blessed to have her as a partner and co-creator as we explore and do what we can to heal the many worlds of the soul and the beings in them. I'm also blessed when we sit on the couch to watch a movie, go out to eat with friends and family, walk in the woods, plant a garden, or do any of the other joyful activities of physical reality.

1. WELCOME

> We are a body with a soul. And we are a
> soul with a body. Now, here we are in the
> physical world trying to figure all of that out,
> too.
>
> — *Tom Blaschko*

My name is Tom Blaschko and I want us to work together to let the world know what it means when we all have souls.

This book is a foundation. It describes what souls are and how we know they exist, how knowing makes our lives better, and how making our lives better helps to heal the world. As you read this book, I believe your life will become more alive, caring, connected, and meaningful. And I hope you will share the benefits with the ones you love.

Why I Wrote this Book

When I look at the world, I see many people searching for meaning. Some are studying healing arts like Reiki and Qigong. Others are practicing martial arts. Many look to religions to bring them closer to God. There are students of shamanism, conjure, Wicca, and older traditions of witchcraft. Native traditions from many lands are drawing new followers. It's a time when material possessions seem less important and things of the soul are increasing. People want to figure out how to connect with other people again with love and understanding.

What I see at the heart of these practices is that they know there is more than the selfishness we find in the physical reality of the Western world. What I don't see is different practices supporting one another. And I think they should.

That's why I wrote this book — to show that all of the people who are searching for meaning and caring can work together. What all of them say, in their own way, is that we all have souls and life force that connects us. I hope we can all learn to see support from others even when they express it differently.

Let me start by saying that I don't have all the answers. Sometimes I don't even know the questions. I'm searching, too. But I do know that proving souls exist is a good place to start. That way we know that our search for deeper meaning and caring has a chance to succeed because we know there really is something deeper.

This book shows the proof. It takes ideas from a lot of different places, finding many ways to understand soul reality. It's more than an idea living in the Mind. As you will see, a lot of the evidence comes from connections between Hearts and Wills. Having a soul makes a difference in how we live out lives.

Some proofs meet the toughest scientific standards. All of the evidence provides support because in soul reality all of these observations and understandings are connected. This book has a model for souls that explains the evidence. It describes how the evidence proves souls exist. It looks at ways we can heal our souls and, beyond that, the world.

Each person has an individual path to understanding. The ideas in this book support all the paths that aim for the highest and best good. When we follow our paths and, at the same time, work together to let others know about soul reality, the world will become a better place. We will find more harmony in our lives.

As you will see, I have a lot of respect for Western sciences. Their discoveries in physical reality have often improved our lives. We need to keep that knowledge and use the techniques to explore more deeply into physical reality.

At the same time, I think Western sciences have chosen to ignore the soul part of our world because they are so focused on the physical. I hope that this book will show how we can keep and respect Western science while we add one more piece that explains soul-reality experiences like angels and energy healing and knowing when someone is staring at you or when somebody loves you. It's time to stop saying these things can't happen and study how they can.

Proving we all have souls is a good place to start.

Who Should Read this Book?

You should! Somehow this book found its way into your hands. Soul reality is like that. When it's your time to do something, the opportunity presents itself. And here you are with your eyes on this very page. I think you will enjoy reading the rest.

If you are new to the idea of soul reality, it might help to look at some of the other reasons for reading this book. Here are 12, in alphabetical order because I couldn't figure out a better way to list them. If you want to do any of these, this book will help.

Assure yourself that souls exist. That's exactly what this book is all about. Knowing souls exist adds a whole new dimension to living.

Combat skepticism. This book has good evidence, a strong model of the soul, and a useful discussion of proof. But I think combating skepticism is a waste of time. It's much more important (and pleasant) to teach the people who want to learn.

Connect with nature and the world. As you will see, there seem to be souls in everything. This book describes how all kinds of souls connect.

Connect with other people. The world can be lonely if you feel disconnected. This book looks at healing your soul to connect more meaningfully with all people and more meaningfully with the ones you love.

Discover what happens after death. This book has good evidence that souls continue after death. It doesn't state an opinion on the afterlife except to say that soul reality is so complex that you will almost certainly be able to find what you are looking for.

Explain a soul experience. Many people have been told that soul experiences like seeing an angel or knowing the future or any of dozens of other things can't possibly happen. This book lets you know they can.

Heal yourself. This book points out several practices to heal your body and soul. Some have been tested scientifically. Others are part of less tested healing traditions.

Help others. This book briefly suggests a few ways you can help others. It points out many paths you can follow and explains why they work.

Improve your practice. Whether it's a healing practice or one of the martial arts, the descriptions of the soul in this book will help you better understand how your practice works.

Search for meaning in your life. As this book proves, we have souls that continue after death. This means that whatever you do in a body, right up to the moment of death, will continue to be important to you and the ones you care about after you die.

Seek the divine. Knowing you have a soul makes the search for the divine seem possible. This book even has a few hints about how to make contact effectively.

Understand your soul. This book is a start. As I said at the very beginning, I hope you will join in the quest to understand even more.

I want to make one more point about who should read this book. This is not a religious book. Even so, Christians, Muslims, and other religious groups will find a lot here to support their central belief that humans were made in the image of the Creator. If you are religious, I hope you will join with us in sharing the knowledge that we all have souls.

When souls get together, good things can happen.

About Me

I wrote this book based on many different personal experiences. Taken together, the experiences shaped the idea that a lot of evidence supports souls, and the evidence becomes stronger when it is combined.

I think it will be useful to briefly describe some of my experiences that led to this book.

Caltech. I have a degree in astronomy from the California Institute of Technology (Caltech). Being there gave me a lot of respect for Western science.

Karate. I started practicing Shotokan Karate at Caltech in 1970. These days, I practice almost every day. I learned about life force (ki) from that practice. Ki creates a connection between opponents so that I sometimes know what attack is coming before it starts, even when I can't see the person because he is behind me or my eyes are closed. It's not possible to do that with the laws of physics we have in Western science.

Ghosts. I have seen one ghost. I'll tell that story here because it helps to show that we don't need anything dramatic to prove we all have souls.

> I was just waking up from an afternoon nap and I thought I saw someone standing at the bedroom door. It was, as best I could tell, a ghost. At first I thought it was my wife (who was out shopping) and I was afraid that something had happened to her. Then I realized that it was not. The ghost was just standing there waving to me. Then he left — not through the door, not disappearing. If I say he went away at right angles to

the rest of the world, it comes as close as I can to explaining what seemed to be happening.

I went, "Huh. That was weird." I did note the time was about 4 p.m.

My brother Bill called about 5 p.m. and said, "I have some bad news about Uncle Malcolm."

I said, "He died about four, didn't he?"

"Yes."

"I thought so. He came to say goodbye."

It's a simple story. But it is also not possible in the view of Western science. Having souls lets us connect this deeply to the ones we love.

Knowing the Future. I have predicted what was going to happen before it did two times in situations where the prediction was unlikely. Both stories are in Chapter 3.

Psychology. I have a master's degree in psychology from the State University of New York at Buffalo. At Buffalo I spent a lot of time learning psychological theories of human behavior. There were many conflicting theories. I want to unify them, which is easier to do when you have a model of the soul that includes separate functions, as the one in this book does.

Emotional Freedom Techniques. These are a set of techniques that have been tested and approved for use at some Veterans Administration hospitals. I have helped people work through problems, including PTSD, using these techniques. They work, but not in any way Western science recognizes.

Shamanism. I spend a lot of time these days with Incan medicine work and shamanic healing practices. Some of the healing I've been part of has been life changing for the people being healed. Western science is skeptical. Results speak for themselves.

Openness. I can celebrate all of the ways we learn about souls. I can synthesize the different ways of looking at the world into an integrated whole. I'm flexible enough to change when someone brings me new information. My way of describing soul reality is not the only possible way. Other people use different words to describe similar observations. Their points of view add to the richness of our lives. I'm awed by how much there is to know and I realize that I'll never understand all of it in this lifetime and probably never in any of my human lifetimes. That doesn't stop me from trying. I won't ever stop learning.

Co-Creators. I regularly work with beings in both physical reality and soul reality. Some are in both realities, such as David Spangler who teaches Incarnational Spirituality. As far as I can tell, no one knows the whole story about souls and our realities. I know I don't. This book is a report of where I am now in my exploring. And our quest continues.

I hope you'll join me.

2. Basic Concepts

> Everything should be made as simple as
> possible, but not simpler.
>
> — *Albert Einstein*

I imagine that you are ready to dive right in and read how we can prove that souls exist and how knowing that souls exist will make your life better. But you probably need some background information before we start. That's what this chapter will give you.

This might be the most difficult chapter in the book. I'm going to introduce you to my way of looking at souls and life force, soul reality and physical reality, the three regions of the shamans, evidence and proof, and other important things. These are all so intertwined that it's hard to talk about one without knowing about all the rest. So this chapter is a quick introduction to each and how they connect to one another. The following chapters will show how these things lead us to proof.

Realities

One of the themes of this book is that we have evidence for souls that doesn't make sense in what we know about physical reality. We'll talk about evidence later. This section is about realities.

To explain the evidence we need at least two realities: physical and soul. Some people use the term ordinary reality for what I call physical reality and non-ordinary reality for soul reality. I don't use those terms because I think both physical and soul realities are ordinary.

When something happens to us, it is important to know which reality it is part of. We prove souls exist with events that can't be explained by physical reality and can be explained by soul reality. Let's take a look at each.

Physical Reality

Physical reality is what we see all around us — buildings, roads, plants, books (or e-readers). This is what our bodies are made of. This is what our bodies interact with. Most of us understand the rules of this reality pretty well, at least the physical part.

In physical reality we know where something is. Everything is in a place we can describe in three dimensions. Scientists often use the term space to talk about the concept of where something is. We also know when something happened, what happened before, and what happened after. Time in physical reality also gives us the concept of now. When we put the two ideas together, we talk about physical reality being made up of space and time. We can also talk about the four dimensions of space and time.

Things change in physical reality because of forces. There are four of them: gravity, electromagnetism, strong nuclear, and weak nuclear.

Gravity pulls two things together. It holds us on the earth and holds the physical earth together. It's a pretty simple force.

Electromagnetism is more complicated. It is responsible for almost everything else in our lives. We see it as light. We feel it as heat. It is how sound waves move through the air. It sends information through our nerves and powers our muscles. Changing electromagnetic bonds is how cells live. The atoms in everything on our world are held together with electromagnetic force.

Inside the atoms are two other forces. Strong nuclear force holds the nucleus of an atom together. It's what powers the sun. When hydrogen atoms combine to make helium, it creates electromagnetic photons, which is what we see. The fourth force is the weak nuclear force. It explains more about how protons, neutrons, and the even smaller components of matter interact. Luckily we can ignore both of these forces when we look for proof of souls. The distance their effects cover is too small to explain the kinds of events that we use to prove souls exist.

Soul Reality

Soul reality is everything that happens outside of physical reality. It's the place where our souls continue to exist after our physical bodies die. It's the reality of angels. It's how we know something has happened to a loved one without any physical message.

For soul reality to work we need to add one more force, which I call life force. Many people talk about this force using words like chi and prana and grace. We'll talk about life force later in this chapter.

The basic layout of soul reality is different from physical reality. In physical reality we have space and time. Most people talk about soul reality as a place with even more dimensions than physical reality. When I think about soul reality, it has no dimensions and no time.

If you are one of the people who prefer the idea of extra dimensions, the idea of no dimensions might seem confusing at first. One way to handle the confusion is to think of extra dimensions that have very different rules for measuring distance and time.

Here's one example using the concept of closeness. Physical closeness is measured in units like inches or miles. Soul closeness is measured in feelings like love and understanding. Both types of closeness are real. The concepts also have almost no connection with one another. It is a little bit easier to feel close in the soul sense to someone who is physically close. That's because it's easier to interact with a person who is nearby.

Another example looks at the way we move around in each reality. When we move in physical reality, we can trace a path on a map. In soul reality it is different. If we know where we are going, we are there. If we don't know where we are going, no one can draw us a map. They can, however, take us there. After we know where the place is, we can get there ourselves. It's all about connections. Taking us to a place in soul reality lets us make connections to the place so we can get there again.

We can also see that time doesn't tick the same way for souls as it does for physical objects. When you are in a hospital emergency room worried about a loved one who was just in an accident, the clock seems to forget about moving. The same thing happens just before the end of the workday for many people. "Time sure flies when you're having fun." People who have had near-death experiences may report that their whole life flashed by in seconds.

There is one place we can even measure that time is moving differently. It happens for an athlete who is in "the zone." Athletes can feel when they are in the zone and it shows in their improved level of performance. It's as if they have more time to act than the person they are going up against. When this has happened to me in karate, I felt like I had all the time in the world to figure out what my opponent was doing and to decide the best technique to counter his move. Feeling this is life changing and time never seems the same again. And think what it feels like to fall in love.

These examples show some of the problems we have when we try to talk about soul reality. We are so used to thinking in physical terms that talking about a place with completely different rules is very difficult. I think the best we can do is to use the models that work for us. Often these models will be the way we look at physical reality. It's okay to use models, but we need to be very clear with ourselves that the model isn't the reality. We're only human. Soul reality is much more complicated than we can imagine.

Multiple Regions of Soul Reality

Let's look at one of the complications of soul reality. Many people who travel in soul reality talk about multiple regions. The Old Norse talk about nine. Siberians have seven or five or three. The most common number seems to be three. I think that's because it's easiest to use a simple model that has us in the middle, something above us, and something below us.

For most of us it doesn't matter if the regions above or below us are divided into more regions, at least at the beginning. It's hard enough to get out of our region and have any meaningful experiences in any of the others.

When shamans talk about soul reality, they describe an upper, middle, and lower region. These sound dimensional, but they are also ways to describe the kind of interactions the shamans have in each region. The lower region is more energy-based. The upper region is more about information. Throughout the book we'll see how we use our souls to connect to each region. Being able to connect to beings in regions that don't exist in physical reality is a way to prove we have souls.

Multiple Worlds

If you read about shamanism, you'll find that the three areas I'm calling regions are often called worlds. Other practices have other ways to talk about areas in their soul reality. Let me explain why I decided to use the term region in this book.

There are many ways to look at the three regions. For example, we can look at it as a human or we can look at it as an angel would. I'm going to use the term world to talk about different points of view. So a human lives in one kind of world and an angel lives in another kind. Both have a soul reality. The human world also has a physical reality that an angel can visit. I don't think there is a physical reality in the angels' world. From either the human or the angel perspective their world has at least an upper, middle, and lower region.

My experience is that we can step between these worlds. There are some places in them that are related to one another, and each has places that are all its own. Where the worlds overlap, there are no clear boundaries between them. We can move between the worlds in the places that overlap by choosing which world we focus on.

I'm reminded of stories of humans walking in the woods. Without realizing it, they shift from the physical reality of the human world to the physical reality of Fairy. It's not that the landscape or the trees change, but suddenly everything is brighter, clearer, and more filled with wonder. Problems arise when the walker can't once more find the place the worlds overlap. She may never get back to her loved ones because her home and family don't exist in the Fairy world.

Living Between

We live in both soul and physical realities. We are affected by all five forces. We have interactions in the upper, middle, and lower regions.

We see this clearly in other cultures. Aborigines who keep the old ways tap into Dreamtime and connect with souls who have changed to another form. One example of this is Uluru, also known as Ayers Rock. Ayers Rock is in physical reality. For the Aborigines it is also Uluru in soul reality. They feel the effects and continued existence of beings that were there when the world was being made. The Aborigine culture honors both realities.

Western culture does not honor soul reality. Still, we can find hints that people in the Western world live in both realities. Sports provide one example. In physical reality physical ability should carry the day. But often the most physically talented athlete is not the winner of a contest. Drive, desire, focus, and concentration are used to explain why that happens. I suggest that these don't make sense as part of physical reality. They sound more like life force to me. But we can't be sure. It's just a possible example of how we may be living in both realities without even thinking about it.

The problem is that many of us don't understand the importance of living in both realities. Physical reality we get. With enough sleep, enough food, enough love and shelter and toys, we should be happy.

But we're not. Soul reality counts, too. We may have a vague feeling of unease or a clear fire of longing. If we don't share love and caring with others, we will never feel whole. If we can't find the spirit of our world, we will never feel at home here. If we don't have higher powers in our life, we will always feel directionless. If we try to explain the world with just physical reality, we will be completely lost.

That's who we are — body and soul combined with a reality for each. If we take care of both of them, it can be glorious.

Bodies and Souls

Bodies are fairly easy to explain. They are all the cells with our DNA that make up each of us. Later in this book we'll talk about whether all of the bacteria that are in and on our body are also part of us.

Souls are less clear. From our place in physical reality, we have trouble finding words for what we find in soul reality. So, rather than try to describe what souls are, I'm going to describe them by what they do.

The top three things: Souls exist before the body develops and continue after the body dies. They connect us with other souls in nonphysical ways. They explain angels, ghosts, and other beings that don't have bodies. To start, we want a soul model that explains the evidence. Beyond that, we would like a soul model that lets us understand ourselves, heal our souls, and do cool things with our lives.

Soul Model

My model of the soul has seven parts I call regions. As you will recall, the world is broken into three regions: lower, middle, and upper. There is a reason I am using the term region for both parts of souls and parts of the world. I think there is a fundamental similarity between them.

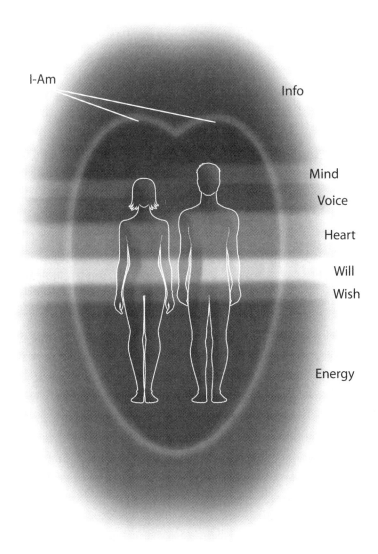

Figure 1: Regions of the soul

When I visualize a soul in physical reality, I stack the regions from below the ground to far above the head. In soul reality, the soul goes from the lower region of the world, through the middle region of the world, and into the upper region of the world.

The lowest region of the soul is our connection to the lower region of the world. I call this the Energy region. In physical reality it would be mostly below the body. The next five soul regions are part of the middle region of the world. In physical reality they are between the genital area and the top of the head. I call these regions Wish, Will, Heart, Voice, and Mind. The highest region of the soul connects to the upper region of the world. I call this the Info region. It connects to the structure of reality. In physical reality it is above the head and connects to information outside us. Surrounding the soul regions is a container that I call the I-Am. I'll say more about this in Chapter 4 when we look at souls.

The other important part of the soul model looks at how each region holds and uses life force. We look at how much life force the region has, how much it can hold, and how well it uses it. Some regions use information more than energy. These are the Mind region and the Voice region. The Wish region and the Will region are more effective with energy. The Heart region seems to use an even balance of information and energy to let us share both with one another.

What Souls Explain

Having a soul gives us a way to feel more fully alive. It lets us know we are part of a greater experience, both with other humans and with everything else in our realities. It lets us love. It gives more meaning to our lives because who we are and what we do continue beyond our death.

From a healing perspective, having a soul gives us a lot of tools to help with sadness and pain. One example is that parts of our soul can be damaged or lost because of trauma. Western medicine may have trouble fixing that loss. Other traditions have better ways to recover lost parts of the soul, remove harmful influences, and increase positive energy.

Because we have souls we can heal ourselves, perhaps with the help of others, and lead happier lives.

We can use the same set of ideas to explain angels, ghosts, and other spirits. They have the same soul structure outside of a physical body. Other things in our world may also have souls. These souls may be more or less powerful than our souls, but they all have a similar structure. If we talk about being made in the Creator's image, this is the image I think we are discussing.

This model lets us explain almost all of the things that we can do that are not explained by our physical bodies. All of the ideas we look at in evidence are covered by this model.

Beyond that, this model can be used to combine many different theories about who we are as human beings. Psychological theories often seem confusing when they disagree with one another. Many of the disagreements seem to be because different models look at different regions of the soul. We'll look at souls again in Chapter 4.

Life Force

A force is something that causes a change. Earlier we talked about the four fundamental forces in physical reality. The life force I am proposing is also a force, but it is different from the physical forces. We need a life force because things happen that can't be explained by any of the currently accepted forces. Chapters 5 and 6 take a longer look at life force.

For example, later in the book we'll look at times life force counters gravity. People, such as St. Teresa of Avila, float in the air. Mothers can lift cars off their children. We will also look at sending information between people who care about one another in ways that can't be explained by the physical forces.

Life force transmits both energy and information. Energy and information can both be positive or negative. They can move between parts of a single soul or between parts of two different souls. Each region of the soul has its own level of life force.

Positive energy makes us feel like we can accomplish something. Positive information lets us know how to do something that increases positive life force. Negative energy and information let us cause harm. When we have too little energy, we may know what we want, but it all seems too difficult. When we have too little information, even if we have enough energy, we often can't figure out what we want to do.

Positive life force is the best for the world. However, you can see the appeal of negative life force over no life force at all. You may be doing something that causes harm, but at least you are doing *something*.

When you think about life force, remember that it has many different names. I believe the Chinese word chi is the most widely known in the West. In my training we used the Japanese form, ki. Another form is qi, as in Qigong. Prana, grace, and many other words are used in other languages. I will use the word that fits best with what I am talking about.

What Life Force Explains

Life force explains a lot of what happens in our world. We see it in action when we know that we really need to talk to a friend because something is wrong. It also shows up in Rupert Sheldrake's experiments on knowing that you are being stared at. Energy healing relies on positive life force to make a change in the client. In martial arts life force determines who will win a fight. In fact, life force may be enough to decide the winner of a fight before any physical blows are thrown.

Connections

In my model, life force connects souls. Each of the regions of a single soul can connect with every other region in that soul. Through the I-Am, every region in one soul can also connect with every region in another soul. The connections can be healthy or unhealthy. The Info and

Energy regions of our souls can also tap into information and energy that are not part of a soul.

Internal connections are how the regions of the soul connect with one another. Each region can send energy and information to another region. Understanding how life force moves between soul regions helps explain why we do what we do. External connections happen between two souls or between one soul and the free energy or information in the realities. This is how we send life force to others and get life force for ourselves. One of the most important parts of connections between souls is whether they are healthy or unhealthy. We'll look at all of these ideas in Chapter 7 on Connections.

What Connections Explain

Knowing about internal connections helps us keep our souls healthy.

External connections explain how we affect one another. We can see why some connections are healthy and some are not. This teaches us how to connect to each other in ways that let us be healthier and happier.

Human connections are not the only ones that are important. We can connect with other worlds in soul reality to learn their secrets. We can connect to the soul of the earth to heal the damage caused by our centuries of not caring. We can connect with higher beings to find better ways to live.

But this is also an area where there are puzzles. One part of connection that I don't understand is how souls and bodies connect. It is all tied up in the interactions between physical and soul realities. That will be an important area for future study. It will not be covered in this book.

Evidence

Evidence for souls includes many things. If something can't be explained by physical reality, it shows we need to add souls and life force. The evidence includes personal experiences, verified reports, and reproducible experiments. When the experimenters are well trained, reproducible experiments are the best evidence.

There are four kinds of experiences related to soul reality that I find compelling: connections we can measure in physical reality, continuation of souls after death and into other physical bodies, using life force, and interactions with soul reality. We'll take a quick look at each as a way to explain the concept of evidence. In Chapter 3 we'll look at the details.

Connections in Physical Reality

My favorite proofs of souls come from simple places. The simplest is that we often know when someone is staring at us. The beauty of this skill is that it works as an experiment. The results show that it is almost certain that people can sense stares. We can't sense stares all the time, but we do it often enough to prove there are souls.

Knowing that something happened to a loved one far away is also evidence for souls. At least it is when there isn't physical-world connection. This kind of event is usually just a report. But it can become a verified report if it is reported to someone else before there can be a physical-world connection. That used to be easy. Before telephones, there weren't quick ways to send information across long distances. Many reports were made and then verified. These days the reports are much less certain. With all our electronic connections, we know what's happening to someone else almost as it happens.

Continuation of Souls

Anyone who has met a ghost knows a soul can continue after death of the body. A soul that exists after the body dies can't be explained with physical forces. Physical forces say that when the brain stops, the personality doesn't exist anymore. There are many reports of encounters with ghosts. The problem with these reports is that they only happen to one person or a small group of people and they are usually impossible to verify. By themselves, they do not prove souls exist.

Better evidence comes from reports of reincarnation. In the best of these reports a young child reports memories of a recent previous life. A researcher checks the details. A child who can describe his or her previous life is pretty good evidence for souls continuing. Physical reality says this is impossible.

There aren't any experiences related to the continuation of souls that are reproducible. Near-death experiences come the closest. But in the end they are only verified by their similarity.

Using Life Force

In karate, we talked about ki as an energy that flows throughout everything. It is one type of life force. The evidence comes in two ways. One is in the interaction of two people during combat. Another is similar to what we feel when we are stared at. It's more intense when the intention to attack replaces the stare. Both of these are reproducible experiments.

Life force is also seen in energy healing. Some healing seems to be soul-based, but usually we only have reports. Reproducible studies show techniques that work. Too bad they can often be explained with physical reality. Energy healing confirms but doesn't prove.

Interactions with Soul Reality

Some of the other beings I want to look at in this book are angels, fairies, and nature spirits. Encounters with other beings are a lot like encounters with ghosts. It's usually one person or a few people and not reproducible. Someone who has the experience is usually pretty sure it is real.

A few reproducible experiments have been tried with other beings. It's not clear that there ever will be totally convincing results. People mishear other beings. Soul-reality beings shape their message for the person. Too many are also known to be tricksters who would prefer to remain mysterious. Others beings probably have better things to do.

These experiences can confirm our thoughts and suggest more things to study. We can't expect proof here.

The one place where there is some evidence is in shamanistic practice. The soul healing that is part of this work can make profound changes in a person's life. I have seen people change as a result of this work. Is it possible to measure the change? Maybe. I haven't found it yet as a scientific study.

Proof

What does it mean to prove something? It's easy to prove something exists — souls, for example. All you have to do is find an example. What's hard is proving something doesn't exist.

Let's say you believe totally black cats exist even though you have never seen one. All you need to do to prove your belief is to find one. If someone else wants to prove that no totally black cats exist, he needs to examine every cat that ever existed or ever will exist. If he doesn't look at every one of them, the next cat just might be the one that is all black.

This leads to a fascinating observation. Skeptics say that the people who believe in souls need to provide exceptional levels of proof. But it is just the opposite. People can prove souls exist with a single example. Skeptics need to examine all the possible locations for souls before they can be sure they don't exist.

To give appropriate credit to the skeptic's position, it is easier to look at a cat and make sure it is all black than it is to look at a soul.

Types of Proof

We will be looking at eight different kinds of proof. These proofs range from proof by authority, where someone tells us what is true, to experiments where a prediction is tested. The first is no proof at all and the last is the gold standard for research.

We have some evidence that meets the highest standard. To get that, we predict what will happen from the model of souls and life force. Then we test the prediction in a controlled experiment.

It doesn't matter that we can't see exactly what happens. In fact that's common. One example from my Caltech years is testing theories about black holes in space. You can't see them, but you can predict what they will do. Whether it's black holes or souls, you test the predictions with observations.

A final idea related to proof is mutual support. What this says is that the more kinds of evidence we have, the more likely it is that we are right about souls existing. We don't even have to agree exactly on what we are seeing. Two people can see the same thing in different ways. We each have personal filters, personal beliefs. It is enough if the observations match up.

The bottom line is not to dismiss other people's beliefs if they help prove your own. It's the observations that count, not the filter (belief) they were seen through. The goal is to find many kinds of evidence that can't be explained by physical forces and use it to prove we all have souls.

Purpose

I think there are six serious reasons why our souls come into bodies. Before we look at those, I want to point out that bodies can be fun and exciting. I don't believe that everything needs to be solemn and serious. We should experience the pleasures in our world.

There are also moments when powerful energies and information are at work. These moments can give us great joy, too. But we need to learn how to act. That balance between silly and serious, between spontaneous and purposeful is something bodies seem to help us find.

I think there are three things that bodies let us experience fully: separateness, change, and thought. There are three other things that we can do better in bodies. They are connecting with others, experiencing and being thankful for our lives, and understanding our reality.

Separateness can't be experienced when we are in a place without bodies. It's hard to know where we end and another being begins. With bodies the distinction between us and others is much clearer. Soul regions are more distinct, too. I think bodies, especially if they have a strong I-Am, also let us move between the three regions of the world more easily.

Change happens in physical reality. We make decisions and see the results. Change in physical reality also happens even if we don't want it to. Understanding and accepting that things are not always going to be the same is a big lesson. We also have time, which gives us a past, present, and future. It motivates us to make changes in the present that will make our lives better in the future. Between lives, where time may not exist for us, it's harder to see the benefits of change.

Thought is something that gets better with a body. I believe that our brains work with our Minds to do things the non-physical Mind can't do by itself. Whoever shaped this world spent a lot of effort on creating brains. We continue that work with our computers and other electronic devices. Sometimes, when we think really well, the results are beautiful.

Separateness and change and thought all work together to teach us about possibilities. We can keep what is good, change what is not, and invent even better ways of being. When we know we have souls, it is a little bit easier to see reasons for making the effort.

Connecting is something we can study better with a body. We come here for separateness. But being separate helps us look at how to connect. We connect with other humans, sometimes with an intensity only bodies can provide. We connect with physical reality. We connect with soul reality. We connect the 10 trillion cells that keep our physical bodies functioning. The last one is something that we can only do when we have a body, so it might be the most important lesson in the connecting set.

Experiencing and thanking are part of many traditions. We have things like sunshine, trees, rain, mountains, and indoor plumbing.

Humans who are alive now create some of the good things, but most of the good things have other creators. We need to experience the good parts of this physical reality. We also need to experience the pain in this world, so we can know the difference. Then we need to thank those who keep it all going for their work.

Understanding goes with having a brain. I think we are supposed to think about where we are and try to understand it better. Even more than that, I think one of our purposes is to improve all of our realities. Some people say we're only in training here. I don't think so, but even if we are, we should work to understand more. As we grow, we can make contributions that add to the experiences of all beings.

We'll look at these purposes in more detail in Chapter 9.

Next Steps

Once we understand that we all have souls, an important decision is how will it change our lives? The last part of this book looks at some of the things you might want to do to celebrate having a soul.

Staying safe is the first step. Before we can do anything else, we need to be safe in where we choose to be. We may need to find better ways or places to live. Then we need to stay safe in what we choose to do. This requires knowing our allies and knowing ourselves.

Healing our souls is the second step. We can't count on being healed automatically when we die. We should take advantage of being in a body to do all the healing we can. Sitting around for half a lifetime waiting to die just doesn't seem comfortable at all. We'll look at the ways you can heal.

Choosing a path is the third step. I'll talk about how you might choose what you want to do next, not your whole life, just the next step or two after you put down the book. I wish I'd known about how souls work earlier in my life. I would have done more on two of the paths (martial arts and some parts of shamanism). But it's never too late to start. What we gain in this life we get to keep in the next life, too.

Healing other souls is one type of path. Many people use what they learn about souls to help others. This seems to have two benefits. One is that healers put something into the community by paying forward the help that they received. The other is that when you are helping others, you can continue to learn more about your own soul. Depending on what feels best to you, you can work with other humans, animals and plants, the land itself, or other worlds and beings in soul reality.

Exploring soul reality has many paths to deeper understanding. They range from learning to love one another better to exploring some very strange worlds. I think it's a good idea to get a taste of several of them to find one that is comfortable for you. But I also think real learning comes from picking one path and following it deeply. At the end of this book we'll look at some of the ways we can learn more about souls. We'll look at places to discover the incredibly beautiful work that others have done and questions that still need to be answered. We'll look at some of the paths others have taken to learn more about their souls and themselves.

Special Terms

I use a few terms that you might not know. Defining them up front makes reading the book easier.

Depossession

Sometimes other souls embed themselves in our souls. The possessing soul may be human, but it is often a non-human being. This is not the best situation for either soul. Depossession removes the possessing soul. Compassionate depossession removes the soul in a way that leads to the highest and best good of all the beings involved. The healer doesn't have to fight the possessing soul. The possessing soul finds a better place to be — and there always is a better place. And the person being depossessed gets rid of something that caused problems.

Highest and Best Good

We should always ask beings we meet in soul reality, "Are you here for my highest and best good?" The assumption, which I think is correct most of the time, is that beings who are not in bodies are not very good liars. Beings in bodies are much better at saying something untrue.

The question is almost always effective in the upper region and lower region of the world. In the middle region, we have to be more careful because many of the beings we meet have bodies. In the upper and lower region, we should work only with beings who give us a definite yes answer. Even when we get a definite yes, we still need to listen to the voice inside us that warns us of danger. In the middle region of the world, things are more complicated.

The question of highest and best good also works when we are choosing whether to do something or not. We can ask a trusted spirit guide, "Is what I plan to do for my highest and best good?" It's good to ask and even better to pay attention to the answer.

Hoocha

Hoocha is a useful concept that I found in Incan medicine. (Some people prefer the spelling hucha.) I think it's different from negative life force. It doesn't cause harm directly. It seems more like the result of bad things happening. It is really good at getting in the way so that nothing can happen.

I see it as a dark cloud of gunk that we create when we are doing things badly whether we have bad intentions or not. It can stay in a place. It can spread through a group of people. It can hang around from one generation to the next.

Hoocha blocks you from seeing possibilities for positive actions. You can't see the nature of others clearly. You can't see your choices clearly. You feel stuck. At its worst, you can imagine it as tar covering you so thickly that you can't move and can't see your hand in front of your face. It's what causes relationships to be so complicated when it seems like they should be simple.

One of the big goals we have when we are doing relationship healing work is to remove hoocha.

Reproducible

Reproducible has a specific meaning in science. It describes experiments that find the same results when they are redone. Some of the evidence we use to prove that we all have souls is reproducible. Evidence that is not reproducible can still be used, but it is evaluated in other ways.

Sovereignty

A sovereign is a ruler of a place. Inside the I-Am, you should be the ruler of yourself. You should be safe and in charge of what you do. I believe sovereignty is one of the gifts we are given as human souls. In compassionate depossession work, I have found that possessing spirits are often willing to move on when I remind them that the person is sovereign.

Problems with standing in our own sovereignty are mostly about separating our wishes from the wishes of others. Heart and Will need to be separate, too, for us to be sovereign. Empaths — people who are especially sensitive to other's feelings — often have trouble with sovereignty because they have trouble with separation.

3. EVIDENCE

> We Forteans can go on in our own narrow,
> separate fields (Ufologists collecting UFO
> reports, parapsychologists studying psi and
> hauntings, cryptozoologists chasing "alien
> animals," "earth mysteries" people running after
> crop formations, etc., etc.) or we can grasp that
> all the different fields of Fortean endeavor may
> be looking at small parts of a much bigger
> elephant.
>
> — *Steve Mizrach*

In this chapter we will look at evidence for life force and souls. We'll start by looking at the types of evidence. Then we'll look at four areas where we find evidence: connections in physical reality, use of life force in martial arts and healing, souls that continue after the body dies, and ways we interact with soul reality.

The most convincing experiences are easily observed in physical reality and can't be explained by the four physical forces. All of us, whether we think there are souls or not, can look at the results. Most of us can even produce effects that show life force. I call these the Sense of Connection. We'll start by looking at a few of these.

The second set of experiences looks at the work that demonstrates souls continue after death. These provide the clearest proof that souls exist outside of bodies. These experiences are rarer, but they are still compelling.

The third set of experiences involves martial arts and energy healing. Many people can see and do these, but not as many as the Sense of Connection. They almost always require years of training. Carefully designed experiments in these areas provide useful evidence. We'll look at a few of them.

In the fourth set of experiences people interact with non-physical beings, such as ghosts. If you have had one of these experiences, you're almost always sure that it was real. People who have not had the experiences are often doubtful. We'll look at a few that support non-human souls.

Each of these experiences supports all of the others because they all make a case for life force and souls. Bringing them together provides much stronger evidence that we need to add life force and souls to Western science. Having life force and souls lets us explain all of the things in this chapter and many more besides.

What I include here are just the highlights of what people have seen. Other books in the **We All Have Souls** series will explore each area in more detail.

Types of Evidence

In this chapter there are three kinds of evidence: personal, verified, and reproducible. When we look at evidence, it's important to consider whether we can trust it.

Personal experiences are convincing when you have them. They may give us new information or confirm something we expect to happen. While the experience is real to the person who has it, a skeptical person can say it was imagined or made up. Personal experiences are best when almost everyone has them.

Verified reports are better. Someone besides the person who had the experience checks to see if it is true. In the best cases the person verifying the report hears what happened before anyone else checks it out.

Reproducible experiments are the gold standard for scientific proof. They often test a prediction to see if a model is correct. Others repeat the experiments to verify the results. In most fields a verified experiment is thought to be proof of what was being tested.

One concern that we have for any kind of evidence is the honesty of the person making the report. We can gauge honesty by talking to other people who know the person. In personal experiences and verified reports it helps if many people report the same thing. We also worry about people who do experiments. We have the same concern for research in physical reality. It's suspicious when researchers get a lot of money or fame for success. It's better when someone else finds the same results.

Connections in Physical Reality

When we are looking for proof that souls exist, it's a good idea to start with something most people can relate to. So let's start with Rupert Sheldrake's work. He has devised several ways to test connections. We will look at two of them: the Sense of Being Stared At and the Telephone Telepathy Test. I group much of Sheldrake's work in the category I call the Sense of Connection. If we connect in ways that can't be explained by the four forces, we have evidence for souls and the life force.

After that we'll look at people who know about something without information from their physical senses. The overall category is Extrasensory Perception (ESP). As part of ESP. we'll first look at people who knew about something far away (Perception at a Distance). Then we'll look at people who knew something was going to happen before it did. Neither of these things can happen in the current view of physical reality. Even so, every once in a while they do. When they do, they help prove that souls and life force exist.

Sense of Connection

The first situation I want to look at comes from Sheldrake's discussion of the Sense of Being Stared At. Sheldrake talks about whether we can tell when someone is watching us. As Sheldrake says, "In informal surveys in Europe and America, I have found that about 80 percent of the people I asked have claimed to have experienced it themselves."[1] We want to know if people can sense that someone is staring at them when there are no cues from the five physical senses.

The concept is really simple and most of us have experienced it. If we stare at someone in a room, the person is likely to look around to see what is happening. When someone is staring at us, it can be very uncomfortable. Often we can look around and find someone looking our way. Sheldrake has several ways to test these effects.[2] We'll look at these in a moment.

I don't know about you, but I sometimes stare at people, kind of with my thoughts drifting, but long enough for them to decide to look around. I'm pretty quick at looking away, so most people don't catch me unless I want to be caught. I suspect you do the same thing. This is important because we may look around many times without seeing someone looking at us. That doesn't mean that it's our imagination.

Next let's look at an example of this connection in a military setting. It's taken from *Iron Ball, Wooden Staff, Empty Hand*, by Caylor Adkins.[3]

> A bunch of us were taking part in the segment of a bodyguard-training course led by former Green Beret dude, Tom Muzila.
>
> Stalking sentries and standing sentry was the exercise. We were taking turns stalking and being stalked and learned that being sharply focused on the sentries soon created uneasiness in them, even when there was a lot of noise from the wind and

the birds. They would usually start to seriously look around. We had already learned how to step with minimal noise and with the ebb and flow of the ambient noise. When we defocused our eyes, just keeping the sentry in our peripheral vision, and mentally including the sentry with the surrounding terrain without singling him out, we were increasingly able to complete successful stalks. A few, however, became more difficult to stalk; obviously their awareness was being enhanced in the same way…. All of us "got it" to a greater or lesser degree.

Tom has also had good success training SWAT team members and sheriffs deputies to sense whether or not there is someone behind a door and, if so, which side they are on. I am very sure that this inherent sensitivity to the attention energy of others is the same that is so successfully trained in various ways by some martial arts experts.

We have two real-life examples, but neither is ideal for testing the effect. Sheldrake figured out how to test the sense of being stared at so we can measure the effect and reduce the chance that the cues are coming through the five senses. He shows us how accurate people are in connecting through what he calls extended mind and what I call the life force. This is what we are looking for. Can we connect one soul to another without going through the physical senses?

Sheldrake is not the first to consider this. Writers from Tolstoy and Dostoyevsky to J. K. Rowling in the Harry Potter books, and many others, have written about it.

If you want to try the experiment yourself, here is the basic procedure:[4]

The experiment is done by pairs of people. One is a looker and the other is a senser. The senser sits at least three feet away from the looker with his or her back to the looker. The senser usually wears a blindfold, but you can try it by having the senser keep his or her eyes shut during each trial.

Sheldrake suggests sets of 20 trials. Lookers either look or do not look at the senser in each trial. The simplest way of deciding to look or not look is by tossing a coin before each trial. Heads means "look"; tails means "don't look." If a random number generator or table is being used, odd means "look" and even means "don't look."

Sheldrake suggests that the looker should record the set of trials on a sheet of paper numbered from 1 to 20. The score sheet should have at least the looker's name, the sensor's name, the place, and the date and time.

For each trial the looker determines whether to look or not and writes "L" for look and "N" for no look.

The looker signals the start of the trial with a clicker, bleeper, or other mechanical signal. The looker should not say anything to signal the start of a trial. It's hard to keep cues out of your voice. As the signal is given, the looker either stares at the back of the senser's neck or looks away and thinks of something else.

The senser then says "looking" or "not looking." The looker puts a plus sign or a minus sign on the line for the trial. Plus means the senser was right. Minus means the senser was wrong. The senser should not think about the answer. It's a feeling that should take 10 seconds or less to decide.

The same procedure is repeated for all 20 trials.

Sheldrake suggests that the looker should record the guess. I think the results would be clearer if a third person recorded whether the looker looked or not and the senser's guess.

In 2005 Sheldrake[5] reported that the experiment had been done over 30,000 times. The average number of correct answers is about 11 out of 20. It's not a lot above what would happen by chance. (Chance would be 10 out of 20.[6]) Some pairs were better than others at sensing stares. They often were people who knew one another outside of the test setting.

One set of results showed that the scores were better when the pairs were strangers.[7] Perhaps this is related to Adkins' experience because the senser felt the strangers were more dangerous. There are some interesting questions here about what makes us sensitive to others staring at us. It doesn't change the evidence that we can sense stares.

When Sheldrake looked at the results in more detail, he found that people are right 12 out of 20 times when they are being stared at. They are right 10 out of 20 times when they are not.

This is still not a huge effect. However, when it is seen in 30,000 tests, the sense of being stared at is pretty much proved. There is 1 chance in 100,000,000,000,000,000,000 that the effect is seen by chance. If the sense of being stared at is not real, it's because the experiment has flaws.

One of the concerns is that many of the tests were run by people who were not trained scientists. To check the results, Sheldrake redid the experiment to take care of concerns that critics raised. Many carefully run experiments, some with one-way mirrors or closed circuit TVs, show the same amount of correct sensing as the first set of tests.

Sheldrake notes that sensers often get better when they are told whether they guessed correctly or not. This matches Adkin's experience with sentries. We get better with training.

Skeptics have conducted some tests that have not found an effect of staring. Almost all of them have had the experimenter doing the staring. Some of the experimenters even said that they didn't try very hard to make the stare work. We saw in Adkin's report that not staring strongly was a good way to avoid detection. The skeptics performed the experiment in a way that got the results they wanted. Some even got results like Sheldrake's and chose to ignore them. We'll talk more about this in Chapter 8 on Proof.

One of Sheldrake's other experiments, the Telephone Telepathy Test, asks if we can tell who is calling us on the phone. There are several ways this experiment can be run. One is to use five people who all know each other. One gets a call from one of the other four people, using a phone which does not display the caller's identity. The person who is calling is chosen randomly.

If we can't tell who is calling, the receiver should be right 25% of the time. In fact, receivers were right 40% of the time. More sensitive receivers in later tests were right 45% of the time. Many of the people said they were more sure about their guesses some of the time. When one person was sure, she was correct 85% of the time.[8]

Physical-reality distance didn't seem to matter. Soul distance made a difference. People guessed better when they were emotionally close to the person who was calling.

Both of these experiments show that we connect with other people in ways that can't be explained by the four forces. They also show that stronger soul connections lead to stronger effects. It's a good start toward proving that souls exist.

Extrasensory Perception (ESP)

ESP means someone knows what is happening somewhere else with no information from his or her physical senses. Sometimes the person knows about the event as it happens. Other times the person senses something before it occurs.

We'll start with a definition of extrasensory perception. Then we'll look at cases where a person felt something bad happen to another person a long way away. Finally we'll look at cases where a person knew something was going to happen before it did.

ESP is important for proving life force exists because ESP can't be explained by the current four forces. Of the four forces, electromagnetism is the only one that might explain it. But this doesn't work because electromagnetic fields quickly get weaker with distance and are blocked by many kinds of barriers. Distance and barriers make no difference with ESP. Precognition is the best evidence because there is no way in physical reality to know that something will happen before it actually does.

Many people (including me) have been in situations where ESP seemed like the simplest explanation. If we can find good evidence of ESP, it helps prove that souls and life force exist. Life force is needed to send the information in ways that are beyond the physical senses. Souls are needed to sense the life force and react to it.

Definition

ESP is a term first used by Sir Richard Burton in 1870. He included telepathy, clairvoyance, precognition, and other effects. Telepathy is information that moves from one mind to another. Clairvoyance is being able to see things beyond what the eyes can see. Some people hear, feel, smell, or even taste something at a distance. As a set these are called "clairs" from the first part of the word. "Clair" means clear in French. Precognition is knowing something is going to happen before it happens.

We can get information through the five senses. We can also figure out what might happen based on what we already know. Cases of ESP occur when a person knows something that he or she can't know in either of those ways.

Perception at a Distance

In 1921 psychic researcher Camille Flammarion wrote about perception at a distance in his book, *Death and its Mystery Before Death: Proof of the Existence of Souls.*[9]

Many stories about sensing an event occur between two people in the same family. For example, Camille Flammarion tells the following story about two brothers.

> Here is a very remarkable example of vision at a distance, in a dream, of a most unusual accident. I take it from the work "Phantasms of the Living" Volume I, page 338, and from its French translation, "Les Hallucinations telepathiques," page 107. Canon Warburton of Winchester wrote under date of July 16, 1883:
>
> I had left Oxford to pass a day or two with my brother, Acton Warburton, at that time a barrister. When I reached his home I found a message from him on the table: he excused himself for being absent and told me that he had gone to a

ball in some part of the West End and that he intended to return a little after one o'clock. Instead of going to bed I sat and dozed in an arm-chair. At exactly one o'clock I awoke with a start, crying out, "By Jupiter! He has fallen!" I saw my brother, who came out of a drawing-room on to a brilliantly lighted landing, catch his foot on the first step of the stairway and fall head first, breaking the fall with his elbows and hands. I had never seen the house and I did not know where it was. Thinking very little of the accident, I went to sleep again. A half-hour later I was waked up by the abrupt entrance of my brother, who exclaimed: "Ah, there you are! I nearly broke my neck. As I was leaving the ball-room I caught my foot and fell full length down the stairway."

Such is the canon's tale; he declares, at the same time, that he has never had hallucinations.[10]

Here is a second story about another pair of brothers from Camille Flammarion's book.

Our next case of mental vision is of the same order. Lombroso published the following letter, sent him by his colleague in the university, Professor De Sanctis:

I was once at Rome with my family, which had remained in the country. As the house had been robbed the year before, my brother was in the habit of sleeping there. One evening he told me he was going to the Costanzi Theater. I had come in alone and was beginning to read when I was suddenly seized with terror. I struggled against it and was beginning to undress, but I remained obsessed by the thought that the theater was on fire and my brother in danger. I put the light out; but, growing more and more disturbed, I lit it again, contrary to my usual custom, and decided to await my brother's return before I went to sleep. I was truly frightened, just as a child might be. At half-past twelve I heard the door open, and what was my astonishment when my brother told me about the panic that had been caused by the outbreak of a fire, which had coincided with the hour of my anxiety.[11]

Camille Flammarion tells similar stories about parents and children, too. Here is one of those:

> A telepathetic [*sic*] vision, in a dream, from Strasburg to Paris has been described to me by an old friend, Madame Dobelmann, in the following words:
>
> I do not know, dear Master, whether or not I have mentioned to you an instance of telepathy which I experienced in January 1901. We were already living in Paris when, at the end of January, we were called to Strasburg, my husband and I, for the funeral of my poor invalid mother. Our son was not able to go also, because of the laws of exception of that place. I was much affected, as can be imagined, by the swarm of memories and by the weather (the air was full of whirling snow), so that I had very agitated dreams at night. One night, especially, I was overcome with sharp distress and dreamed that I saw my youngest son caught between two rows of planks which had fallen on him, unable to free himself and calling me, "Mama!" I spoke of it to my sister, while I was still very much oppressed by this nightmare. But neither she nor I dreamed of attaching any importance to it. A few days later, on our return to Paris, the servant who received us said: "Monsieur Julien is much better, he is at his work." — "What, has he been ill?" — "Why, yes, he had to stay in the house several days, for he hurt his leg. Didn't he write you?"
>
> On my son's return we questioned him, and he told me that he had had an accident, for a pile of boards had fallen on him; but it had been nothing serious, and it would have been useless to frighten us. "But I knew it," I said. "I dreamed about it all one night and the curious thing is that the place did not at all resemble your wood-yard. You were in the midst of planks, unable to get up, in a great unfamiliar yard, and the sun was shining brightly." — "That's correct," replied my son; "the sun was shining on that day and it did not happen in my place but in a neighbor's yard, which is just as you have described it

without having ever seen it. But I have no recollection of having called you."

Had my son called me at night in his sleep? It is not impossible, for he was accustomed to dream out loud.

I must add that this is the one and only time that such a thing has happened to me.

Valerie Dobelmann,

(Letter 2320.) 12 rue Linne, Paris.

We see what variety exists among all these sincere, simple, and authentic tales. They reinforce one another and prove to us that our body does not contain all the reality that exists.[12]

The three stories provide three different levels of connection. In all three cases there was sufficient connection for the receiver to receive the information. Let's take a look at each.

In the first story we have a very detailed view of the location, the accident, and the time it occurred. For the time it took Canon Warburton's brother to fall, the connection was near 100%.

In the second story, we find far less detail about place or actions. In fact, all that really came through was the feeling of fear and an impression of fire. If the theater-going brother was sending sight and sound information about the whole scene, it seems like the other brother got only a small part of it.

With the mother and son we have something in between the first two stories. The mother had a pretty good picture of the accident, but she did not receive it until the night after it happened. We can guess that what she saw was her son's dream the night after he was hurt. So, the connection varied for this pair. It was not strong enough to get the mother's attention when the accident occurred. However, they had a good connection later when the physical-reality situation of the mother was not as hectic.

Striking instances of perception at a distance seem to have two major features. The first is that there often is a connection between the people prior to the perception. Green's[13] search of reported cases found that most cases have a loving relationship between the two people. Heart connections between souls are often the strongest and easiest to sense. The communication is often about death or a serious illness or accident because these are things that really matter. The second feature is that having a non-sensory perception is often a life-changing event. In his survey of elite scientists McClenon[14] found that when scientists believe in ESP (and that's not very often), they usually had a personal experience that convinced them.

None of the cases described could have happened in physical reality. If there is a flaw, it is in the honesty and memories of the people making the reports.

We can add the story I told in the introduction about my Uncle Malcolm visiting me when he died. I trust that memory. In the same way I trust the honesty and memories of these three people. Some of the details might be wrong, but they at least had some knowledge of an event that was outside the range of their senses. So I count these as more evidence that souls and life force exist.

Before we go on to the next kinds of examples, I want to show you how to collect evidence for yourself. It's the first of many exercises that will help you understand how your soul works and what you can do to improve your connections with others.

Most of these exercises can be done in a minute. They are designed that way so you can easily try them while you are reading the book. They're mot much work and they will definitely help you understand souls better. I encourage you to try all of them.

Some may seem uncomfortable, though, so we have the sovereignty rule. If anything you are doing doesn't feel right, stop. Only do the ones that feel like they are for your highest and best good.

This lesson looks at the Hawaiian Huna practice of ho'oponopono. I think you will find it improves connections with loved ones. One part of the technique changes who you are. That, by itself, can change how you interact with others. The other part of the technique changes the connections between you and the one you love. You observe the changes and store what you find with your other evidence for souls.

Lessons

Ho'oponopono makes thing right between two people or groups of people. The practice involves saying four basic phrases:

I'm sorry. What do we have to be sorry for? Here are some thoughts: I got to this place where there is a misunderstanding or conflict. I did not see a way to keep this from happening. I was unaware or asleep. The Huna practitioners say I did not do this consciously, but my unconscious knew what was going on. My unconscious knew this problematic pattern and did not fix it. When something isn't working, I take my share of the responsibility for the problem.

Please forgive me. What can we ask to be forgiven for? Some possibilities: I was unaware of what I did to hurt or trouble you. I didn't realize what I was doing. I could have done better. I could have cleaned up this pattern before we ever met.

I love you. The Huna point of view is that the essence of God is love. When we say I love you, we move toward God. They speak of the new pattern of this age as Aloha. It translates as many things, including love. I see saying, "I love you," as recognizing and connecting with the spark of the Creator in the other person. Along with all the other possibilities for love, we recognize each other as part of the divine. Then we love that in each of us.

Thank you. Saying thank you is how each part of the healing is sealed. For me it's like this: I recognize the change, I welcome the change, and I acknowledge accepting the new way I am. I do this with gratitude.

The basic technique is actually quite simple. You repeat four phrases: *I'm sorry. Please forgive me. I love you. Thank you.* Specify why you are sorry and what you want to be forgiven for. There is no particular order to the phrases. You just pick the phrase that works for what you are feeling in the now of the healing. Whatever shows up for you, including your own resistance, is what you say these phrases about. You can expect it to take several minutes to clear up the misunderstanding.

I need to make one point very clear. Don't do this exercise to help an abusive relationship. If you are being abused, find someone to help you. If they guide you in using ho'oponopono, they will let you know that you must not take the blame for the abuse and you do not forgive the abuser when you say you are sorry. You can say (to yourself) that you are sorry for being in a place where another person chooses to abuse you. Then you make sure to get completely away. There's more about getting to a safe place in Chapter 10.

Whether to say these phrases aloud or to yourself depends on the situation. Both may work. But there will be times when you do not want to say them to the other person. This is especially true when the other person will use what you say against you in the future. One young woman I know apologized to her mother for everything she had ever done that the mother didn't like. But she didn't say a word to her mother. It was all done privately. And it really helped the young woman free herself from the mother-daughter conflict.

There is also a question about who receives these phrases. I direct them at the relationship. Specifically, I phrase them for the person I have the conflict with, even if I am saying them to myself. This may also be a conversation with the divine. You can work with your God to clean up the troubling aspects of yourself. Regardless of whom you direct the phrases to, you definitely want to ask the divine for inspiration in figuring out what to say.

Ten-Minute Exercise

Use this technique on a conflict you are experiencing with another person. Start with someone you love. In ten minutes or less, if you really apologize, you will have a better relationship with that person. For this exercise only say it to yourself.

In other situations you can do ho'oponopono so that the other person hears your words. You can decide which to do by asking what will be for your highest and best good.

If it works for you, you can use ho'oponopono for all sorts of conflicts. A good practice is to review your day before you go to sleep and do ho'oponopono for anything that concerned you during the day.

Going through your relationship with another person will take about 10 minutes. This is 10 times longer than most of the exercises, but it will do you about 100 times as much good. I hope you will give it a try.

Knowing the Future

So far we have been looking at examples of the life force that comes from outside of us. Now I want to look at one of the things that happen because the life force is part of us. We can sometimes know the future. The current scientific view of space and time says this can't happen.

In physical reality we have the concept of causality. Causality means that we always agree on the order of events. From the order we can infer that one event caused another. Almost all of physics is based on causality. Causality, in turn, is based on the law that information can't travel faster than the speed of light. This means that all observers agree on the order of events. Observers in different places may see events happening at different times. They may also see different times between events, but the order of events will not change.[15]

To know something is going to happen before it happens breaks causality. It can't be explained by physical reality. Sometimes we do know the future, though. It's more evidence for soul reality. Here are some stories:

Over Christmas break in 1973 I was planning to drive my van from Buffalo, NY, where I was going to grad school to San Gabriel, CA, where my parents lived. Before I take a trip, I almost always spend a few minutes trying to feel what the trip will be like. What I do is think of myself getting in the car (plane or whatever), starting off, and following the route I plan to take. I look for possible trouble spots or problems I should avoid.

Usually there is nothing. Occasionally I'll have a feeling that a plane ride is going to be bumpier than normal. Sometimes there seems to be some other kind of problem. If I change the timing of the trip I am envisioning, the problem usually goes away. Getting into an accident means you have to be in an exact place at an exact time. Even a few seconds before or after may be enough to make a difference. Usually there is no way to tell what might have happened.

This trip from Buffalo was different. It was cold. I didn't have enough anti-freeze in my radiator, and the heater wasn't working because the line to it was frozen. When I envisioned the trip, I kept reaching a point where I was lying on the ground looking underneath the front end of the van. The engine was running and I could see radiator fluid dripping onto the ground. Bad news, I thought.

I needed to get to California and I had promised to pick up friends along the way. So I went past the moment when I was looking at the dripping radiator and tried to envision the rest of the trip. This happened a long time ago and I don't remember exactly what I saw, but I was sure that I would somehow get home safely. So I decided to go anyway.

Somewhere around Erie, PA, maybe a little sooner, the heater thawed out, so I stopped at a service area to shed a few layers of clothes and check the radiator. No leaks. Okay, I thought. I guess I was wrong.

No such luck. It was snowing. The roads were icy. The van didn't handle well. I had the wrong kind of tires for the conditions. I was a lousy snow driver. And did I mention that this was the last time in my life that I rode in a car without wearing a seatbelt?

The van skidded and I wasn't able to correct it. I don't remember hitting the bridge abutment (which was the only solid object for about 10 miles in either direction.) because I was knocked out for a few seconds. When I came to, there I was lying on the ground (no seatbelt), looking under the van. The engine was still running. The front end was smashed in. Radiator fluid was dripping out of the broken radiator.

I spent the night in a Toledo hospital. They sewed up the cut on my forehead and made sure most of my brain was functioning. The next day I caught a plane out of the Toledo airport. I had a relatively pleasant trip back home, at least as pleasant as you can have with a bandage wrapped across your forehead.

A year or so later my higher-order cognitive abilities were mostly back to normal. For example, I could write coherently again. Getting knocked out, even for a few seconds, is not good for a person's brain.

Some of you may be thinking that this was just a coincidence. Maybe you're thinking that I remembered this time when something bad actually happened and forgot about other times when nothing happened. I have always been careful not to make that error. In fact, when the heater started working, I was ready to say that my pre-trip vision was wrong. It wasn't though. I think what I saw was close enough to what happened to say that when things are bad enough, sometimes we can see the future.

My story isn't an isolated one. I read another on alt.folklore.ghost-stories by a fellow named Haunter (R. P. Murtha)[16]. He had a dream where he was making a left turn on a dark road. Suddenly, in the dream, he heard a loud noise, was looking at the ceiling of his car with pretty sparkling things flying all around.

Fifteen days later he had a photography assignment that took him out on a lonely road before sunrise. He remembered the dream about five miles before he was supposed to make a left turn. Just like in the dream, there was a car following him. Just like in the dream, he put on his blinker, slowed down, and watched the car pull around him. He checked and rechecked his rearview mirror and there were no lights for miles. So he stopped to wait for a convoy of trucks coming the other way before he made the left turn, just like in the dream.

Just before the first truck was even with him, WHAM! A drunk driver with his lights off smashed into his rear end. His seat collapsed and he was staring at the ceiling as the broken glass from the rear window bounced around the inside of the car.

Here's one more story. In 1977 I was living in Boulder, Colorado, and working for the National Center for Atmospheric Research. Usually I worked on the University of Colorado campus, but on this day I was riding my motorcycle up the hill to the main building in the foothills west of Boulder. There was a housing tract on one side of the road. About eight blocks before I got past the housing tract, I had a feeling that something wasn't right. So I slowed down. About 20 seconds later a car came out of a street to the right. It pulled onto my road about a block ahead of me, without even slowing down. Of course, I can't be sure that the car would have hit me if I had continued at the same speed, but it would have been awfully close.

Usually when a person pays attention to their feelings, they have no idea if it makes any difference. (It actually makes me feel foolish sometimes.) This time I think it did make a difference. I certainly could have been hit if I had been going a little faster.

So, three stories. Many other people have had similar experiences. If we accept the experiences as real, then there is something besides causality. We have more evidence for souls and life force.

Life after Life

More evidence comes from reports of souls that continue to exist even after a person has died or nearly died. In this section we will look at three topics: reincarnation, ghosts, and near-death experiences (NDEs). Reincarnation gives us the best proof of souls since we see the same soul in two different bodies. Ghosts are human souls that are seen outside of a body. Some of the reports offer useful evidence. NDEs support some of the other findings, but they are not strong evidence on their own.

Reincarnation is one way to show that souls exist. The best cases are when a person remembers his or her last life when he or she is in a new body. This shows that something exists between lives. When we find accurate memories of earlier lives, we have evidence that souls exist. The biggest concern is that memories might be from a source in physical reality. We'll take a look at some of the best research.

Belief in ghosts exists in almost every culture. Many have ways to make sure that ghosts pass on to the proper places. Most people don't want ghosts hanging around and bothering the living. Hungry, confused, or angry ghosts are the worst. Human souls that come back to visit after the body has died are similar to ghosts, but they are usually welcomed because they offer comfort.

There have been so many reports of ghosts that you would think they would be accepted as real in Western culture. For a long time they were. But the current emphasis on physical reality has moved ghosts out of what is possible. Now sightings of ghosts are thought to be hoaxes or imagination. We'll look at some useful evidence.

NDEs have been examined in great detail in the West. I'm including them here because there is so much interest in them. I don't think NDEs provide conclusive evidence that life continues after death. They may help us understand what it is like between lives. I think what they really offer is information about the connection between the physical brain and the Mind region of the soul.

Reincarnation

Reincarnation is the rebirth of a soul into a new body. In its simplest form reincarnation says that the soul of a person survives after the death of a person's body. The soul spends some time outside of the body and then creates or joins a new body.

Ian Stevenson's Work

I believe the best evidence for more than one life comes from the work of Ian Stevenson. He and his coworkers have been studying this since 1958. They currently have over 2,500 cases that show links with past lives.[17]

They have looked at many possible explanations. They believe the best explanation is that personality continues after death. They usually avoid the term "soul" because it is tied to religion. And they never claim that they have "proved" that a current life is tied to an earlier one.

They find four kinds of evidence important. The first is markings on the current body that match wounds suffered by the previous body. The second is memories of the past life. The third is unusual behaviors that are like the previous personality. The fourth is recognizing people that the person knew in a past life.

Stevenson's research is almost always with young children. They have found that children who remember past lives show glimpses of the past personality almost from birth. The children may remember many things or only a few. Often they demand that their parents take them back to their "real" families. This is especially true if the person in the past life died as a child.

About 75% of the children remember how they died in the previous life. Of those who remember, about 70% died by unnatural means. This included being shot, run over by a bus, or drowned. Others who remembered died suddenly from natural causes.

This is clearly not a normal sample of how people die. It is likely that sudden death helps a person remember a previous life. Sudden death may also be important in how quickly a person comes back or whether a person comes back at all.

Another factor in remembering may be a wish to take care of unfinished business from a previous life. One case was a four-year-old boy who tried to kill the person who (he said) killed him before. Other cases include people who came back because they loved the family they left behind. In Stevenson's studies the average time between death and return is 15 to 16 months. Other sources suggest less traumatic lives are separated by about 70 years. I think the kinds of cases explain the difference.

Stevenson has also found that the memories of the past life fade over time. By the time the child is six, the memories are much weaker than they were at three or four. About half of the children will have completely forgotten them at that age. As teenagers, they usually don't remember anything about the past life unless there was ongoing contact with the previous family. Even if they remember, they may want to cut ties. One teenage girl was annoyed that the previous family kept visiting. She was ready to get on with her current life.

In 1978 Stevenson's group did a survey in the Agra District in Uttar Pradesh, India. For every 1000 people, they found 19 people who remembered reincarnation.[18] If you assume six people per family, that means that one family out of eight had someone who remembered a previous life. That kind of evidence helps convince me.

Let's look at two reports. The first is from Stevenson's *Where Reincarnation and Biology Intersect.*[19] It is about the four-year-old boy who was looking for revenge.

> Metin Köybai was born in the village of Hatun Koy, near Iskenderun, Turkey, on June 11, 1963. Even before his birth, he had been provisionally identified, on the basis of dreams his parents had had, as the reincarnation of a relative (Haim Köybai), who had been killed some 5 months before, during a postelection riot in the village.
>
> At his birth Metin was found to have a birthmark on the right side of the front of his neck. It was a small area of increased pigmentation. No informant told me to what wound this birthmark corresponded, and I did not know until I examined the postmortem report on Haim Köybai. This showed that the bullet which killed Haim had entered his head behind the left ear and almost exited on the right side of the front of the neck. It did not, however, fully penetrate the skin; as sometimes happens, the resistance of the skin stopped the bullet before it exited. The pathologist had made a small incision and extracted the bullet. The birthmark therefore corresponded to the pathologist's postmortem wound. As for the bullet wound of entry, I could see nothing distinctly corresponding to that behind Metin's left ear. Nevertheless, I photographed the area and on the developed photograph found a round area of increased pigmentation. I believe that

this corresponded to the wound of entry. (Perhaps I had failed to see the mark because of insufficient light when I examined Metin looking for it.)

Like many other children of these cases Metin showed powerful attitudes of vengefulness toward the man who had shot Haim. He once tried to take his father's gun and shoot this person, but was fortunately restrained. He later became more pacific.

The second report is from Jim B. Tucker's *Life before Life*.[20] It looks at memories of a previous life.

Ratana Wongsombat was born in Bangkok in 1964 Her adoptive father meditated once a week at the War Mahathat, a large temple with more than 300 monks on the other side of Bangkok from the family's home. Ratana began asking to go there. When she was fourteen months old, her father took her for the first time. While they were there, she seemed to show knowledge of the buildings. After they returned home, her father asked her where she had been before this life. She began talking about a previous life at that point and eventually told the following story. She had been a Chinese woman named Kim Lan and had stayed at the temple, where she lived in a green hut with a nun named Mae Chan. After eventually being driven from there, she moved to a district of Bangkok named Banglampoo. She said that she had had only one daughter, who lived in Kim Lan's old hometown, which she named, and Kim Lan had returned there at the end of her life where she died after surgery. Ratana expressed displeasure that after she died as Kim Lan, her ashes had been scattered rather than buried.

Ratana's father was not familiar with a woman named Kim Lan and he apparently made no immediate attempts to verify Ratana's statements When Ratana was two years old, he again took her to the temple. When they passed a large group of nuns there, Ratana appeared to recognize one and called out "Mae Chan" to her. The nun did not respond to her, but Ratana told her father that she had lived with that nun in her previous life. Ratana's father returned to the temple a few days later and spoke with the nun: Her name was Mae Chee Chan Suthipat (Mae Chee is an honorific for nuns in Thailand meaning "mother nun"), but some people, including the previous personality, called her Mae Chan. She confirmed that almost all of the statements that Ratana had made, including all the ones listed in this summary, were correct for the life of Kim Lan Prayoon Supamitr, who died one and a half years before Ratana was born.

Kim Lan's daughter also confirmed Ratana's statements, including even the matter of her remains. Kim Lan had wanted her ashes to be buried under the bo tree at the temple complex, but when her daughter tried to honor her wish, the roots of the tree were so extensive that she ended up spreading the ashes rather than burying them.

Some people doubt these stories. The biggest concern is that the adults may have given their children the information. The researchers try to rule that out. They usually make a good case for the memories belonging to the soul. They always ask if there is contact between the old family and the new family. The cases are only used when there is no reported contact before the initial reports are taken.

I believe the people are remembering correctly and telling the truth. These reports do not benefit the families, except by giving them more understanding about their child. The lack of monetary benefits helps their credibility.

Other Beliefs

Let's also look at the broader picture. These are not isolated cases. Many cultures accept reincarnation. We usually think of Hindus and Buddhists, but other cultures believe in reincarnation as well. They include some Shiite Muslims, some groups in both West and East Africa, Brazilians (mainly those with ties to Africa), native tribes in the northwest part of North America, Trobriand Islanders, native tribes in central Australia, and the Ainu in Japan. In the United States and Europe approximately 25% of the people believe in reincarnation[21].

Belief in more than one life can be found in several places in history. In India before 1000 BC, it was included in the later Vedas. The belief continued in India as we can see from the Bhagavad-Gita, which was written between 200 BC and 200 AD. In that sacred writing Krishna tells Arjuna

> You and I, Arjuna
> Have lived many lives.
> I remember them all:
> You do not remember.

We know that the ancient Greeks believed in more than one life. Pythagoras (530 BC) taught reincarnation and said he remembered his previous lives.[22] While there is no way to know for certain, I believe that people made reincarnation part of their culture because they saw it happening in themselves and the people around them.

All of the cultures mentioned believe in reincarnation, but the exact method of reincarnation is viewed differently in different cultures. In the West we generally think of reincarnation as being affected by karma. This is the idea that your actions affect what happens to you later in this life or, more often, in the next life. The concept of karma comes to us from Hindu and Buddhist teachings.

I believe that karma may be influenced by the caste system and used to justify a higher caste treating lower castes as less than equal. The justification goes something like this: "They deserve to be treated badly. They were not as good as I was in their previous life so they should be punished for it in this life."

However, it is not clear that this interpretation of karma is supported by the holy writings of the Hindus. For example, the Brihad Aranyaka Upanshad says this about a person who has just died:

> Through his past works he shall return once more to birth,
> entering whatever form his heart is set on. When he has

received full measure of reward in paradise for the works he did, from that world he returns again to this, the world of works.... According as were his works and walks in [the previous] life, so he becomes. He that does righteously becomes righteous. He that does evil becomes evil. As they said of old: Man verily is formed of desires; as his desire is, so is his will; and as his will is, so he works; and whatever work he does, in the likeness of it he grows.[23]

In this passage I see three important aspects of reincarnation. First, when we are reborn, we choose where and with whom. ("Whatever form his heart is set on.") Second, our reward comes between lives ("in paradise"). Third, we are not rewarded in our next life. Our basic personality continues on. If we work hard at being good, we will continue to improve from one lifetime to the next. However, there is no suggestion here that our place in life will necessarily be better because of our good works. It all goes back to the first point — that *we* decide where and when. Nothing forces a bad person into a difficult life situation.

Other cultures also believe in free will for choosing a new life. None of them hold the belief that our action in this life affects our status in the next life.

The Shiites who believe in reincarnation say that we are given a series of lives. Some are better than others. In each life we do our best to live correctly. At the end of all of the lives we are rewarded with heaven or hell for the rest of eternity based on how well we lived.

In West Africa there is no belief in a connection between morality and reincarnation. They regard life as pleasant and better than the limbo between lives.

The Tlingit of southeastern Alaska also do not believe there is a connection between how we live and the status of the next life. They do have another interesting belief: that they can choose the family they will be reincarnated into, either before or after they die. This matches the concept of soul groups. We form close-knit units and take turns being parents and children, brothers and sisters, husbands and wives to others in our group.

I accept reincarnation as evidence for souls. Memories that go from one body to another can't happen in physical reality.

Further Studies

If you look more deeply into reincarnation, you will find out that it's really complicated. Time for souls is not the same as time on earth. Some people think we can be in more than one body at a time. What was presented here is the simple evidence to show that souls exist. The complications aren't required until we try to figure out the connections between physical reality and soul reality. That's a subject for another book.

Speaking of books, the best two books I have found on reincarnation are Ian Stevenson's *Children Who Remember Previous Lives: A Question of Reincarnation* and Jim B. Tucker's *Life before Life: Children's Memories of Previous Lives*. Dr. Stevenson summarizes his beliefs about reincarnation based on his group's study of over 3000 cases of children who seemed to remember previous lives. He includes a description of his research methods. They try to rule out physical reality connections. Dr. Stevenson has also written books with detailed information about cases. Dr. Tucker is continuing Dr. Stevenson's work on reincarnation.

A good general book on reincarnation is Head and Cranston's *Reincarnation*. It looks at reincarnation from many perspectives. The information on different cultures in this book comes from that book.

Ghosts and Human Spirits

When a human dies, the soul continues. Ghosts and other human spirits give us evidence for souls that exist beyond the death of the body. In this section I want to look at three areas related to ghosts and human spirits.

The first is what most people usually mean when they talk about ghosts. These are souls that remain near where their bodies died because they can't or choose not to move on to the next phase of their existence. They are stuck.

The second involves places that hold an imprint of a past event, such as a battlefield. We are affected when we go into a place where a traumatic event has occurred. I'll look at whether we are affected by the place or the ghosts tied to the place.

The third area includes souls of people who have died and have moved on. They are returning, usually to offer comfort or counsel to people who are still alive. They are not stuck because they can choose where they want to be.

All of these areas provide evidence that something continues after death. It may be a soul or memories held by a physical place. Both of these show that there is more to life than physical reality can explain.

Ghosts

When I discuss ghosts, I will be discussing human beings who died. We'll look at other kinds of spirits later. For some reason ghosts can't leave, so they are still hanging around on earth in places and forms that living people can sense. They are able to interact with their surroundings to some degree.

Most often they are simply "sensed" as "someone looking at me" or "making the hair on the back of my neck stand up." One of the most common experiences is feeling cold. Sometimes the ghosts are heard, either as voices or as footsteps or creaking floors. Other times they are smelled. Perfume and tobacco smoke are commonly reported. Less often they are seen, usually as shadows or hazy outlines. Occasionally they appear as fully formed and clothed figures. The most clearly sensed ones were often part of traumatic events.

Let's look at three examples of ghost reports.

The storyteller has stopped on a farm road on a dark night. He sees a person carrying a lantern walking toward him. The storyteller watches as the man with the lantern comes closer, looking from side to side as if he is searching for something. He gets close enough for the storyteller to see he is wearing clothes from the 1800s and seems to have a dazed expression on his face. The storyteller asks if there is anything he can do to help — and the man, lantern and all, disappear.

This is strange enough that the storyteller does some checking in the area and finds out that in the 1800s, somewhere near the place he stopped, an Indian raid killed a family of settlers — all except the father. The father has been seen ever since carrying the lantern, looking for his family.

Let me start by saying that when I read this, I understood it was a story and not a report. There is a difference in the reliability of information. Still, I reacted to this story because I could understand the father's concern. I reacted because the ghost behaved just as I would expect a lost, confused soul to behave. The story is also more credible because many people have reported seeing the same man.

This story is similar to stories about white ladies, the second example here. These are souls that many people see going through a ritual set of actions. A typical example would be walking along a garden path and through a gate, but disappearing once they were through the gate. Patrick Harpur says

> Hauntings of [white ladies] are mostly attributed to events long past. They have become legends, usually involving some crime or unexpiated guilt which has caused the ghost to *walk*. It may have been murder or suicide, for instance, but the ghost has to walk until the crime is pardoned. The crime usually connected with white ladies is a crime against love. She is the ghost of one who has suffered a breach of faith, such as adultery; or of one who had been shamefully abandoned or murdered. We might expect the guilty party to walk, but in fact it is the victim who walks.[24]

Credibility comes from the number of people who report the story. I find it interesting that it is the victim who walks and not the person who caused the harm. I suspect that the person who caused the harm is tied to physical reality in another way. Perhaps the victim can't move on until she receives some of the compassion shown in the next story.

The third example of a ghost report takes place in a family home. Some time in the past a girl who was about three died when she dove through the railings at the top of the stairs while chasing a doll she had dropped. As with most ghost stories, she was dressed in outdated clothes, in this case crinolines and lace. She disappeared just before she hit the floor. This went on once a year on the day she died. She would go to the top of the stairs, watch something down below, drop the doll, chase it through the stair railings, and fall, presumably to her death.

Several years later, the eldest daughter had a date. The mother came downstairs, too, to meet him. His first words were something like, "Ma'am, I just caught your daughter when she fell off the balcony." The family was amazed, of course. Whoever thinks of catching a falling ghost? The young girl is reported to have said, "Thank you, sir. Please put me down now." The girl was never seen again.

That sort of interaction is useful for the ghost. The man's compassion was felt by the girl and her soul seems to have moved on.

There are many reports of ghost encounters. Usually they talk about a ghost that seems focused on one event. The ghost is almost always frightened or distressed. Occasionally, the ghost is described as angry and seeking revenge. I think those may be closer to the human spirits described in the next section because they seem to be choosing to stay on earth.

Often there are reports of people helping the ghosts move on to another place. As in the story of the little girl, the person helping the ghost move on is compassionate and caring. Souls really aren't happy being stuck here as ghosts. They have better places to be.

All of these stories provide evidence that we have souls that continue after our death. The question is, can we believe the reports? I think we can when the reports have these features: Several reliable people report seeing the ghost. The ghost is tied to a known event. The ghost behaves in a way that makes sense. The ghost interacts with the people who see it.

And reporting the ghost causes no great gain in the fame or fortune of the people who report it.

I think there are too many stories and too many people who are too sane and too careful about their observations for all of the stories to be explained away. Some are weak observations, some are lies, but I am pretty sure that some (perhaps most) are true.

Places with Memories

Another kind of haunting is usually called a residual haunting. In these sightings the ghost always appears at the same place and always does the same thing. Actions are repeated over and over, sometimes for many, many years. There are two possible ways to explain what is happening in these places: life force from the event staying in the area and severely traumatized ghosts.

Life force staying in the area means that events can be stored in a physical object at the haunting site, much like a movie is stored on film or a DVD. Most people say that the negative life force from the event burns the image into some part of physical reality. It's possible. However I think it's more likely that there is a soul in everything, buildings and rooms, hills and valleys included. If that is true, then the soul of the place stores the event.

People who visit battlefields often feel these kinds of residual hauntings. In North America, major battles from the US Civil War have left a mark. Sites of battles between the armies of White settlers and Native Americans also hold the trauma. A classic example is the Civil War battle at Gettysburg, PA, which was extremely traumatic and highly charged. The negative life force that resulted is still felt in the land. People often claim to see Civil War era soldiers marching on the battlefield, but the life force shows up in less dramatic ways, too. If you want to see the effect, visit anywhere a major battle took place. Stand outside the battlefield gate and observe how much the visitors' moods change from the time they enter until they leave. Then go in and watch your own mood change.

Could this be caused by the knowledge of what happened there? Perhaps, but I find the effect far more profound. I had a similar reaction in Spain when I saw a room full of religious objects made from the gold the Spanish Conquistadors stole from the Americas in the 1500s. I couldn't stand to be in the same room as the gold. The rest of the building was not a problem. I believe the suffering of the natives was captured in the gold, just as the suffering of soldiers is captured in the land of a battleground.

Residual hauntings aren't the only possibility, though. These could be ghosts who have been through a very traumatic experience. Being tortured and killed can do that to a person. As we know from living people who have PTSD, it is hard to let go of the event. Imagine you have been killed. All contact with things outside you is cut off so no one can help you. You might become very preoccupied with your current fate and replay the scene over and over in your mind. Perhaps these ghosts are trying to find a way to change what happened. Perhaps they are psychologically unable to think of anything else until they deal with the trauma. Unfortunately, playing an event over and over in your mind, whether in the body or outside the body, is *not* the way to move on to something else. It just ties you more strongly to the event.

I think it's possible to figure out whether a haunting is a ghost or residual life force. We can learn to touch the souls of both ghosts and buildings. On the one hand we have the strength of the ghost in a fugue — locked into a single memory. On the other hand we have the memory of the event captured by the building, which will have many other memories, too. They feel different in intensity and singleness of focus.

Castles should be especially good at capturing events and holding the information for a long time since they are made of especially dense and long-lasting materials. In 1993 my wife and I visited a haunted hotel, the Manressa Castle in Port Townsend, Washington. This was once the home of Charles Eisenbeis. After serving as a Jesuit school, it was converted into a hotel in 1968. There are supposed to be two haunted rooms.

We spent the night in one of the non-haunted rooms. We talked to one of the people who worked there who told us stories of glasses that mysteriously shattered, the priest who committed suicide by hanging himself in the attic, and the woman who committed suicide when she heard the man she wanted to marry had been killed at sea. We got to look in the attic at the place where the priest reportedly hung himself. Neither my wife nor I could pick up any feelings there. In fact, the story didn't match very well with the layout of the attic. Of course, the attic might have been remodeled, but the layout we saw was not set up so the hanging could have been accomplished easily. We didn't sense a ghost there or feel any memories stored in the building.

The next morning we asked if we could look at the haunted rooms. My wife and I wanted to check whether there was anything to the hauntings. The first room we went into was a suite just below where the priest was supposed to have hanged himself. Our plan was to stand in different parts of the room and look around for a spot that seemed haunted. On a signal we would both point to the location of the spirit.

There were two doors into the suite, so we entered through different doors and looked around. On the signal we both pointed to exactly the same spot, about six feet off the floor, right over the bed. I had a hard time describing what I felt there. Whatever it was, it was very small, maybe three inches across, and very intense. It was not sending anything out. If anything, it was pulling life force in. I had a sense of a three-dimensional whirlpool spinning rapidly and pulling life force into its center. It had the feel of a ghost or some other focused entity. It was not something stored in the room as a whole.

And it was right over the bed! We were pleased that we had been able to sense this strange entity — and we were more pleased that we had *not* spent the night in that room!

The other room was a standard hotel room in which a woman who lost her lover at sea had committed suicide. The plan was for me to walk over to the window before we took a look around. Apparently I walked right through a ghost that was on the floor just inside the door. I never noticed; it's what my wife said. I didn't even think to check when I walked in the room. It was a lesson in always being aware.

Overall the experience was enough to convince me that there was something to this haunting business. It certainly was not, nor was it intended to be, a formal investigation. I just wanted to convince myself that there was something that I could sense. Formal investigations could be conducted to see if other people felt the entity in the same place. That type of evidence is useful in demonstrating that souls exist.

Human Spirits

Human spirits are different from ghosts because human spirits are generally aware of themselves and their surroundings. They are souls that once were in human bodies. Where ghosts may be lost, human spirits usually make choices about where they are and what they are doing.

Of course, since they are humans, the choices aren't always good ones. They are not all-knowing. Their reasons for doing something may be no better than they were when the person was in a body. In many ways, these human spirits are similar to the beings we'll look at in the evidence for interactions with soul reality.

One common interaction with human spirits is with loved ones who have recently died. They may come to say goodbye, as my Uncle Malcolm did. They often come back later to give assurances that they are okay in the afterlife.

Other people have loved ones or ancestors who are guides for them. These spirits are there much of the time for comfort or for providing advice on issues that concern the living person. If people are wise in a body, they usually are wise after they leave their body. If they didn't know what they were doing before, they probably don't know now. As with all advisors, choose ones that are looking out for your highest and best good. Also choose ones that actually know what they are talking about.

Interactions with human spirits show that souls continue after death. The problem with this type of encounter is that it usually happens to just one person. They don't happen very often either. It's hard to find two people who met the same spirit. On a personal level, these experiences can be very convincing. They just don't add a lot to the proof for those who haven't had the experience.

Further Studies

One of my favorite books on ghosts and a lot of other things is Royall Tyler's *Japanese Tales*. It contains stories from Japan that were first written down between the 700s and 1578 AD, most between 1100 and 1350. It offers wonderful stories and reminds us that these stories are part of all cultures and all times.

There are dozens of ghost investigators throughout the world. Some are worth working with. If you are interested, I suggest finding those that treat ghosts as lost humans and work to send them on to better places.

Many people do similar work in the shamanistic traditions, helping ghosts and other spirits move on. I've worked with Alida Birch, Betsy Bergstrom, and Ana Larramendi and recommend all of them if you want to consult about the spirit of a loved one in your life or you want to learn how to work with spirits who need to heal and move on.

Near-Death Experiences

Many people say near-death experiences (NDEs) prove that heaven exists. I think NDEs are valid, but I don't think the reports of heaven provide very good evidence that souls exist.

Because we are so tied to physical reality, we tend to experience everything as if it were physical. Heaven just isn't physical. In an NDE, we may see a lighted tunnel and open gates, but those physical objects aren't really there. The path is real in soul reality, and the tunnel is how our minds represent the life force that is there.

The other problem with NDEs is that they are highly personal. There is no way for another person to experience the same thing. People who experience them are often totally convinced. Other people can be doubtful.

However, one aspect of NDEs may be good evidence of souls: these events often occur when the brain is totally shut down. When people who experienced an NDE report on something that happened in the operating room while their brains weren't working, we're looking at pretty clear evidence that the soul region called Mind is not the same as the physical brain. If there is no Mind, there is no way the person could be storing those memories. The timing of the event related to brain function can often be verified by the medical team. In that way NDEs offer support for other evidence.

Using Life Force

We use the life force and related experiences in many places in soul reality. We're going to look at two: martial arts and energy healing.

Martial arts provide situations that can be tested because we can look at the same situation many times. That lets us test what the life force can do. Energy healing is harder to reproduce, since you can't heal the same person for the same thing more than once. However, we can look at healing success rates with groups of people and changes in a healed person. I've seen cases where the results were clear to me, but I understand that there are other ways to explain what happened.

I also want to look at a few cases where life force has given people extraordinary powers, such as lifting a car off a baby. Love and caring are often the motives for these beyond-physical abilities. If you've done one of these feats or seen it being done, it's convincing, but it's seldom reproducible. These cases show us what our abilities might be once we accept that souls and life force exist.

Martial Arts

My first experience with the life force was in martial arts. In 1970 I was a Caltech undergraduate studying to be an astronomer when I joined the Shotokan Karate class led by Mr. Tsutomu Ohshima. For the first year or so, it was a basic introduction to moves, forms, and sparring. But later on, it was different.

We were introduced to ki pretty early in the training. But, in the beginning, it just seemed to be another way of saying, "Punch harder." I don't remember when my idea of ki started to change. I do remember being in Colorado in the mid-1970 when our group of four Caltech graduates started to look at ki very differently.

It was clear to us that there was something there that could not be explained with physical reality. We could sense attacks coming and move out of the way, even with our eyes closed. We could feel the start of the attack, just as the attacker started to move, even when the attacker was behind us.

We knew that there was a possibility that we were hearing breathing or a slight movement. We did all we could to remove any physical hint of the attack. But we were still feeling the intention to attack. We also practiced ways of increasing the life force we were sending at the opponent to see how it changed a fight. Fights changed based on the life force connection. The person with more life force had a big advantage. These started as personal experiences, but they were verified by asking the other person what he or she was feeling. When the other person reported feeling what I was doing, it helped to show that something exists. This experiment is reproducible.

There are ways to test ki more rigorously. A simple experiment is to have two people both facing the same way. One person is about 15 feet behind the other. The person who is behind holds a sword pointing up in the air. The sword is slowly lowered until it points at the back of the head of the person in front. I have seen this done with people who have a lot a martial arts experience. In most of the cases I saw the person in front reacts just as the direction of the sword is pointing at the very top of his or her head. It can be quite dramatic.

This can be a scientific experiment if we vary the timing of the sword movement. One possibility is to have the sword point at the person's head any time within a ten-second window. The test would be whether the person moved in the correct second. Chance would result in the person being right one time out of ten. Anything above that would indicate some ability to sense the threat of the sword.

Some people put a screen between the two people so they can't see each other. Others let the attacker see the defender, but the defender can't see or hear the attacker. The question is, can the defender sense the attack in a non-physical way?

A similar test is for the person in the back to point to a particular body part. The person in front names the part. Let's pick eight possible parts: head, left shoulder, right shoulder, upper back, lower back, hips, left leg, and right leg. If the part is selected at random, there is one chance in eight of getting it right. If the person is right more than that, it suggests a life force effect.

These tests are reproducible experiments. If we can sense an attack when there is no way of sensing it in physical reality, we have proof of the life force. We are more sure because skilled martial artists are usually better than beginners. There are sensitive beginners, but the theory behind life force says that we get better at sensing it with training.

You can try these ideas out. Just remember that when you are the person in back, you need to make the strongest feeling you can. Keep track of how well you do. I believe you will find that for most pairs you will be better the one-hundredth time you try this than you are the first.

Energy Healing

Energy healing is the result of a healer using life force or some part of the soul to heal a client. The healing can be physical or emotional. Examples are acupuncture, acupressure, Reiki, Qigong, and related techniques. I also include work with chakras and healing with prayer. Another set of techniques that might use soul reality are Rolfing and other deep tissue massage. Emotional Freedom Techniques (often called EFT or tapping) and eye movement desensitization and reprocessing (EMDR) fit in here, too. I'll talk about shamanic healing as part of a later section on Interactions with Soul Reality.

These healing techniques help many people. So try them and continue with them when they work for you. But I have trouble using them as evidence for souls and life force for two reasons.

The first reason is that all of these techniques are closely tied to the physical body. It's difficult to decide whether the effect is from life force or from some part of the physical treatment.

The second reason is that the healing these techniques provide is hard to measure. For example, when I use EFT, I know it is very important to have the client tell me their level of distress before tapping. The beauty of EFT is that it removes the distress. The problem with documenting EFT is that often it also removes the client's memory of feeling the distress. Clients may report no change even when I can see a lot of difference. They don't remember how big the problem was before. Having clients report a level before and after helps them remember the change. I suspect forgetting happens in other techniques, too.

Even when we know how much change happens during a session, it doesn't prove the long-term effect of a technique. Healing needs to help for months or years. I haven't found much long-term information for clients. When researchers decide we all have souls, I expect it will be more common to gather long-term reports. Until then, these techniques can be used for healing, but not for proof of souls.

Special Powers

When I want just one thing that proves life force exists, I choose floating in the air. Gravity (unless you are one of the people who walked on the moon) always pulls us down to the earth. A floating object that is not held up by a physical force or physical object is pretty convincing proof.

This proof seems to exist. There are people who have been seen floating in the air. One of the best known is St. Teresa of Avila. She described the moments she felt closest to God by saying, "... the Lord catches up the soul ... and carries it right out of itself ... and begins to show it the features of the Kingdom He has prepared for it."[25] In those moments it wasn't just her soul that was swept off the ground. Her whole body was lifted up, too. Her sister nuns usually succeeded in holding her down, but this conduct was so extraordinary that her confessor made her write down her experiences to make sure they weren't the work of the devil.

This was a real effect witnessed by dozens of people at a time. She wasn't alone in levitating. More that 100 Catholic saints have been said to have the experience.[26] Non-Christian traditions have similar stories.

Gravity doesn't let you float off the ground. Neither do the other currently accepted forces. If we want to explain what happened to St. Teresa and all of the others who have defied gravity, we're going to need life force.

Another kind of story about special powers describes mothers who save children who are in danger. On the Internet you can find many stories about women who have lifted cars off a child. You can also find people who say this is just an adrenaline effect. I don't know the answer and I don't suggest putting babies under the wheels of cars to see if mothers can lift them off. I offer one story from 1979.[27]

> SAN DIEGO (AP) — "I don't know how I did it. My body hurts all over now," said 44-year-old Martha Weiss.
>
> Police say the 5-foot-3, 118-pound woman helped rescue a child from beneath a 4,500-pound Cadillac Wednesday by lifting the front end.
>
> "Things like this have happened before," said police spokesman Bill Robinson, "but I can't recall it being done by anyone so small."
>
> The Tijuana woman reacted after a car went out of control near an elementary school as parents dropped off their children. Eight-year-old Berta Luz Amaral of San Diego was struck by the car and dragged more than 20 feet.
>
> Ms. Weiss said one of the wheels ran over the child and was resting partly atop her when the car came to a stop.

"The mother started screaming and attempted to pull the child from under the wheel," Ms. Weiss said. At that point, she rushed to the front of the car and began lifting.

"I could feel the car moving when I was pulling up. I lifted it up enough for the lady to get the little girl out," she said.

Traffic investigators said the woman had grease, "all over her from where she picked up the car. She had tire marks on her slacks."

The child was taken to a nearby hospital, treated, and released, police said.

People with special powers don't show them to just anyone. Until our world changes and it's safe to show these abilities, we won't find much public evidence.

Interactions with Soul Reality

Soul reality is the realm where souls and life force are used instead of physical forces. We'll look at what we can do in this realm later. In this section we'll just look at the evidence that it exists.

I start this section with inspiration because it's fun. Even though it offers little useful evidence, it is an important part of soul reality.

Next I look at some of the evidence that comes from other beings. As with ghosts, these are often one person's report. They help by expanding souls and life force beyond human to show us where we fit in a larger universe of beings.

Finally, I look at shamanic practice. There are two contributions from these practices. One is that we can heal our souls using these techniques. While the healing is seldom measured scientifically, it can be easily seen. The second contribution is that there is more than one level to the world. Shamans usually speak of three regions: upper, middle, and lower. These regions are critical for understanding the structure of our souls.

Inspiration

Artists describe the work they do in many ways. Exactly who or what inspires them in their greatest works is often a question they ask themselves. Often they say it is from something outside themselves. Scientists often say the same thing about their great discoveries.

The Romans talk about works of genius. Western culture thinks of these as coming from within the artist. On the other hand, the Romans thought a genius was a separate creature that briefly visited the artist, philosopher, scientist, or performer.

This creature would offer a great insight to the person it was visiting. The person, if he or she was quick enough, could capture the insight. And then the genius would head back to its spot in the wall of the house. Geniuses don't necessarily have to live in walls of houses. We hear stories of artists being inspired in many ways and in many places. Irish pipers, for example, catch melodies in fairy glens.

Here's a story from our times about catching a genius. It was told by Elizabeth Gilbert in her TED Talk on genius.

> I had this encounter recently where I met the extraordinary American poet Ruth Stone, who is now in her 90s, but she's been a poet her entire life and she told me that when she was growing up in rural Virginia, she would be out working in the fields, and she said she would feel and hear a poem coming at her from over the landscape. And she said it was like a thunderous train of air. And it would come barreling down at her over the landscape. And she felt it coming, because it would shake the earth under her feet. She knew that she had only one thing to do at that point, and that was to, in her words, "Run like hell!"
>
> And she would run like hell to the house and she would be getting chased by this poem, and the whole deal was that she had to get to a piece of paper and a pencil fast enough so that when it thundered through her, she could collect it and grab it on the page. And other times she wouldn't be fast enough, so she'd be running and running and running, and she wouldn't

get to the house and the poem would barrel through her and she would miss it and she said it would continue on across the landscape, looking, as she put it "for another poet." And then there were these times — this is the piece I never forgot — she said that there were moments where she would almost miss it, right? So, she's running to the house and she's looking for the paper and the poem passes through her, and she grabs a pencil just as it's going through her, and then she said, it was like she would reach out with her other hand and she would catch it. She would catch the poem by its tail, and she would pull it backwards into her body as she was transcribing on the page. And in these instances, the poem would come up on the page perfect and intact but backwards, from the last word to the first.[28]

My favorite part is in that last phrase, "from the last word to first." What is that all about? This thing roaring across the countryside, whatever it is, does it have a direction? A time sense? Does it have a beginning and an end? Apparently so. If you catch it by the tail and pull it through you backwards, it comes out backwards. We humans are clever enough to catch these things sometimes. In this case the poet was even able to turn what she caught right end front.

Music is another place where inspiration plays a part. All of the cultures that respect soul reality seem to use music as one of the ways they enter it. I've done shamanic work supported by drums, rattles, and flutes. Aborigines play the didgeridoo, the bullroarer, and the gum-leaf. Singing and dancing are parts of ceremonies for Native Americans and many others. In fact, music seems to be everywhere.

At another level we have the stories about fairy music or fairy dancing shoes. These tales involve inspired dances by humans who are not that talented. The bad part is that, once they hear the music or put on the shoes, the humans can't stop. Inspiration is not always pleasant.

I think there is useful evidence here. Many of the people who have been inspired say that what they did came from somewhere outside of themselves. When it happens to me, it's hard to deny. We are not likely to find reproducible experiments here, but we do find repeated experiences. Ruth Stone is one example.

Other Beings

When I talk to people, the three experiences they are most likely to have had are knowing when someone is staring at them, seeing ghosts, and a belief in other beings, such as angels. We've looked at the first two. Now let's look at these other beings.

There are so many of them! There is no way we can look at all of them in this book.

The evidence we get from other beings has two aspects.

The first is that having an encounter with another being is almost always convincing for the person who experiences it. It's not as convincing for someone who just hears the story. When two people meet the same being, either together or separately, agreements between the two stories can be evidence for the reality of the being. Showing that non-physical beings exist goes a long way toward proving that there is something besides physical reality.

The second aspect of the evidence is that the more powerful of these beings can tell us what soul reality is like. We can work with them in our studies and play with them in our games. Being both proof of souls and partners in life makes these beings something special.

I divide the beings into three groups. Each group has a wide range of powers in a continuum from very powerful to very small. There are beings at every level of the continuum. And a particular kind of being, human for instance, may have powers that cover a wide range of the continuum. We'll look at a few examples so you understand the range of beings I am talking about.

Beings Who Make Magic

Beings who make magic are very powerful. They are the beings that create and continue to shape reality. The Christian tradition has God, angels, and demons. Shamanic traditions have gods, angels, and devas.

The devas are beings who are in charge of large parts of soul reality. Other powerful spirits oversee parts of physical reality. Other traditions, such as Shinto and Western traditions of nature spirits, see beings in all things. In those traditions powerful beings guide groups of less powerful beings.

Gods and goddesses are described as beings with special powers or abilities. When there is a single God, He or She is described as the Creator and ruler of the universe (although the Devil sometimes decides to put up a fight). Other gods have more limited skills. People pray to God, gods, and goddesses for blessings, boons, grace, and all matter of satisfying outcomes. Gods are creators. They bring about reality.

Below the gods are angels, guardians, devils, and demons. They usually have more contact with humans than gods do. They are powerful. Their varying mixes of good and evil define their nature. Miracles are within their power, where miracles are defined as a change in physical reality that can't be explained by physical forces. Creation is probably more than they can do.

Angel is one name given to these spirits. When angels are described, they usually have great beauty and radiate goodness. They are intelligent beings. They bring messages or perform tasks while being fully aware of what they are doing and able to adjust to circumstances.

Guardian is another name for a great spirit. One role is to guard humans from powerful, evil beings. They are also here to teach us about physical and soul realities. People usually describe meetings with guardians as positive, even when the learning experience is difficult.

Guardians, like angels, are often sensed in dreams and out-of-body experiences. Sometimes they come into the human world, such as in times of danger. Guardians are often seen as a grander form of humans. They are intelligent and decide how to best teach humans. Shamanic spirit animals usually act as guardians. Guardians often work on their own development with the goal of moving on to more complicated worlds after their tasks in the human world are done.

If angels and guardians are the messengers and teachers of what is good for people, devils and demons are the ones that instruct us in evil and tempt us to do things that are bad. They are every bit as intelligent as angels and guardians. They may be every bit as powerful, too. But I think that good is always just a little bit more powerful than evil. This has to do with the results of good and evil actions.

From our vantage point here on earth, here's how we can tell what is really good and what is really evil. Being able to love another is a measure of good. Another measure, "An it harm none, do what ye will" is used in witchcraft.[29] Jesus said, "Do unto others as you would have them do unto you."[30] Some beliefs speak of not harming the earth or the creatures on it. Others say that all beings have the spark of the Creator. Not acknowledging that spark is what evil is all about.

Here's the distinction: Actions which do harm to others or make them weaker are evil. Actions which help others to grow and gain more life force are good. And that is why I believe good is more powerful. With good, everyone helps the others to have more life force. With evil, life force is stolen or lost. One person is more powerful, but the group is not.

A related question is, what are these evil entities all about? Why are they here? I find the explanations of these negative entities among the strangest in all the stories of creation. The explanation I like best is that they don't really belong in our world. They are scared and grab power or cause harm because it makes them feel safer.

Elementals are another kind of powerful being. They represent powerful forces of nature, such as blazing fire or flooding water. Because they have very different reasons for being, they do not seem to understand humans very well. Elementals are not known for moderation. Working closely with them can be dangerous unless we are ready to use real, force-of-nature levels of power.

I believe that humans can sometimes reach the level of power described in this section. We can make magic. Miracles are within our grasp. When Buddhists call a person a bodhisattva, they seem to be saying he or she is in this category. So are saints in the Catholic tradition. Later in this chapter in the section on shamans and other magic workers, I'll look at other humans who reach the status of beings who make magic.

Beings Who Use Magic

This set of beings has a wide range of powers, but none as powerful as the creators I described above. These are beings that can use the magic the creators have made. Different traditions call these beings different names.

For example, in the fairy traditions, these are called the Sidhe. These are beings very much like humans who live less in physical reality and more in soul reality. One example is the elves in the *Lord of the Rings*. There are also less powerful creatures in fairy lore that I'll talk about in the next section.

Shamanic and nature traditions have beings of places. The beings in charge of power places, such as the Apus in the high mountains in Peru, belong to the creator group. Beings who are in charge of a forest, valley, or town probably belong in this group.

One characteristic that I believe is important in this group, as well as in the more powerful group, is that these beings practice what they do. This is one of the things that separates these groups from the group of small beings. Beings in this group are working on getting better. They do magic while the smaller beings are magic.

I have a couple of stories about beings in this group.

The first one is about the Sidhe. One day an Irish servant-girl was sitting with some other girls by the gate of the "Big House" when she heard some horsemen approaching. She sprang up to hurry back to the house because she thought the riders were "quality" [rich friends of the master of the house] and she would be needed there to help.[31]

> She had not run far when the party of riders came in sight, eight of them, men and young women, in bright clothes and with colored bridles and saddles, the girls aside, the men

astride, and all laughing and talking gaily. They were no more than forty yards from her when they swung to the right over a grassy bank, across a small field, and into the side of a thorn-ringed fairy fort. Horses and all, they trotted into the earth as coolly and casually as humans would pass through a stable gate.[32]

Disappointed, the girl returned to her companions and said, "Ah, 'twas no quality at all. 'Twas only a pack of fairies going into the fort."[33] The story was told in 1932 although it is clear that the experience occurred when the woman was much younger. In her day — not all that many years ago — fairy sightings were a natural occurrence, and not even a very exciting one. Think about the tone of voice the girl must have used. We'll find a place we can use that tone of voice in Chapter 8 as a response to proof by authority.

According to David Spangler's sources,[34] when our world was created, humans and Sidhe were the same. At some point humans moved more into the physical while the Sidhe moved more into the non-physical. While the two groups worked together for a while, the split eventually became too great and the groups mostly separated.

Every culture that I know of has some set of beings that are almost like humans, but magical instead of physical. Most of us know about djinns (Arabian genies). Mermaids, fox spirits from Japan, coyote and raven from the Native Americans, and sirens from the Greeks might all be part of this group. I think of Bigfoot as a hairy fairy, so I think they belong here, too.

Many people think of the Sidhe and their fairy allies as much more powerful than men. But this isn't so. In the wars between fairies and men, the battles were not one-sided. Both sides won battles, especially when they were fought in physical reality. We don't fight any more because the Sidhe left our world. They live in their world now, where few humans go. Some fairies will still work with us, but others think there is no hope of ever working with humans again. I would like to see the problems worked out. The human world needs to reclaim its magic and the fairy world can help us get it back.

As with humans, a fairy is a mix of good and bad, clever and foolish, beautiful and ugly. None are totally safe, just as no human is totally safe. We need to be respectful when we walk in their worlds.

The second story is about a nature spirit that I met. In September 2015 I was in Albuquerque, NM, for a recreational therapy conference. One afternoon I took a walk out in the desert and came across a tall rock on a cliff face. It was about 20 feet high and about 40 feet up the cliff. From one angle it had a very human-like appearance, with a clear head and upper body. It was looking out over a large valley that was Native American land.

It offered me its job.

It turns out that its job was watching over the valley, not so much doing as just observing, reporting, and, perhaps, gathering the life force there and sending it to other beings that needed it. Positive life force was being created there all the time so there was a lot of life force to send.

It was a very tempting job.

I did point out that the climate there was too hot for me. The Rock pointed out that it was a rock. It didn't care about how hot it was, or how cold either. It made some slightly disparaging comment about humans and their body-centeredness. I had to agree. We talked some more about the joy the Rock had in looking out over the truly beautiful place, both physically and spiritually. "Talked" isn't quite the right word. It was more like being shown what the job felt like.

I believe that the job offer was real. I could have taken the place of the being in the rock, but that wasn't really why the Rock made the offer. (It actually liked what it was doing.) The offer was a way to seriously get my attention. It showed me other possibilities of life and love for beings who work with magic.

The encounter also answered a question I have had for years about the creation myths of the Australian Aborigines. They believe that beings in Dreamtime, probably before humans came around, settled in places as features of the geography. The beings became the caves and rock formations. Before I met the Rock, I didn't understand what those beings intended. I think the Rock was one of those beings and I now understand their intention.

In the end, I declined the job. I decided that for now I needed to be active in a human way. In this life I am here to share these kinds of reports with other humans in the hope that we can learn to honor the earth and all the beings associated with its creation.

This particular job was in Arizona, but there are other spirits who oversee all of the places on earth, even the densest cities, even the on-line communities of the Internet.

One last question I have is whether members of this group of beings, either physical or non-physical, aspire to become more powerful beings. More simply, do they and we wish to be gods? I don't, at least not yet. If you do, plan on doing a lot of hard work to get there.

Beings Who Are Magic

Finally there are beings that live on a much smaller scale. The beings discussed up to now seem free to roam the earth pretty much at will, unless they have a job that ties them to a location. The little ones seem to be tied to a particular place. Some of them roam throughout a small region. Others are tied so tightly to their surroundings that they do not leave a particular tree.

They have less power than we do. In the fairy tradition many have specifics abilities or tasks. This group also includes nature spirits where there is a spirit for each plant, each blade of grass, each drop of water, or each grain of sand. Some say there is a spirit for each physical object down to the smallest parts of an atom.

They are *everywhere*. Everyone knows about the many varieties of Celtic faeries. Some of the names in the traditions of the United Kingdom include boggarts, boggles, borrowers, brownies, elves, gnomes, knockers, moon-dancers, knickers, nippers, noggles, pucks, and sprites.

Other cultures also have their little people. The Japanese Shinto religion worships numerous gods and spirits that inhabit specific places or things. The American Indians speak to spirits, often in the shape of sacred animals, who help them with hunting. Both the American Indians and the West Africans have tales of tricksters. The ancient Romans made small food offerings to house gods to keep them from upsetting their domestic lives. The Australian Aborigines have "little-bit Dreaming" beings that have been there from the beginning.

And if you think contemporary Western culture doesn't have its own varieties of little people, consider this: When Charles Lindberg flew across the Atlantic, he spent much of the time talking to vague shapes, in the form of a cloud-like vapor, that had the power of speech. Lindberg said that they were quite friendly and offered to help him navigate. He called them gremlins. The creatures had been seen by pilots in World War I. Generally the pilots didn't talk about them, partly because they didn't want to break the good luck they were having, but I suspect it was mostly because they were afraid their superiors would think they were crazy and ground them.

The striking thing about these little people is that they are *not* all the same. The little people in Celtic countries are usually quite playful, or at least filled with a *joie de vivre* (joy of life). Sometimes they are helpful; sometimes they are harmful. In Scotland they are more often dour and less often friendly than in Ireland. In Australia the beings are never playful. The Roman house gods and the Chinese house spirits always seem to need food. The American Indian spirits are more likely to provide food. The Arabic djinns are asked to provide great wealth (and provide tricks instead, much like Western stories of dealing with the devil).

Perhaps each human culture creates the spirits it finds appropriate, so naturally, the spirits match the culture. Or perhaps the spirits in an area affect the humans living there so that the human culture changes to best work with the available spirits.

Here are three stories that represent the kinds of evidence we have that the beings who are magic exist. As you might expect, the events are convincing to the people who experience them.

The first is from Dora van Gelder, who had experience with nature spirits and little people in many places. There was an ancient tree in a garden in Java that could not be trimmed because every time someone went to cut the tree, something happened to the worker. Eventually no one would even try. "They attributed the accidents to the malignant influence of the old Kashmir nut tree spirit.... He did not like human beings at all, for he remembered a time when he was surrounded by trees and not by houses, and he blamed human beings for his isolation and loneliness. When he projected himself toward people he looked rather like a thin grey-faced ape of huge dimensions, perhaps fifteen feet tall."[35] Van Gelder was writing before Bigfoot was widely known, or she might have made the connection.

The second story happened to me. One day I couldn't find my wallet. This is kind of normal for me, because I read in bed and my wallet often falls out of my pocket, sometimes onto the floor. However, on this particular day I couldn't find my wallet anywhere. I searched the bed and the floor at least twice, the second time more carefully than the first. Before I searched a third time, I mumbled, "Okay, please bring it back." When I went back into the bedroom after checking some other possible places, there was the wallet on the floor, by the bed, in plain sight. No one else was in the house. Sounds like a brownie to me. And I did say, "Thank you." This is similar to a story told by another person who was a little more directive: "No more fooling around! I don't have time for this! I want those keys back *right now!*" And there they were in plain sight in a spot already well searched.

The third story, which was told by Azathool on alt.folklore.ghoststories,[36] has much richer detail.

> The grandfather of Azathool, at the age of ten, was going to spend his first night alone in the mill, which was owned by several farmers. This was an old-fashioned mill that needed to

be tended constantly to feed the grain in, to sack up the flour as it was produced, and to make sure that nothing went wrong. It took some time for each sack to fill so he sat down to rest. Of course he fell asleep.

He woke up when he heard a sound at the door of the mill. Just as he looked over, he saw a little man dressed in gray with a woolen cap going out the door. He looked around and discovered that all of the grain had been ground and put into sacks, which were left around the spot where he was sleeping.

Just about then the great-grandfather comes in. The grandson is an honest boy. He tells the great-grandfather that he fell asleep and has no idea who has made the flour. The great-grandfather smiles and says it is the mill-man, a little gnome who lives in and watches over the old mills. To repay the mill-man's kindness the grandfather gives it a bowl of sweet porridge, some bread, and a jug of mead.

I told the author how much I like the story and asked if the story was true. Azathool said, "Thanks, Tom, and yes, it is a true story. At least my grandfather said so."[37] The grandfather in later years found it entirely natural to be surrounded and helped by little folks.

Of course, we always wonder what was gained or lost in the telling and retelling. Each version is a little bit different. However, the heart of the story has a pretty deep mystery: the boy fell asleep and the grain was ground. Sacks don't move and fill themselves. Regardless of the changing details, the central occurrence provides evidence for something outside of physical reality — unless we choose to believe the great-grandfather came back to do the work that night. And that doesn't explain the help the grandfather got in later years.

When we talk about even smaller beings, such as the spirit for a grain of sand or a drop of water, the picture changes. These are not beings that appear as small humans. The way I think about them is that they are the soul reality equivalents of our physical laws. They help us understand how soul reality works, but they really don't provide conclusive evidence.

Evidence from Other Beings

The evidence we get from other beings is much like the evidence from inspiration. Many similar experiences let us know that something is happening. Beings who make magic make changes we can feel in soul reality and physical reality. So do beings who use magic. On a smaller scale, beings who are magic make small changes, such as returning keys. All of these are convincing for the person who experiences them but not for doubters.

Another piece of evidence comes from seeing the beings. We have many reports of sightings. When several people see the same being, especially if the being is doing magic, we have even stronger evidence.

Shamans, Witches, and Other Human Magic Workers

There are many terms for humans who work with magic and many ways that they practice that magic. I'm going to give a few simple examples, so you have a feel for this range of practices. I know it's not complete. Later books in the **We All Have Souls** series will look at some of these practices in much greater depth.

Some shamans journey with spirit animals for information and healing. Other shamans contact the spirits of mountains and lakes to gain knowledge. Witches work with both soul and physical realities in our world or work through ritual magic. Sorcerers work to gain power over people and things in the environment. There are practitioners of Celtic magic, African traditions, and Voodoo and the traditions of conjure that came from these roots. Native American and First Peoples have their own set of traditions. Australian Aborigines work in Dreamtime. Mystics and alchemists seek true nature and purest forms.

Basically, magic is everywhere. In this chapter, we are not trying to understand any particular form of the magic. We are asking if magic is evidence for soul reality.

I believe the change in health that comes from some types of magic is possible evidence. The views that magic traditions have about other beings and other types of reality support what we have talked about already.

Three Regions of the Worlds

Most traditions talk about multiple regions in their world. Usually there is the region we live in, another region above us, and a third region below us.

Most of this book looks at what we can find in the middle region where we live. I think this region has been covered enough. But let's look at the other two regions in more detail.

The upper region is almost always seen as a place of spirit and information. It is where we find angels and other guardians. The Creator or creators, in whatever form he, she, it, or they take, live in this upper region. It is often described as a place of great beauty and perfection. Many people describe it as a place with beautiful music and say that music is one of the best ways to reach the gods.

This matches my view of the soul because I see the top region of the soul reaching into this upper region of the world. The top soul region works with information and inspiration. It is the part we use to gain insight into the reality beyond what we see.

In the Incan traditions this is the realm of the condor. It is a place for spiritual wisdom and global vision. We move from subjective experience into an objective and inclusive view. Just as the condor looks down from his flight, we can see the big picture and avoid becoming bogged down in small details.[38]

Witchcraft, Voodoo, and other conjuring traditions see this as the home of the protectors. Where these practices have merged their beliefs with Christian tradition, they call on God and the angels in this realm.

The ancient Greek philosopher Plato's said this is the place where the true form of things can be found. The alchemists also work in this region to find the pure forms that they seek. Mystics travel here for inspiration.

Most people say that the upper region is a place where we find pure goodness. I can go along with the pure part. The upper region is a place of clarity. I disagree with the goodness part. As you will see later in the book, I think the upper region can be a place where pure evil exists, too.

The lower region is more chaotic. Most traditions see it as a place where we can find both good and evil, and I agree. My view is that it is a place of energy. We go there to gather the kind of energy we want. It can be used to heal or to harm.

In the Western version of shamanic healing, this is where people go to find spirit animals and energy sources. These are used for positive purposes. On the flip side, a sorcerer who is looking to control others also moves through the lower realm. People who work with demons to gain their power call them from the lower realms, too.

The conjuring traditions have a similar mixed view. Some parts of the lower region are part of the natural process of decay and rebirth. For example, in conjure culture Daddy Death is the helping spirit from the world of the dead who connects us to the wisdom of the ancestors and the graveyard. In contrast, there is also Daddy Down-There, who is purely evil. He is composed of all the anger and hatred from everyone who has died and been buried. You want to avoid him. As the conjurer Orion Foxwood says, "To any readers who think they are big and bad enough to take him on — you are delusional."[39]

The Incan traditions see the lower region as the realm of the snake. In this place anything is possible. Everything exists in a primary, volatile state between spirit and matter. This is the hub of creation, where physical manifestation can occur. Pachamama is the connection used in these traditions to tap into the energy of the lower region.[40]

The evidence here comes from the wide consensus of people who have experienced these regions. Each region is strikingly similar across many traditions. The evidence fits well with my proposed model of the soul to give us a foundation for further, careful exploration.

Healing and Harming

All of these traditions exist to cause a change in physical reality by using information and energy from soul reality. When we are looking for evidence, the question is can we show there was a change? And can we show it was caused by life force?

I think in some cases we can.

I've been part of a conjure to bring rain. It rained about half an hour later. But is this useful evidence? Probably not.

There are so many conflicting and intertwining forces in nature that it is nearly impossible to separate out the effect of human conjure. Any kind of controlled experiment would require making rain or clear skies on demand. The model we are using says that we can do that. But it also says that there are nature spirits in charge of making the rain or clearing the skies. I think those spirits would just ignore us because our purpose of trying to prove our power is meaningless to them.

Luckily there are meaningful ways we can see a change. I have done shamanic soul retrievals and depossession. The positive changes I've seen have been striking enough that I'm sure something significant changed. The people have reported that their friends also notice a change, even when they don't know about the soul work.

This evidence is enough to convince me. But some changes in the usual process would make the evidence better. We'll talk about those in Chapter 8 on proof.

This kind of work has the support of our guiding spirits because it is meaningful and for the highest and best good. Proving that soul work is healing may not seem all that important to those spirits, so we explain that this kind of proof will lead to more people getting more healing. The spirits seem to like that idea.

The magic traditions also have ways to harm other people. Evidence could be gathered there, too, but why would we want to? All of that is rooted in our fear and pain. Harming others only makes the pain worse. If we want to be healthy, powerful, and make the world better, we need to accept our dark side and deal with it, not make it stronger by harming others.

4. SOULS

When they are seen as fields of energy,
human beings appear to be like fibers of light,
like white cobwebs, very fine threads that
circulate from the head to the toes. Thus to the
eye of a seer, a man looks like an egg of
circulating fibers.

— *Carlos Castaneda*

In this chapter we'll look at a model of the soul that explains the evidence for soul reality that we looked at in Chapter 3. It will also help us know ourselves better. I believe that knowing about souls will also help us have better relations with each other and everything else in our realities.

One of the most important things about souls is that we are all separate beings. I think this defines our reality. We are here to learn about boundaries between ourselves and others. In a body it is difficult to join closely with others and easy to see our separateness.

This separation is also one of the great dangers of this reality. As Orion Foxwood points out, we may feel this as isolation and abandonment. He feels that the primary wound in the human soul is this abandonment pain.[41] When we look at souls, one of the most important points is how we balance these two aspects of life. We need to be separate to learn lessons, but we also need to join with others and connect to the wholeness of life. To ignore either part is to lose the lessons we are here to learn.

I call the aspect of the soul that handles the functions of separateness and connection the I-Am. It holds the middle five regions of the soul and is specifically built to interact with the middle region of the world in both physical reality and soul reality. It may extend to cover the top and bottom regions of the soul when we travel into the upper and lower regions of the world. It divides what is outside us from what is inside us by defining self and other. It allows us connect closely with others when we choose to. You can refer to the diagram of the soul on the inside back cover.

The lowest region of the soul is our connection to the lower region of the world. I call the first soul region the Energy region because it connects to the energy in the world. It seems to me like the roots of a tree that extend into the energy around us. In physical reality it would be mostly below the body. It connects with such powerful forces that most of the time it is not completely under our control.

The next five soul regions are part of the middle region of the world. In physical reality they seem to be between the genital area and the top of the head.

The second soul region is the Wish region. It deals with what we hope to have and what we hope will happen. Our Wish region is how we filter the kinds of energy we need for our goals from all the other energy that is available.

The third region is the Will, which is responsible for powering our actions and keeping us moving forward to achieve our plans. It deals mostly with energy.

The fourth region is the Heart. This is the part that connects us with one another in positive and negative ways. It deals with a mix of energy and information.

The fifth region is Voice. This is how we transmit ideas and feelings and how we give thanks for what we have received. It deals mostly with information.

The sixth region is Mind, which we use for processing information. It works with all the other regions to make our plans. It helps us integrate information we receive from the upper region of the soul.

The highest region of the soul connects to the upper region of the world. I call this the Info region. It connects to the structure of reality. In physical reality it seems to be above the head. Some of the information comes from more powerful soul beings. Like the Energy region it connects with things that can be more than we can handle and is not entirely under our control.

The top and bottom soul regions are outside the middle region of the world. How far they go depends on where we want them to go and how much power we have to send them out. People use these two regions of their soul to journey in soul reality.

While the top and bottom regions both work with soul reality, their effects can also be seen in physical reality. When we interact with someone who has little connection with the lower region, we often say she isn't grounded or he has his head in the clouds. Someone with weak connections to the upper region might be called low-minded. This model of the soul makes it clearer what those terms mean.

If you know about chakras, you'll notice some similarities. My model has some important differences, though. First, I prefer to think of souls as a continuous thing with one region blending into the next. The colors of a rainbow have colors between the seven colors we call primary. I think soul regions blend their functions, too.

Another problem I have with chakra models is that they often describe chakras as small spots tied to a particular organ of the body. I think a healthy soul is bigger than the body, so that we are bodies inside souls instead of soul chunks enclosed in parts of a body.

Turning the connection so that bodies are inside souls, let's us sense what is going on in our soul by feeling it through our body. I usually stack the regions from the belly to the head, as shown in the table below. I think the locations make some sense for body-soul connections. For example the Voice region, which controls communication, contains the areas where we hear and speak. The Heart region is about connection. It is in the part of the body that connects with every cell through the blood and lymph systems. Soul-body connection is an area that needs more research, but it is not crucial for proving souls exist. We'll leave it for another time.

For the rest of this chapter, I want to look at each of the regions of the soul. At the end we'll tie them together with the I-Am and look at the soul as a whole.

Table 1: Regions in the Soul and Associated Body Areas

Info (7)	above the head
Mind (6)	head
Voice (5)	neck
Heart (4)	chest
Will (3)	belly
Wish (2)	lower belly
Energy (1)	below the feet

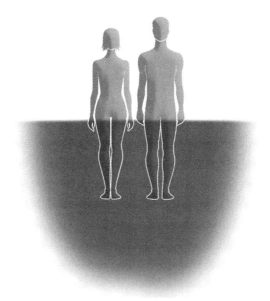

Energy Region (1)

The Energy region of the soul is our deep connection to a mix of positive and negative energy we tap into to create, destroy, or move through our realities. People who speak of chakras call this the root chakra. I agree with that interpretation. This is a root in exactly the same sense as a tree root. It brings vital nutrients — the soul energy we need to live — into our souls.

The place where this region of our soul exists is in the lower region of the world. Along with the Info region, it is our connection to soul reality outside of the middle region of the world. It resides in an area of very powerful energies. These elemental forces are not something humans should think they can control. If we are not careful, the energy we tap into will control us more than we control it. Like the root of a tree, the Energy region works with the Wish region to sort through what is there to bring the kind of nutrients we want into our system.

There seem to be three thoughts about the purpose of this region.

The yoga traditions see this as where we get energy, but they generally want us to escape from the influence of this region. They call this the root of our wicked impulses.[42] Their goal is to focus on the Mind and Info regions.

Tantric tradition says this region contains the realization of greatest joy, natural pleasure, delight in controlling passion, and blissfulness in concentration. They accept the energies that are here and work to bring them into harmony with the rest of life.

Shamanic practitioners, native healers, Aboriginal hunters, and many others live in this land of energy or visit this land of energy as part of their spirit journeys. In this place they meet other travelers. If a spirit journey takes them down, they are working through the Energy region in the lower region of the world.

I believe one of the reasons we are in bodies is to learn to process this raw energy by ourselves. When we are not in bodies, I think it is buffered by all the other souls around us. In a body we need to learn to tap into the energy and stay connected with it. This provides a deeper understanding of what the energy is all about. When people try to ignore or "conquer" this region, they are missing the reason we are here.

When most people take journeys into the lower region of the world, they create the landscapes they are traveling through. The raw energy is there, but they need to impose some basic structure on it to be able to act inside the experience and understand how to gather the energy. I usually do that, too. But sometimes I sit there with my spirit guide in the shiny black of the lower world letting it be without form. We watch other journeyers create a tunnel of form with animals and plants and geographic features as they move nearby.

Life Force Processing

This region is much more concerned with the energy component of the life force then the information component. The rest of the soul system does the information processing to decide which type of energy to connect with. The Energy region just carries out the energy requests of the other regions of the soul. Useful energy is gathered and energy that is not useful is left behind.

Another purpose of the Energy region is to ground us. We gather life force energy from many people and places as we go through our day. It doesn't all come from the lower region of the world. Some of the life force is useful for what we want to do. Other life force makes our lives harder.

I expect we've all experienced days when we can't concentrate on a task because we are too full of good feelings and joy of being alive. It is possible to have too much positive energy. It's like floating in a cloud instead of having our feet on the ground to take us where we want to go next.

There are also days when we absorb so much negative energy from the world around us that is feels like we can't even think. To actually move forward with some task is unimaginable.

The root nature of the Energy region works both ways. It can take the energy we don't need and put it back in the lower region. Some people say back into the earth — same thing. We're sending it out of us to a place that can hold it. Then we can get on with what we need to do using the energy we need to have for the task.

When the soul is working at its best, all the regions agree on the task to do. They send the message of the kinds of energy that are needed to the Energy region. The Energy region gathers the energy and sends it to the other regions as required.

Lessons

We can draw enormous amounts of energy through this region. Some of us are better at it than others. It is something that we can practice and improve on. Here is a quick exercise for you to try. For this exercise and any of the others, if something feels wrong, stop. Bring yourself back to your normal way of being. Ask yourself or people and spirits you trust if what you are doing is for your highest and best good. If not, ask how to change what you are trying to do so it is.

One-Minute Exercise

This one-minute exercise for the Energy region involves searching into the earth for something physical. If you want to make it more interesting, find the spirit of what you are searching for, too.

Put the book down (after you read the exercise, of course). Place your feet so your soles are touching something below them. If you are sitting, put your feet flat on the floor. If you are lying down, roll onto your back and bend your knees so your feet are flat on what you are lying on.

Close your eyes.

Feel roots or tendrils growing out of the bottoms of your feet.

Go down into the earth, and spread the tendrils out until you can wrap them around a rock. Study the shape of the rock for about 10 seconds.

Now move the roots around until you find an earthworm. Say hello. Feel the earthworm move. You have about 10 seconds here, too. Say goodbye.

Next look for the roots of a tree. You have roots and the tree has roots. Feel the shape of the tree roots. Feel how the tree's roots take nutrients up into the trunk, branches, and leaves of the tree. Ten seconds. Time to move on.

Next move farther out until you find a river. Feel your tendrils move in the flow. Ten seconds here, too, then move on.

The last place is a cavern. There might be one near you, or you may have to go a long way away. You're looking for an open space under the ground. A mine will work, too. Let your tendrils move into the space and expand to fill it, at least as much as you can in 10 seconds. Find the edges of the space and try to figure out how it came to be.

Bring your roots back up into your feet along with any energy (and wisdom) you managed to gather.

If you want to spend more than ten seconds in any of those places, good. That's the point of these short exercises. Practice is fun. It doesn't have to be difficult. To really understand something, you have to do more than read about it. To understand something enough so it changes your life a lot may take more than a minute, but even one minute makes some difference. Working on changing has to become part of your life. You can check on how much you have changed by doing this exercise every few months to see how your ability to sense energy has improved.

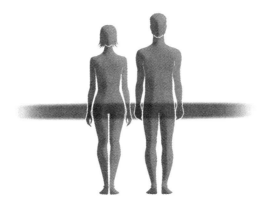

Wish Region (2)

The Wish region is what we come into the world with. Any wishes we have from the time before we are born or from previous lives are found here. These wishes express who we want to be. The rest of who we are grows out of these wishes.

Another reason it seems appropriate to call this the Wish region is because what we bring into a life really is just a wish. It can be comforting to think that everything happens to us for a reason, but I don't see evidence for this.

So many things happen to change the course of our lives that it is hard to believe there is anything like a master plan. At best we are here with others who have connecting wishes. Chances come along and we pick the options that seem best at the time. Problems arise and we solve them with what we have available.

The Wish region provides us with an anchor for making decisions. We do best when we remain true to what we want. This is not to say that our wishes stay exactly the same throughout our whole life. They don't.

What we wish for changes as we learn and grow. When we are hurt by something in life, our wishes change, too. But I think there is a core set of wishes that don't change much. To understand who we are and live a life we think is successful, we need to find that core.

Traditionally, this region has been called the genital chakra. It is usually associated with desire, including sexual desire. In many reincarnation books, authors suggest that less spiritual humans spend lifetimes returning just for sexual pleasure.[43] I think these authors are missing the point. Sexual interactions are one of the best places to look at how we connect and stay separate.

Sex is one of the benefits souls get from having bodies, but there are other wishes that are equally important. One of our important lessons is meeting those wishes. They are the way we signal that we are not meeting the basic needs for staying alive. The psychologist Abraham Maslow[44] described five levels of needs. The first two levels include food, water, sleep, shelter, and sex. If we are missing any of these, our Wish region focuses our energy on getting what we need to stay alive.

But Wish goes beyond that. It includes our wishes for relationships with other people, which are on Maslow's third and fourth levels. Sometimes these go across lifetimes. Wish also includes any goals that we bring with us into the world. I believe that each of us is part of some plan that includes more than our life on earth. Our current life may not let us follow the plan. We may forget the plan while we are here. But there is hope. I believe we can find our plan when we reach deeply into our Wish region and use it to connect to soul realities outside of physical reality.

We often think of wishes as a desire to create something, but sometimes we desire to take something apart. Removing something can be a positive wish, too. It's like taking down an old building to replace it with a newer and better building. The underlying wish is for the new building. Taking the old one down is just a step in the process. As we'll see in the discussion about life force processing in the Wish region, even destructive wishes have a place and must be acknowledged. Wishes become a problem when they are only looking to cause destruction or some other kind of harm.

Many of our wishes are crushed by our lives. The ones we are most likely to keep are the basic ones that involve physical survival and pleasure. It is sad when we lose the other ones that define our purpose. Most of our culture denies that our souls exist. Even the parts of the culture that talk about souls don't have much to say about how you find *your* wishes. Your wishes don't have to be the same as what is written in a holy book. Rediscovering the wishes you brought with you into this life means cleaning up the damage your life has done to your soul. Knowing you have a soul and that it might need some repair is a really good place to start.

Life Force Processing

A wish is like a seed. When we have a wish, it first grows roots. They go down into the Energy region and reach out through the lower region of the world to gather nutrients, water, and energy to power the wish.

Then the wish grows up, just as a seed grows, into the middle region of the world. First it grows into the Will region where we decide if we will make it so. A wish that becomes reality needs the Will's help to stand strongly against the forces of the outer world. The wish brings the energy through its roots into Will to give Will enough energy to protect the wish.

If the wish needs to connect with other people to become real, it grows into the Heart. The Heart connects with others to bring the wish into the world. It can grow in physical reality or soul reality. Important wishes grow strong in both. The Heart is especially important if our wish is to get back together with someone we loved in a previous life. Then the Heart helps pull our two lives together so we can meet again.

Wishes run into problems that need solutions. For example, how do I write a book to tell you that we all have souls? When the wish reaches the Mind, the Mind calls on its sources of information in the middle region and upper region of the world to find ways for the wish to work through problems it has run into.

In my personal example, I search for the right words to explain what I mean. I try to say them with love. I know that there will be many forces working against the message that we all have souls, and I prepare to stand up against them. Why do I do this? Because I have a wish that humans know about souls so we can live well with all the beings in physical reality and soul reality.

When the Wish region processes life force, the information content is quite simple, usually a single action and an object: eating food, loving a friend. The Wish region remembers the wishes we have had and whether they were met. It is also the gateway to energy because it calls on the Energy region to provide life force for very specific purposes — your active wishes.

The process can be blocked at any of the levels. The Will may say it isn't strong enough. The Heart may receive messages from others that the wish is wrong. The Mind may say that the wish makes no sense and should be forgotten. But the worst is when it is blocked in the Wish region. When that happens, it means there is no energy for us to be who we want to be.

Sometimes the Wish region can let a wish go by releasing it. That's all right when there is an even better wish that can be followed. It's not all right when the wish stays just a wish and never makes it into the world. The Wish region holds it, but the other regions resist it, so the soul is never satisfied. This happens to so many people. For the soul to be satisfied, the wish must be acknowledged and changed into something that can grow.

Changing wishes leads to the topic of dark wishes, wishes that will cause harm to you or someone else. We all have them. They are our shadow side and it is important that we understand our shadow.

As with all wishes, dark wishes need to be acknowledged. If we don't admit we have them, they sprout up and cause harm that we can't control. We can't stop dark wishes, but we can change them.

A wish for harm to someone almost always includes "because…". It could be because the person harmed us, or because the person was in the way of something that we wished for. For example, think of Andy applying for a promotion at work. If Betty gets the promotion, Andy's dark wish is for Betty to fail "because I deserved the job more."

Harming the person just continues the cycle of bad energy. We are often harmed in return and don't get any closer to our real wish. If Andy actively tries to harm Betty's work, he will hurt both of them. We don't solve the "because" part of the wish and often make it worse.

A better answer is to acknowledge that we want harm to the person, but go beyond that to look at why. The next step is to figure out a way to get what we want without causing harm. That was the real wish that caused the situation and the Wish region will realize that when it is given the possibility. In the example, what Andy wanted was a better job. Trying to harm someone else is unlikely to work. Both the Heart and the Mind will point out better options if they have the chance. Then it is Wish's job to listen.

When we see our shadow, we see what we really wish for much more clearly. And we have a much better chance of getting our deepest wishes.

We can sum up the life force processing this way: The wish grows in the Wish region and pulls life force energy up from the lower region of the world to power all of the other soul regions as they work to make the wish real. The Wish region filters the energy we need to accomplish our goals.

Lessons

In the lesson for the Wish region we will look at how a wish moves through the other regions of the soul to become reality. It's a good way to start to look at whether your whole soul is working together. Life is smoother when all the parts of you agree.

One-Minute Exercise

We are going to use this exercise to look at how wishes move from the Wish region to the other regions of the soul. Let's take a wish that almost everyone has: spending time with your best friend.

There are seven soul regions and the I-Am to consider. For each region, write down one or two answers to the question being asked. To finish the exercise in a minute you have seven seconds for each region. Don't think too much about your answers and write quickly.

Start by thinking about the favorite thing you do with your friend. For the one-minute exercise, you probably need to concentrate on just one interaction. You can always do the exercise again with other people and with other types of interactions. And, as always, feel free to take more than a minute if you want to. Going through the questions again at a later time will show you how you have changed.

- Energy: What kind of positive and negative energy do you feel?
- Wish: What other wishes are satisfied when you're with your friend?
- Will: What parts of the interaction are you in charge of?
- Heart: What feelings are you sharing?
- Voice: You probably talk about wishes. What have you said about this wish?
- Mind: What do you think about while you are spending time with your friend?
- Info: What feels right about being with your friend?
- I-Am: How is your interaction with your friend different from your interactions with everybody else?

Usually people say there are no right or wrong answers. But that's not true here. The right answers show that each of your regions is acting in a way that matches the friendship you wish for. If not, you can think about how to get your whole soul working together. Repeating this exercise in a few weeks will show you if your soul regions are in better agreement.

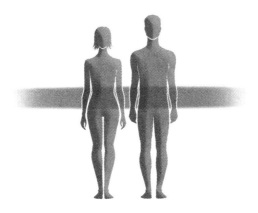

Will Region (3)

The Will region is how we turn our wishes into reality. The Wish region seeks different states of being. The Will region takes the wish and decides what we can do to reach it. Possibilities for actions may come from the regions above Will, but the decisions are coordinated by Will.

The Will region is how we focus on actions. For example, I may be a little overweight. So my wish is to be the right weight.

The Will region decides what to do. The wish could be met at least two ways. I could lose weight or I could grow taller. The Mind region figures out that growing taller is probably not a likely option. The Will region decides to work on losing weight. With more help from the other regions, Will sees that I will lose weight by exercising more and eating only to satisfy my physical hunger.

The Wish region needs to get this right, too. It must learn that physical hunger requires food. Eating as a substitute for other needs, such as love, is best handled by finding ways to get more love. If Wish and Will do their jobs in a healthy way, our needs will be met more accurately.

The Will region does more than control our actions. It is also the part of us that gives life force to a group when the group wants to accomplish something. There are two ways this can happen. One person's Will can dominate the group or the whole group can combine the life force from their Wills. I believe sharing all the life force is usually better. Let's look at both cases to see their advantages and disadvantages.

When one person dominates the others in the group, the person is very likely to meet resistance. Very few people like to be dominated. Those that do are probably not well aware of their Wish region. If someone is powerful enough to dominate a group, good things in the group may be lost. Others in the group will not share their feelings or thoughts if they conflict with the leader. Most of the energy goes toward doing what the leader wants. Negative energy is suppressed, but comes out as resistance anyway. It may be all right for one person to take over a group when everyone agrees about the wish, but the group can't decide on the actions.

When the whole group combines the life force from everyone's Will, other life force is brought into play. All the Heart regions can add their cooperative connection between people. All the Mind regions can add possible solutions. If all the soul regions in the group work together well, the group has the most possible resources to work with. Sometimes the group chooses a spokesperson, such as Franklin Roosevelt, who represents the combined Will of the group to the rest of the world. This is different from a leader who is trying to dominate a group. It lasts as long as the spokesperson reflects the combined Will of the group accurately. The downside happens when the Wills do not form a solid set of actions. We've all seen committees where there is a lot of talk, but nothing gets done. Either the wishes are not clear or the Wills are not working together. If the Wills can't join together, there is no advantage to sharing them.

A related situation is when one person sets out to dominate someone else. This is bad for both people if the dominating person is trying to cause harm. The traditional Incan medicine people use the term hoocha for the bad stuff that gets created when harmful actions happen. Dominating someone else to cause harm makes a lot of hoocha. The power from this region is not usually negative. That only happens when what we are willing into being is harmful.

Let's look at some of the positive uses of Will. In healthcare situations Will can be positive. Energy from the Will region of the healthcare provider can give the patient enough will to get better. Will can also be used by parents to teach children how to use their own Will. Children who don't know the abilities of their Wills get lost in lives they can't control.

It's worthwhile to look at what other traditions say about this region. Many consider Will to be the center of our power. I think they are considering power in the sense of a person causing something to happen. In that sense this is where the power is expressed.

Chinese Qigong practitioners think that this region takes sexual energy and converts it into chi. That chi is used by the rest of the body. Martial artists think this is the center for making strong techniques. Sorcerers say the greatest power comes from the belly. It is used when the sorcerer changes reality. All of these are talking about using power gathered by the Energy region.

In our Western languages we also recognize the importance of the related area of the body when we want to do something difficult. Here are some examples: It takes guts to do the hard stuff, as in "No guts, no glory." We talk about people not having a "stomach for it" if they are afraid to do a difficult task. We get butterflies in our stomach when we are afraid. And it takes a strong stomach to watch unpleasant things without getting upset or feeling ill.

We need to feel a fire in our belly before we are ready to work on something that is difficult. This is another example of how important this region is in getting things done. Note also that this is the only region that is considered a good place for a fire.

There are few things more dangerous or powerful than a parent whose children are being threatened. We looked at some of those situations in the Evidence chapter. The Will can give us superhuman strength. I suggest that fire in the Will region also powers the Heart's superpowers. I'll talk about those in the Heart region discussion below.

Another aspect of the Will region is the concept of a gut reaction. Most people like to believe that they think decisions through with their Minds. That's being rational. But research shows that we often make decisions in non-rational (emotional) ways. I think these decisions are being made by the Will. Then we use our Minds to find rational reasons for our decisions.[45]

Life Force Processing

The information processed by the Will region is pretty basic. It usually comes in the form of orders like "Do this!" or "Follow me!" The commands have a verb with an object. Our Will region reacts to commands from the Wills of other people. We remember the command and how successful it was, but not the details of what happened.

Our Will can be directed at ourselves. Sometimes I am not successful in getting myself to do what I tell myself to do. I usually have problems when Will is not in sync with Wish.

The energy handled by the Will can be large. One place we find this is in martial arts. An example is stopping an attacker just by looking at him. I have done this, at least in practice.

If we expand this idea to a battlefield situation, we can look at the power a leader has in controlling the actions of his warriors. The Scotsman William Wallace (Braveheart) led his fighters against the British army. With his Will he convinced his men to stand against the charge of the British cavalry. Of course, they had a plan, but good plans notoriously get forgotten when Will isn't strong enough to carry them out.

The Will is there to use the energy we pull in with the Energy region for making our wishes happen. It uses information from the Heart, Mind, and Info regions to decide on the best actions.

Lessons

The exercise for the Will region looks at how our Will affects us and others when we need to choose between conflicting wishes.

One-Minute Exercise

For this exercise we'll look at how you use your Will region in three situations. Will acts to bring about wishes. So pick a wish to think about when you are doing this exercise. It's best to pick one of the basic wishes: safety, food, water, sleep, or sex. The directions use sleep, but you can choose a different wish. Here's how you can do a quick check on your Will. You have about 20 seconds for each part.

- Remember a time when you needed to work on a big project or get ready for a test the next day. You were really sleepy, too. It doesn't matter which choice you made. If you chose to sleep, did worrying keep you awake? If you chose to work or study, did sleepiness keep you from finishing what you needed to do? Write down how well you carried out your choice.
- Remember a time when a friend wished to do something with you, but you were really sleepy. Describe how you and your friend sorted out your conflicting wishes. How did your Will protect your basic wish for sleep?
- Remember a time when you wished to sleep but your boss expected you to keep working. Did you find a way to get enough sleep? How?

The first situation looks at how well you choose between your personal wishes. Do you honor or ignore your basic wishes?

The second situation looks at how you handle conflicting wishes when one of the wishes comes from a Heart connection with a friend.

The third situation looks at how you handle conflicting wishes when one of them comes from a Will connection with your boss.

To stay alive, you need to fulfill your basic wishes. Your Will needs to protect them from internal and external forces. In this case you need to be sure you get enough sleep. Your answers to these questions will give you an idea of how well your Will works for your basic wishes.

You can try this exercise again with a different basic wish or a non-basic wish that you can't seem to accomplish. Compare the results of the basic wish and the non-basic wish. If they are at all similar, you probably want to use the basic wish to practice making your Will stronger. That way your Heart and Mind will raise fewer objections.

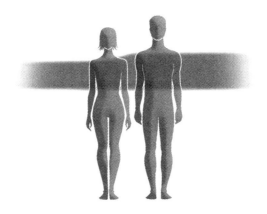

Heart Region (4)

The Heart region powers our connections with others. In a positive situation we feel love for others and for ourselves. Gaining positive connections gives us joy. Losing them leads to sorrow. When the connections are negative, we feel anger and hate. And we feel joy when negative connections go away.

The Heart is special in two ways.

One is that the Heart has feelings. The Heart's feelings are responsible for both friendship and romantic love. Things that might look a little like feelings can come from other regions. Sexual desires are part of the Wish region. The Mind region has thoughts about others, but thoughts are not the same as feelings. The interactions other regions have are all different from the feeling interactions of the Heart region.

The other difference is that the Heart brings about connections. These can be positive or negative. It's best when we connect to other people in positive ways. We keep the idea that we are two separate beings, but we share an understanding of one another that goes beyond words. Love is one of the great positive forces in the universe. It is there for all of us to access through the Heart and to use when we are helping one another. All the great healers I have known send their healing energy through this region.

When we love someone, it's important to feel this sharing connection. Any feeling of domination or being dominated by Will is a bad sign for love.

Heart connections can be positive or negative. Love is the positive side. We have many sayings about the power of love. John Lennon[46] said, "All you need is love." The Bible has a longer passage. First Corinthians 13:8 says, "Love never fails. But whether there are prophecies, they will fail; whether there are tongues, they will cease; whether there is knowledge, it will vanish away." Thinking about regions of the soul we can say: Prophecies from the Info region will be gone. Words from Voice will be gone. What our Mind knows will be gone. Love from the Heart will remain.

As the philosopher R. Buckminster Fuller[47] puts it, "Love is metaphysical gravity." Sets of souls travel together through lifetime after lifetime. It is love (and its opposite) pulling the souls together. Creating positive connections and cleaning up negative connections is one of the most important tasks we have in this life. When we have positive connections, our lives are happier because we travel with the ones we love.

The Heart has a dark side, too. Those who would destroy us also send their life force through this region. The Heart can overpower the Will and cause us to act in ways that are not for our highest and best good. Nothing hurts more than betrayal by a loved one. We may die for many reasons, but we usually kill ourselves because of something related to love.[48]

Our Hearts need to be ready to ask any being that wants to work with us, "Are you acting for my highest and best good?" If the answer is no, in either physical reality or soul reality, do your best to walk away. If you can't escape, find the best protection and protectors you can and power up your Will to protect your Heart. Leave when you can. Working with someone who does not have your best interests at heart is not a healthy way to live.

The Tantric tradition says there are two parts to this region. So far we have been talking about the first part (anahata). The second part (hrit) is even more amazing. It lets us use superpowers. Here is how Susan Shumsky describes them: [49]

1. The ability to transform your body size to that of an atom.

2. The power to decrease your physical weight or levitate.

3. The power to increase your bodily size or stature or become mighty.

4. The capacity to fulfill desires and go anywhere at will, described by the ancients as "touching the moon with your fingertips."

5. The ability to pass through earth, walk through solid walls, or not be immersed in water, and to assume any desired form.

6. The greatest power and dominion over the five elements … earth, water, fire, air, and ether, and the subtle sense objects … of which these elements are made, odor, flavor, form, touch, sound. This is also the power to attract and enslave others by enchantment.

7. Mastery over the appearance, disappearance, and aggregation of the five elements and objects in the material world [physical reality]. With this [accomplishment] you can transcend all human limits.

8. Resolution — the ability to determine the five elements and their nature and to transform them at will. It is also the power to conquer or subordinate others.

I have to say that I have never done any of these things in physical reality. If you are looking for someone who says he has, I suggest reading the later books by the sorcerer Carlos Castaneda. Many say Castaneda is nonsense, but what he writes agrees with the Tantric tradition. He says that sorcerer's powers flow out through the belly. I haven't found a place in his writings that say where these powers originate.

There are other stories of great (and not so great) people who had some of these powers. Jesus walked on water, changed water into wine, and rose up to heaven. D. D. Home[50] and St. Teresa levitated. In the Zen tradition there is a story of two monks who met one another as they were about to cross a river. After a brief discussion, one monk tossed his hat into the river, stepped on it, and rode it to the other shore. The other monk said, "If I had known you were that sort of person, I would have killed you on the spot." Apparently in the Zen tradition it's not acceptable to show these superpowers.

It would be interesting to know if the Zen monk who objected to the other monk's use of his hat to cross the river would have objected to the mother using a similar power to save her child. (Probably not.)

We have many stories of vampires and other mythic creatures, Jedi warriors, magicians, and spirits who have superpowers. Many wish they had these powers. Those who believe in only the four physical forces work very hard to stop belief in anything beyond physical reality. They fear that rational thought will be lost. It may be true that the Mind needs to shut down for superpowers to work. But that isn't a certainty.

For those who believe the world is coming to an end, perhaps this is the end we will see. The Heart will reclaim its ability to change the world in ways that seem like superpowers. This time the Mind may be able to hold on to the experience so we can share it among all of us.

Life Force Processing

Of all the regions, the Heart is the most balanced between energy and information. Somehow, that's fitting, since it is the center of the soul.

The information that the region handles includes relationships between people. In some sense, the information can be represented in simple sentences. Some positive examples include:

I love you.

You are safe with me.

I am here for you.

We are together in this.

God cares for you.

The messages include two beings and the connection between them. One being or both beings can also be represented by a group, as in "My buddies have my back."

The Heart region remembers who we are connected to, the strength of the connection, and the directions of energy flow. It won't remember events or the words that were spoken. It holds our feelings about what happened between us and someone else.

The information seems simple, but there are deeper meanings in the energy flow. When Voice can't describe love, it's not a problem of saying the words "I love you." The problem is the energy flow. Words are a pale reflection of it. The flow can be extremely powerful, with both positive and negative energy. Words simply can't convey that to someone who hasn't felt it. If the same words are heard by someone who has had the feeling, they will know what is going on.

The energy from this region can be very strong. We have a saying, "When he came into the room, the temperature dropped by 10 degrees." We know that the room is not really 10 degrees cooler. We are measuring what the soul feels. We translate the feeling to physical reality because we have better words for it there.

The Heart also holds the superpowers. The energy required to perform some of those feats has to get into physical reality. Levitating requires canceling gravity. Another example is soldiers who drove into enemy fire. They got out of their Jeep, picked it up, and turned it around. Their extra strength acts like an electromagnetic force in physical reality.

The superpowers also include transforming matter. Nuclear forces are needed for this. The energy comes from the Energy region. Information comes from Mind or Info. The Heart region handles both. The lower regions do not have enough information. The higher regions would burn out from too much energy. In fact, Kundalini experts warn about this energy problem. They say that energy from below can travel to the Heart, but it should never be forced up into the Mind.

The final set of superpowers involves mastery over others. This is the dark side of affiliation. There is a connection so strong that energy from the Heart overwhelms the Mind or Will of the other person. The Good People, also known as fairies, are said to be skilled at this sort of enchantment.

I've talked about the lessons on connection and separation that we can learn in physical bodies. With all its powers and superpowers, the Heart is the place we practice those lessons.

Lessons

The lesson for the Heart region looks at how our Heart connects us to others. For our lives to be meaningful, we need to connect in positive ways.

One-Minute Exercise

In this exercise we are going to take a look at what flows into and out of our Heart region.

Seeing the flow may take some imagination. I suggest reaching out and looking at what flows from your hands. Then turn your hands around and see what you catch coming back. When you are scoring the strength of the feeling use a scale of 0 to 10. If there are no feelings, write down "none." We'll look at three situations. Take about 20 second for each.

First, think about a friend. In your mind, reach toward the person.

- Name one positive feeling flowing from you. How powerful is it?
- Name one negative feelings flowing from you. How powerful is it?
- Name one positive feeling flowing to you. How powerful is it?
- Name one negative feelings flowing to you. How powerful is it?

Next, think about a group of people you see almost every day. It could be some of the people you work with or go to school with. It won't be everybody you see in a day. Pick a set of people who would feel all right about sharing a group hug. In your mind, put your arms around the group.

- Name one positive feeling flowing from you. How powerful is it?
- Name one negative feelings flowing from you. How powerful is it?
- Name one positive feeling flowing to you. How powerful is it?
- Name one negative feelings flowing to you. How powerful is it?

Now think about yourself. In your mind, reach from your Heart inward toward yourself.

- Name one positive feeling flowing from you to you. How powerful is it?
- Name one negative feelings flowing from you to you. How powerful is it?

You can do this exercise again with different people and different groups. You can list a larger set of feelings. When looking at yourself, negative feelings usually come from a wish that is not being met. Write down the wish. You can do this exercise every few months to keep track of changes in how you relate to others and to yourself.

It can be enlightening to try it with a person or group you don't like. Look especially at the negative life force that is coming towards you personally. It may not be as strong as you think it is. If it really is strong, ask yourself why you are still connected to these people. In the section on healing souls in Chapter 10, we'll look at ways to cut connections.

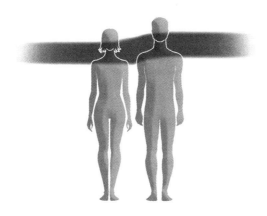

Voice Region (5)

The Voice region lets us send messages to and receive messages from other beings in physical reality and soul reality. We have many ways of communicating in physical reality. Words are one. We also have tones of voice, facial expressions, and body language. I think the Voice region has a part in all of these. This region works with the mouth, throat, ears, and other areas that send and receive messages, such as hands and eyes for texting or gesturing.

Body language also communicates. I think the Voice region deals with our body language as part of expressing emotions.

This region is also responsible for communication in soul reality. One example is sensing when something is staring at you. It also lets us speak with angels and know what is happening to a loved one who is far away. You can use this region to talk to God, but it is not the same as knowing God. That happens through the Info region. When you pray to God, words are not enough. You also need to reach out and touch Him or

Her with every part of your soul. Or as St. Teresa of Avila said, "Prayer is nothing else than being on terms of friendship with God."

Non-Western traditions have their thoughts on what the Voice region does. They say there are two parts: expressing emotions and handling voice functions.

Those traditions say there are 12 emotions: respect, contentment, offense, self-control, pride, affection, sorrow, depression, purity, dissatisfaction, honor, and anxiety. When I first looked at this, I thought it was a strange set. Then I read Paul Ekman's work on facial expressions.[51] He describes six basic emotions: anger, disgust, fear, happiness, sadness, and surprise.

Most of the emotions in the region relate to Ekman's set. Dissatisfaction and pride fit in Ekman's disgust category. Purity and honor might fit also, if they are based on avoiding things that disgust us. Sorrow and depression are parts of sadness. Offense is part of anger. Anxiety is part of fear. Contentment and affection might be included in happiness. Respect and self-control are showing feelings at the right time. Ekman's work helps us make sense of the Voice region.

The vocal functions include the sounds we speak and the musical notes we sing. Voice may also hold language skills we bring into this life. It would work with the Mind region to help us use and understand language.

The Voice region expresses what is happening in the rest of the regions. It might speak for the Heart when it wants to express love, anger, and hate. It is also responsible for letting others know what you figure out with your Mind or see in a blinding flash of angelic inspiration.

Poets tell us that there are no words to describe inspiration and love. At best words point the way. If the people you are talking to have had similar experiences, they will be able to understand. They will be able to translate your words back into what they have known.

If they haven't had the experience yet, your words can act as signposts. As they go through life, they will look back on the words you said. Then they might say, "Oh, now I understand" or "Oh, now I know how he felt." If you were telling them something you wanted them to do, they will know that they are on the right track. I have had this experience many times in my karate practice. Things I was told to look for years ago still show up now and then to let me know I am headed in the right direction.

This region also expresses Will and Wish. Adolph Hitler was an expert at expressing his wish to change Germany. Watching his speeches, you can see how he moved his followers beyond what his words said. He used Voice to tap into the Wish regions of the people listening to his speeches. He also spoke to, united, and shaped his followers' Wills. Leaders in all times use Voice to affect public opinion.

None of the other regions have a physical-reality way to communicate. Voice has many ways to communicate — words, voice tones, facial expressions, body language, along with its soul-reality connections — but there can still be problems. Voice does the best it can, but when the other regions disagree, especially if it's Mind and Heart, Voice's task may be impossible.

An important point to understand is that the body and soul are not tied together in parts. All of the body is available to all of the soul. A kiss is more likely to be from the Heart region than the Voice region. The hands and arms are tools that all of the regions use. We will discuss this again when we look at how bodies and souls are tied together.

The Voice region can be used for good or evil, depending on the life force behind the message being conveyed.

Life Force Processing

Voice is the dominant region of our current culture. We have tossed out thinking about political issues, for example. Instead, we spend our time throwing thoughtless words back and forth. We have little time for Heart interactions even though we spend hours texting words to one another.

Information is sent through the Voice region. It can be quite detailed, but it is never as complete as the information in our Mind. It may use less complex symbols. It may be more restricted in time and content. It may use fewer spatial and time dimensions. We work to improve the information with photos, movies, holographs, surround sound, and other technology. Even so, Voice is always less than what is in reality or the Mind.

Similar problems occur when the Voice region tries to work with Heart region energy. The Voice region can't send or receive as much energy as the Heart region. Connecting with Voice instead of Heart leaves us feeling alone and unenergized when we interact with others. We must use Mind and Heart instead of relying on just Voice when we connect.

Lessons

I'd like to take a look at why we should use our Minds and Hearts instead of Voices. If you are used to using Voice most of the time, these exercises might feel uncomfortable. The question is which way conveys the most life force, not how comfortable it feels. With time you can learn to process more life force comfortably. Remember that you can stop at any time.

One-Minute Exercise

The hands and arms can be used by any of the soul regions. Imagine you and another person like each other a lot. You want to share that good feeling. This exercise looks at two ways to convey what the Heart is feeling. You have about 30 seconds for each part.

- One way is to use the hands to send a text message. This uses Voice to describe what Heart is feeling. Write a quick message you would send. Write a quick message you would like to receive. On a scale of 0 to 10 rate how much of the Heart life force was included in each of the messages.

- Another way is to hug the person. Imagine doing that. On a scale of 0 to 10 rate how much of the Heart life force was included in the hug.

Compare how easy each method is and how long each takes to send the Heart's message. Voice is valuable, but it is not suitable for everything.

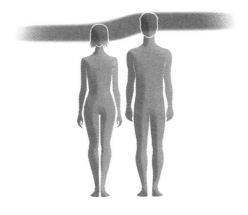

Mind Region (6)

The Mind region combines sensing and intellect. It has the ability to see and hear the world, to make sense of things, sort them out, and figure out how they fit together. It also answers questions for the lower regions when they have a problem they can't solve.

I think the overall purpose of the Mind is to figure out how to achieve our wishes in physical reality. Sometimes it takes a skillful Mind to even figure out what our wishes are. Physical reality can be very confusing. To understand the Mind we have to look at its three processes, sensing, sorting, and thinking.

Let's start by looking at sensing. When I talk about sensing, I include all of the senses, including the third eye. When New Age people look at the Mind region described by Eastern traditions, they focus on the third eye. They believe it is how we mystically understand the deep connectedness between all things. That leads to problems. Concentrating on the third eye suggests we run all of our connections through one spot in the soul. It isn't that simple. Every part of our soul connects with every part of every other soul.

The mystery of using the eyes to see, the ears to hear, or the skin to feel is wonderful. The senses pass information to all the other regions of the soul. We need to get away from the current Western idea that the senses are just mundane physical things while the "third eye" is totally spiritual and, somehow, more special. All the senses are special and represent aspects of our souls.

We need to feel Heart connecting to Heart, Will connecting to Will, and all the rest. To know our place in soul reality, we need to look at all of these. If the third eye has a special function, it is most likely to be the part of the Mind that brings connections between regions into our consciousness. The physical-reality sensing that brings the outside world to all of the regions of our souls is more important.

Assigning the eyes and ears to both the Mind region and the Voice region, as I have done, might seem confusing. The Mind region is more traditional. But the Voice region seems better if we want to send and receive with the same region. I think the best answer is that the senses are in the blended region between Voice and Mind. Both regions use them.

In my model the second process of the mind is sorting. Zen and other traditions believe that consciousness sorts the raw sensory data and passes some of it on. They call it a sixth sense organ. I prefer to leave it separate from the senses as a process of its own. Either way, the result is that only part of the information from our senses gets used in the Mind's thought process. Other sensory data get used in the processes of the other regions.

The third process of the Mind region is thought. Dreams are part of that process. When we sleep, the senses are shut off. It gives the other regions of the soul a chance to bring their concerns to the Mind. We need sleep to give the other regions of the soul a chance to access the Mind. One reason dreams seem so chaotic is that the realities of the other regions of the soul are very different from the Mind region's view of reality.

The Mind processes the information given to it and, in the end, suggests actions for the other soul regions to consider. I think the final decisions on what to do are made in the other regions of the soul. For example, we don't think about what we should do in a relationship, we typically follow our Heart. We are usually better off, though, when our Heart is informed by our Mind.

I use the word Mind to refer to part of the soul. I use the word brain to refer to the nerve cells in the head. We probably should add nerve cells in other parts of the body. There is evidence that the 100 million nerve cells in our digestive tract may be responsible for what we call gut reactions such as deciding what to eat and how to react to a threat.[52] There are similar nerve cells near the physical heart. They seem to be activated by emotions.

Thought happens when the Mind region of the soul and the physical brain work together. We have a very powerful physical brain that lets us think much more precisely than Mind alone is able to. We may have worked for billions of years to evolve it, or God may have given it to us, or both. Either way we should try to use it.

There is clear evidence that the Mind is connected with the brain. For example, when our brain is damaged, we don't think as well. It's another case where the physical is an important part of who we are. We need our physical brain to live in physical reality. There is also evidence that the Mind does things that can't be explained if the Mind is only in the brain. Let's start by looking at a fairly typical story of an out-of-body experience.

Phyllis Rodin[53] told me that when she was driving an open-top sports car, probably too fast, she went off the road on a sharp turn. She was thrown from the car and knocked out. At least her brain was knocked out. Her soul, including her Mind, was standing off to the side watching what happened. She went with the emergency crew as they took her body to the hospital. Later, at the hospital, her soul made the decision to go back into the body. From the medical team's point of view she woke up. Of course, from her point of view, she was aware the whole time.

There are books about near-death experiences that tell similar stories. Astral projection and shamanic soul journeys, where the soul travels away from the body, are similar. All of these reports show that the Mind is more than the brain.

Another way we can see that Mind is more than brain is by looking at memory. Western belief is that memories are stored in the brain. Scientists may talk about ideas like holographic fields and neural networks to explain how memories are stored. But people who have created artificial neural networks are extremely skeptical of any claims that the physical brain and/or the neural connections in it are responsible for memories.

For example, Mark Lawrence wrote about an experiment with caterpillars and butterflies.[54] Caterpillars were taught to avoid an odor. When the caterpillars turned into butterflies, the butterflies avoided the same odor. When Mark sent out his newsletter, several people said it was amazing that the caterpillars could store that kind of information in their nervous systems as they became butterflies. The only problem is that there is no nervous system when the change happens. Everything is broken down into primitive compounds. There isn't any physical structure to store memories. It's a place where biology based on physical reality is running into problems. However, if we allow butterflies to have a butterfly soul, then there is a place to store memories.

A fair question at this point is, how does the Mind store memories? But there actually is a better question: Do we believe that only the Mind region stores memories? I think the answer is a clear no. Regions store information that works with the life force they process. How are they stored? I don't know.

What I do know is that the Mind region senses, sorts, and thinks. It connects us to physical reality. It also suggests possibilities for the lower regions when they need help with their physical reality interactions.

Life Force Processing

The Mind region holds the most complex information and symbology that we can handle. We build up systems to help us plan our actions and predict outcomes. The systems aren't as complex as the ones we find in insights from the Info region. Still, we can make them complete and self-consistent if we try hard enough.

Our Mind stores and analyzes patterns. Our consciousness, which is our thoughts about ourselves, is handled by this region. This is where we hold memories. Mind and the physical brain work together for what we call thinking.

In addition, the Mind region reaches out into the world with the senses to gather information. All regions store their own types of memories, but the Mind memories are the ones we usually mean when we talk about remembering something.

The Mind region is able to send and receive some energy. We talk about people having a great mental force. When we say someone can give others creative insights, it probably means the person can transmit life force that contains Mind region energy along with clear information. Compared to the lower regions, this is not a lot of energy, though. The Mind region deals mostly with information.

Heart and Mind

Western culture is split on the relative importance of Heart and Mind. Will is sometimes mentioned, too, but usually because it makes Heart or Mind stronger. I think it's worthwhile to take a moment to compare the two.

Mind is the region intellectuals prefer. They use their Minds to understand the world. They think the Heart and its emotions get in the way of living a life that makes sense. For them, if the Mind can't deal with something, it isn't important.

What they leave out is that the Mind can ignore a lot of what is out there. As anyone in love knows, Mind can't process love. Love only works with the Heart. In fact, any kind of connecting and cooperating needs the Heart.

Others favor the Heart as being more important. They distrust the mind because it is isolated in one person. They think connections are what matters most.

I believe the best plan is to use both because each has a distinct purpose. Sandra Ingerman and Hank Wesselman point out that[55]

> In shamanic literature, the words "shamanic seeing" refer to seeing with our hearts rather than with our eyes. The shamans and visionaries of all the world's traditions know that the spirits make contact with us through the doorway in our hearts, and what we receive through that channel is sent to our higher mind, our intellect, our egoic soul or self, which then thinks about it, analyzes and integrates it, and makes decisions about it….
>
> Everything that happens or is perceived in a shamanic journey is part of the answer to the question we have asked, and the intellect's job is to assign meaning to the symbols that we have perceived and to figure them out. The heart and the mind are thus in relationship.

It's not just Heart and Mind. I think all of the soul regions are vital for understanding who we are as creatures living between the energy beings below and the inspiration of the gods above.

Lessons

The exercise for the Mind region looks at how we deal with information. There are many possible exercises. We can choose from sensing, sorting, and thinking. For this book, I want to look at dreaming.

One-Minute Exercise

Dreams process the questions of other regions of the soul. For this exercise think of three recent dreams. It's best to use dreams while you are asleep, but daydreams count, too. If you can't remember a sleep dream or if you can't find three dreams of any kind, see the note after the exercise.

Write down four pieces of information for each dream.

- A brief description of the dream.
- The wish behind the dream.
- The region of your soul that asked the question.
- Mind's suggestion for what should be done.

Here's a way to capture dreams if you can't remember any. You can also use this method to start a long-term exercise to find out more about yourself. Keep something to record your dreams beside your bed. When you wake up from a dream, write down the four pieces of information. Add how long you have been asleep. Then go back to sleep.

The question about how long you have been asleep is because I suspect there may be some kind of order to the soul regions asking their questions. I'm hoping you will write down 20 or so dreams and send the information about the region and how long you have been asleep to me. I don't want to know the description, the question, or the answer. That's private.

Info Region (7)

The top region (above the head) is the soul's connection to the structure of the universe. Perhaps it's a connection to God. Maybe it's the way people speak with angels. Most of all, it's our connection to sources of information that are normally beyond our ability to understand.

We started with the Energy region. That is outside the body and rooted in the energies that surround us. The next five regions connect us with our fellow journeyers. Some of those are people, animals, and spirits with souls like ours, whether they currently have bodies or not. We also connect to plants and trees, rocks, mountains, lakes, and seas.

Now we come to the Info region. While the Tantric tradition puts the topmost region above the head, I think it may be even farther from us than they suggest. We are not capable of completely understanding everything in the universe. The Info region is a place we can visit and draw information from. But there is more in that region than we can handle. We can't store all of that information in our Minds and use it in our daily lives.

Many people talk about gathering information through this region. Scientists speak of blinding flashes of inspiration, and so do poets. Musicians hear the music of the spheres. Scientists might disagree, but I think all of these come through the Info region. This knowledge is not within us. It's not from anyone we contact through the other soul regions. Inspiration from the Info region just feels different.

The times we reach into this region and access information from it are brief. Those times are glimpses of how a small part of the universe functions. Our Minds are not capable of holding all the information that is available there.

The theosophists[56] talk about the akashic records. Akasha is a Sanskrit word meaning "sky" or "space." The akashic records are believed to be records of the past that are written somewhere in the soul space around us. The theosophists believe that we can access the records stored there. There is something to their idea, but I think it would be more correct to say that the universe *is* the record, all time is available to us, and we can tap into everything that is there. We may not actually store memories. We just keep our connections through physical-reality time to when the events happened.

The Brahman traditions emphasize this region. Perhaps it is related to their thoughts about castes — social levels. Their highest social level works with thought and inspiration. They believe the "higher" regions are better than the lower. It seems to me like they choose to live in the higher regions while cutting connections with the lower regions. Some Westerners have similar beliefs. For example, Christians suggest that the ideal is to be one with God while giving up all earthly desires. Other traditions seem to choose a more balanced approach to the aspects of the soul.

Usually people think of this region as a connection to the divine. I agree but still have a question about what we mean by divine. The Hindu religion has many gods. Some are associated with building up, but others are associated with tearing things back down. The Norse gods have a trickster god (Loki) who works hard to undo the efforts of the other gods.

Most of the other systems with a pantheon of gods also have a trickster. In religions with one god, such as Islam, there is usually a devil who is responsible for a similar kind of destruction.

Some think that this region connects to good spirits and the bottom region connects to evil spirits. They would say God is in heaven above and the devil is in hell below. I don't think that is right. The Energy region in my model has nothing to do with deciding between good and bad. It is a place we gather energy to achieve our wishes. I suggest that the Info region is the home for both gods and demons. We go there to be inspired about ways to carry out our moral choices.

One important question is whether this region really is part of our soul. It feels to me like it is above my head. Does the soul extend outside the body? How far above the physical body does it go? Do we control this region or is it just a connection to spirits?

I choose to believe that the connection is part of me, but in the end it may not matter. To believe we control our access to God is usually dangerous. Believing we can deal with the devil seems to lead to even more problems. And we should never be certain that we remembered our flashes of inspiration completely or even accurately. They are more than our Minds can handle.

Life Force Processing

For humans the Info region is all about information. There is much more information in the Info region than we can handle.

Connections to this region are usually brief and weak. If we work hard at it, we can connect more deeply. Then we might be able to tap into a small part of what is there. As humans, some of us can see a small part of the totality well. We will never see the complete picture. This explains why one person's visions of the divine do not match up with visions other people have. Each is seeing only a small part of the whole.

When we discover truths, our Minds need energy to hold what we found in the Info region. It takes even more energy to tell others what we found. Thomas Edison's famous quote speaks to that: "Genius is one percent inspiration and ninety-nine percent perspiration."

A brilliant fellow named Carl Jung had one of those insights. He called it the Collective Unconscious.[57] Jung saw it as a place where the archetypes — perfect representations of characteristic types — reside and as a place where everything is deeply connected with everything else. I think he would place the Collective Unconscious in the Energy region, but I may be wrong about his thoughts. I think it is more likely that the archetypes are here in the Info region. This is the region of perfectly realized forms.

When I think of the energy of the Info region, I think of gods and lightning bolts. There is a lot of energy in a lightning bolt. Gods have the reputation of being able to generate that much energy on a regular basis. We are not gods. I think humans are unable to send or receive any energy through the Info region. For humans the connections made with this region are all information and no energy.

Lessons

There are many possibilities for exercises with the Info region. We could explore contacts with the beings who live there. We could go there for insight with a shamanic journey. But those might be too advanced for people who are just starting to work with their souls. Let's try a simple exercise that makes the world a better place every time you do it.

One-Minute Exercise

This is a blessing called The Cloak of the Angels, which I learned from Orion Foxwood.

I call down the cloak of the angels.
Fall down as a waterfall of light.
Guiding, guarding, blessing me,
By day and by night.

The physical movements for the first two lines are raising your hands up above your head — into the Info region of soul reality — and bringing a cloak down out of the sky. In the next line place the cloak over your shoulders. In the final line, wrap the cloak around yourself by touching your hands together in front of your heart.

Notice any change in how you feel. My reaction is often to feel safer and calmer. It can be hard to step into soul reality enough to have this work. At first it feels like pretend, but with practice it's just reaching into another place that's also real.

If you can't tell a difference with your first blessing, here are some things to try. As you reach up, sense the transition between the middle region and the upper region of the world. Some people describe it as moving through a soap bubble that doesn't break. Others say it's something like rising out of water into the air. Only your hands need to move into the upper region for this exercise.

Imagine taking hold of the cloak more strongly and feel it, maybe as a tingling. See the cloak as shimmering gold with silver sparkles. Watch it move down onto your shoulders. Feel the softness as it goes over your shoulders and then around you. Note especially how your Heart region feels.

You can also do this for others after getting their permission. For one person, stand in back of the person. All the movements are the same except that you put the cloak around the shoulders of the person (or a community or the whole world). Close your hands in front of the person's heart. Fill in the blank with the receiver of the blessing.

I call down the cloak of the angels.
Fall down as a waterfall of light.
Guiding, guarding, blessing _____,
By day and by night.

You can do this in person or at a distance. If you are with the person, you can ask him or her if there is a difference. Orion suggests you can send this blessing to everyone you care about. I think it's better to ask permission first.

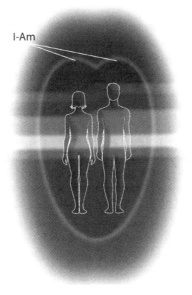

I-Am

I-Am

The I-Am provides the boundary that separates each of us from everything else in soul reality. It surrounds and flows through the middle five regions of the soul and expands to cover the Info and Energy regions, if we have enough life force. It provides protection for soul regions when we interact with anything outside of ourselves and helps coordinate soul regions inside our soul. It can join with other I-Ams.

Other people writing about souls use terms like subtle body and energy body. They often have seven or more layers. I think it is less complicated than that. One I-Am that contains the soul regions seems like enough.

How the I-Am appears in soul reality is directly tied to the amount of life force in the soul. In a healthy, powerful soul, the soul regions and the I-Am are larger than the body. Sometimes the I-Am is much larger. When we say someone is larger than life, we are describing someone with a powerful personality. In soul terms, we are talking about a very large soul.

We also know people who barely make an impression. I believe this is usually because their souls have very little life force. The I-Am and the soul regions it contains may be small enough to hide inside the physical body. This is not a healthy situation because it leaves the body open to danger in both realities.

Sometimes I look at the need for a soul that is larger than the body from a martial arts perspective. I want to thank my karate friend, Mike Panian, for his insight on the three zones.

The outer zone is beyond the area where I can be physically harmed. The outer edge of my I-Am is starting to connect with the outer edge of my opponent's I-Am. The engagement has started in soul reality although outsiders might not see anything in physical reality.

The middle zone is where we can start to physically interact with one another. This is where most people would say their I-Am exists, but I think it can extend farther. It's also the closest distance we feel comfortable standing when we are talking to a stranger.

The inner zone is right next to my physical body. It is the closest I can let an opponent get physically and still be safe from harm. At this distance there are strong interactions between my soul and my opponent's soul. The interactions have been going on ever since we noticed each other, but they are much stronger at this distance.

I think the I-Am needs to cover all of the zones. If the I-Am doesn't reach out past the body, it can't act in any of the zones. Harm can reach us without any protection from the soul. A person with a small I-Am is easy to run over. For a healthy body and soul we need to have enough life force so the I-Am is powerful enough to extend out from the body and protect it.

The I-Am is also important for friendship and love. When we are in love, the I-Am is more open to the other person. Some couples feel best when all the regions of the soul are deeply shared. Others want limits on how close they feel. The I-Am can handle any of the combinations as long as both people agree.

It's important to remember that sharing is all right, but domination isn't. In this life we are here to be separate and connected at the same time. Letting someone else dictate thoughts, feelings, or wishes is not part of the plan. Pay attention if your I-Am is warning you about this kind of problem. You are looking out for your highest and best good when you get out of that kind of situation. Your I-Am will try to separate you from the unhealthy situation. Find help from other people if you need it.

Before leaving this idea, I need to talk about one more case. Sometimes people who make no impression are very powerful. That kind of person has an I-Am that is very large, but it has the ability to cloak the person so the person can't be seen. This is especially useful when doing shamanic work because it makes it very hard for evil beings to track us and cause us harm. Many spirit beings have this kind of cloaking.

Another aspect of the I-Am's protection is that it keeps soul regions from being harmed. Shamanic traditions know that traumas can break pieces off of the regions of our soul. We also lose pieces of our soul when we choose to give them away. For example, we have the idea of giving our Heart to someone else.

Losing pieces of our soul, whether it's from trauma or by choice, is not a good idea. Soul pieces that are lost can stay scattered throughout soul reality until a soul retrieval is done.

We are better off when we keep all of our soul together. For example, it's better to keep all of our Heart so we can continue to send life force from it to the person we care about. The I-Am can contain the soul in a way that lets the life force out while keeping parts of the soul from leaving, too. A healthy I-Am protects our souls from losing pieces of itself.

Let's look at what some other people think about how the I-Am provides separation and protection.

One person thinks of it as a flying teacup with a lid on top. If you know the comic strip Rose Is Rose, think about Pasquale's dream ship.

The cup can be sealed off for protection, but it usually allows energy to move into and out of it.

Another person thinks of the I-Am as a set of control rooms. There seems to be a level for each region of the soul. He travels to the control rooms to work with people-shaped beings who are in each soul region. When he goes outside of the control room, he is in soul reality. He sees connections with others coming into each of the control rooms. Sometimes the connections show up even when they aren't wanted. With effort, he can open and close the connections to keep himself safe.

This is an important aspect of the I-Am. Inside that area of soul reality you are in charge of yourself. David Spangler uses the concept of standing in your own sovereignty.

The other function of the I-Am is to coordinate the soul regions. Each soul region has its own functions. It also needs to share life force with other soul regions for both energy and information. I think the I-Am is the pathway between the regions. That means the I-Am does more than wrap the soul regions to protect them. It also flows through them to give them a way to connect.

Let's look at an example. People who do acupuncture use energy meridians that connect parts of the body. What they observe is that working on one area of the body can heal other areas. The way the I-Am connects soul regions is how my model would explain this. I think some of the connections are permanent while others form and dissolve as required.

With all of its functions, the I-Am creates the totality of what we are. As long as the soul has enough life force, the I-Am can accomplish all of its functions — coordination, integration, separation, protection, and sovereignty.

Life Force Processing

Some I-Ams may be rigid, brittle, full of holes, torn, broken, shattered, or even nonexistent. Those leave the soul unprotected from dangerous life force. On the other hand, an I-Am may be so tightly closed with shields and protections that no life force can get in. That's not healthy either because our souls need life force to live.

The best sort of I-Am does three things. It is strong enough to protect us from danger. It is open to receiving positive life force for all the regions of our soul and reaches out from the Energy and Info regions to gather life force in the upper and lower regions of the world. It lets our soul regions send life force to others without losing parts of our soul in the process.

The best I-Am is resilient, flexible, and as open or closed to the life force around us as it needs to be for our highest and best good. It can shield our soul when it needs to and gather positive life force when it is available. It gives the soul regions enough space to feel comfortable and makes enjoyable contact with the I-Ams of other people.

Having a healthy I-Am is required for having a healthy soul.

Lessons

The lessons to learn about the I-Am are related to its ability to protect us when we need protection and still let in the life force we need to live. We'll look at one example here.

One-Minute Exercise

This exercise looks at the openness of your I-Am.

Find a safe place where there is a lot of positive life force. It will probably be outside in a natural setting. For this exercise it's best to be away from people and their confusing mix of positive and negative life force.

Stand or sit tall. Breathe deeply so it feels like your breath is filling your whole body. One by one open the part of the I-Am surrounding each region of your soul and pull some positive life force into that region. For each region write down how much life force you were able to pull in. Use 3 for a lot, 2 for some, 1 for a little, and 0 for none. Here is a list of the regions: Energy, Wish, Will, Heart, Voice, Mind, and Info.

If you have regions where it's hard to pull in life force, there are two possibilities. The I-Am might be blocking it or the region might not be able to accept life force. It doesn't matter which it is. What you want to do is measure this every month or so to make sure you are making progress in being able to receive life force in every region. You may even find that what you think of as a lot of life force changes. What seemed like a lot when you started might not seem like as much later on. Make a note of that in your records, too.

This exercise can also be done another way. Find a chaotic place with a lot of negative life force. Make it someplace where you body will be safe. A TSA screening line at a busy airport comes to mind. Riding in a car stuck in rush hour traffic is another possibility, especially if the driver is seriously irritated. Go through each of the regions and write down how much of the negative life force you are able to block out. This is also good as a monthly checkup.

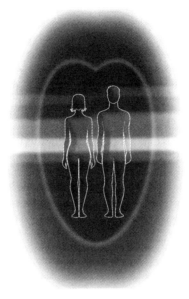

Soul as a Whole

As humans we stretch between the Info region and the Energy region, not quite fully in control at either the top or the bottom regions of our souls. Some beings are in control of their Info region. They can use that region with energy. Beings with an Energy region they control can use that region with information. They can create new things in the world. We're usually not that skilled.

Let's look at how this model compares with some other models of the soul.

Many martial arts groups talk about the importance of what they call the center. This is usually placed in the lower abdomen. It's in the regions I call Wish and Will. Some groups also talk about centers of movement in the upper back, part of the Heart region, and centers of perception at the base of the skull, part of Mind.

The Incan medicine people emphasize the Belly (Will), Heart, and Mind. They recognize other regions, too, but these three are the most important for them.

There are other groups who also speak of different regions. All of them see the advantage of looking at who we are in all our complexity. If a model is too simple, it doesn't explain all we need to know.

Next let's look at how important souls are in our lives. Here are five things this model of the soul gives us.

1. Having a soul gives us a way to feel more fully alive. It lets us love. It lets us know we are part of a greater experience, both with other humans and with everything else in our realities. It gives more meaning to our lives because who we are and what we do continue beyond our death.

2. From a healing perspective, this model gives us a lot of tools to help with sadness and pain. When parts of our soul are damaged or lost because of trauma, Western medicine usually can't fix that loss. But this model shows that there are ways to recover lost parts of the soul, remove harmful influences, and increase positive energy. Because we have souls we can heal each other and ourselves to lead happier lives.

3. The ideas in the model can be used to explain angels, ghosts, and other spirits. They have the same soul structure without having a physical body. Other things in the world also have souls. These souls may be more or less powerful than our souls. Simple souls may not control as many of the regions. But they all have a similar structure. If we talk about being made in God's image, this is the image I think we are discussing.

4. This model lets us explain almost all of the things that we can do that are not explained by our physical models. All of the ideas we talk about in evidence are covered by this model.

5. Beyond that, this soul model can be used to combine many different theories about who we are as human beings. Psychological theories often seem confusing because they disagree with one another. I think this model helps explain why the models disagree.

Different theories describe different parts of the soul. Each is correct within one region, but can't explain everything. When we combine the theories as being true for part of our soul, they make a lot more sense.

Understanding ourselves is a big step in knowing how to love one another and make ourselves and the world better.

When we learn to feel the souls that are in all of us — in everything — we escape from the illusion of isolation. We can connect with others. We can heal and grow.

Lessons

The soul works best when all the regions are working together in harmony. The exercise below has some things for you to look at.

This can be a difficult exercise for some people. So remember the rules for every exercise: If something feels wrong, stop. Bring yourself back to your normal way of being. Ask yourself or people and spirits you trust if what you are doing is for your highest and best good. If not, ask how to change what you are trying to do so it is.

One-Minute Exercise

This is an exercise to check out how well the regions of your soul agree with one another. You will be asked to consider the goals for each region of your soul. Before reading on, find some way to write down your answers — pen and paper, notes in an e-book, or whatever. The important thing is to write everything down. If you don't, your Mind will trick you and you'll forget answers from the other regions that your Mind doesn't like.

This exercise looks at what each region of your soul wants you to pay attention to. There are seven regions and the I-Am, so to keep this exercise under a minute you have only seven seconds for each region. Write down up to three answers. Don't think about it. Just write fast.

- Energy: What do you do that leaves you with more energy than when you started?
- Wish: Where do your daydreams take you?
- Will: What do you feel like you should be doing right now?
- Heart: What do you love to do with your friends?
- Voice: What are your favorite things to talk about?

- Mind: What do you think about all of the time?
- Info: In the best of all possible worlds, what would be happening now?
- I-Am: What is the outside world pressuring you to do?

The first time you go through this exercise often gives the answers that are truest for you. It doesn't have to be that way. Getting true answers when you know what is going to be asked is possible. You give each region permission to speak as it is answering. It is useful to do the exercise every once in a while to see how you are changing.

No great analysis is required. You're just checking to see if all the regions have compatible agendas. For most people they don't. You can work toward better agreement by paying attention to every region and what it wants. Use your mind to reason out what will work for you. The other regions will usually go along if they are listened to. Your life will be better as you learn more about yourself and heal.

One interesting test, especially the first time, is to set the list aside for two days. Then try to create the same list again from memory. Don't ask the regions again — make the list from what your Mind remembers. Knowing how well (or badly) your Mind really remembers the goals of the other regions explains why we need to listen to all the parts of the soul. If we don't, we spend a lot of time fighting ourselves.

Blending Soul Regions

It helps explain who we each are when we look at how our soul regions work together. While it's not always true, the cooperation is often in regions that are next to one another. I think it's similar to the way colors in a rainbow change smoothly from one primary color to the next. For example, between blue and green we can see many types of blue-green. Let's take a look at pairs of regions to show how this works in souls.

When Energy and Wish regions work together we see a person with a lot of energy to devote to a cause. The energy may be positive or negative. The cause may be healing or harmful. If the cause is getting enough food to eat, we can expect the person to use any energy that is there. Others may be hurt. If the cause is helping others, there is a better chance that the life force will be positive. We don't see this kind of directed energy very often. We're clear about wishes that are related to what our body needs. We are not as good at finding the soul wishes that we bring here from before we are born. They seem to get lost.

When we look at the blend of Wish and Will, we see want. This is a combination of something we hope to get while having the life force to get it. I'm using the word want to describe something a person is ready to act on. Both the wish and the knowledge of how to act need to be present for the person to act.

When Will and Heart blend, we get something that looks like teamwork or group spirit. The Will provides the focused life force to accomplish something. The Heart gives us the connection to do it with others.

Voice doesn't seem to have a lot to do when it isn't blended. Usually it blends with Heart and Mind at the same time. If it's mostly Voice and Heart, we are expressing emotions. If it's Voice and Mind, the blend is trying to help someone else understand an idea. It's usually all three together. Mind clarifies what is said and Heart makes sure the message is presented so the other person can hear it.

Mind and Info combine for inspiration. If complete understanding is anywhere, it is in Info. Mind is the part of it we can hold. When Mind and Info blend, there is a moment when we feel a real depth of comprehension. Sometimes our Mind grows enough to hold a lot of what we have discovered. Other times most of it is lost. It's the reason we should all write down our good ideas when we have them. It may seem like we will remember them forever. That's what inspiration feels like. If we record them, it's easier to get back to the inspiration point.

There are many other ways that soul regions blend. It's not important to name and describe all of them. In fact, it's probably a way to make everything more confusing. What you should remember is that the soul regions do not have rigid tasks. It's important to look at how the regions blend together when we are trying to figure out what is going on in a person's soul.

Souls in Everything, Evolution of Souls

I want to make it clear, if I haven't already, that I think there are souls in everything. My favorite is the souls I find in the sacred stones the Incan healers call *khuyas*. I work with these stones for part of my practice. While they are very different from human souls, they are definitely beings with their own personalities.

Other people talk about the souls in nature. Souls are in plants and animals. Most people who consider souls find an overriding soul that is the soul of the whole earth. She goes by many names including Gaia and Mother Earth. Many people recognize other spirits that go by names like angels, devas, Sidhe, and djinns.

One question that I still wonder about is how souls change as we move through lives. The best I can do right now is say I don't know. We might become different kinds of souls if we work to heal ourselves and grow stronger. Considering the details of souls beyond our human ones is something I'm leaving for another time.

5. LIFE FORCE

> When you are in rhythm with the symphonic
> pulse of the universe, you can feel the
> electrifying current of the life force, a hundred
> thousand gigawatts of light bursting out of each
> and every cell.
>
> — *Christine Pechera*

Now that we've taken a look at souls, it's time to look at the life force that powers them. There are many places that we find life force. It's hard to explain all of what we see in either physical reality or soul reality without it.

Life force goes by many names. In Japanese it is ki and shows up in martial arts (ai-ki-do, for example) and healing (Reiki). Chinese use the word chi or qi, as in tai chi or Qigong. The Hindus call it prana. Christians say grace or, perhaps, the Holy Spirit. It has sometimes shown up on the fringes of Western psychology, for example as Wilhelm Reich's Orgone energy. The Incan medicine people use the word *kausay*. There are many more words. But they all talk about aspects of the same thing: life force.

I am proposing this life force as an addition to the four physical forces. Those are gravity, electromagnetism, and the strong and weak nuclear forces. I believe those forces were created as part of making physical reality. In our lives, they exist. Life force exists, too, but we often get too caught up in physical reality to see it. This is especially true in the last 400 years where we have made great advances in defining what goes on in physical reality.

Most people use the term life force or any of its other names in two different ways. Usually it doesn't matter. But because I want to say life force is like the physical forces, I want to make this clear. Life force that transfers something from one place to another is like a physical-reality force. Life force inside a soul is more like physical-reality energy. So we have life force (as a force) sending life force (as an energy) from one place to another. I haven't found any words that are clearer than life force, but I welcome suggestions.

I don't think I need to say more about the physical forces here. To prove we have souls we only need to talk about the life force. Let's start by looking at hoocha in more detail. Then we can look at the two things life force sends: energy and information. We'll look at how life force can be positive or negative. After that we'll look at how life force explains some of our experiences better than anything else.

Hoocha

Hoocha is everywhere.

When we fight with our family — hoocha. When we get drunk or stoned and do something stupid — hoocha. When we pollute the air or water because we don't care — hoocha. When we suppress, oppress, terrorize, or otherwise harm other nations — big hoocha — and probably a lot of negative life force, too.

One of the best places to find hoocha in something like normal life is reality TV. The dysfunction that the director plays up for the show is hoocha. I don't watch, but I think one of the big attractions is that you can watch someone with even more hoocha than you have. The problem is that the hoocha, being part of the soul reality, spills out of the TV and gets all over the people watching. If we see or hear something, it becomes part of us.

There are better choices when we care about our souls. I'll know the message that we all have souls is getting around when I hear reality TV called hoocha TV and hear about people avoiding it.

So what does hoocha feel like?

Let's say you want to play the guitar. Hoocha is like having chewing gum on the strings. Let's say you're looking for an off-ramp on the freeway. Hoocha is like fog keeping you from seeing where you are going. If you want to hike along a trail, hoocha is like the mud that clings to your boots. If you are flying in an airplane, hoocha is like volcanic ash getting into your engines.

It's stuff that gets in the way when you want to do something. There can be a little bit or a lot. It can stop you completely or just be a minor annoyance. The fog can be a thin mist or so heavy you can't see the front of your car. The mud can be in a few spots or a continuous slog through gunk up to your waist.

Notice that hoocha is not negative life force trying to do you harm. It's just stuff that is getting in the way. I sometimes catch myself using the term hoocha to describe a situation full of negative life force. It's not a good idea to do that, though. Dealing with hoocha and dealing with negative life force require different techniques. Not knowing which situation we are in can lead to dangerous mistakes.

One significant aspect of hoocha is that it hangs around until something removes it. I have found beings in the world that can do that. My sense is that they turn the hoocha into positive information, as in, "Now I see why I can't get along with my _____." I ask for their help a lot.

If you want them to help you, you can ask, too. One possible image is thousands of little star-like beings flying around nibbling on hoocha and shining brighter with every bite. This image works really well when you have hoocha in the way of information. Less hoocha gets in the way and you have more light to see your path.

If you have hoocha stopping you from getting energy, you might think about earthworm-like beings eating through the hoocha. The hoocha goes away and your roots have tunnels to reach the energy you need.

It helps when you can see your hoocha and direct the appropriate being to a particularly troublesome chunk. At the very least say please and thank you to them.

Now we can move on to look at the components of the life force.

Energy

Let's start by looking at the energy part of life force. The energy part brings energy into regions of the soul. The regions use the energy to act. With energy a region can do something. Without energy it can't do anything.

I know of two ways for energy to get into a soul region. It can be pulled in freeform from the universe or it can come from other soul regions. When it comes from soul regions, it can come from regions in the same soul or from regions in another soul. I'll talk more about the details as part of the discussion about connections in Chapter 7.

I'm not sure, even for myself, whether we get more energy straight from the universe or from other soul regions.

I know that energy is shared between regions in my own soul. I can feel it coming up through the Energy region and moving through the rest of my soul. I also know I get energy from being around other people. I find many things, especially difficult karate practices, that are easier when a group of us shares our energy. This is probably Will combined with Heart to make a feeling of teamwork.

Energy from the universe is less clear. I believe everything that exists has a soul. For example, when I'm properly dressed and sometimes when I'm not, I love to walk in the rain. I think each of those raindrops has a bit of soul. So is the energy I get from walking in the rain from the souls in the raindrops (among other things) or is it from the universe as a whole? In this case, I believe it's the raindrops, trees, clouds, wind, and whatever else is around.

My Energy region connects with Pachamama, who is a very powerful spirit of the earth. So energy that comes from her is coming from another soul. My Energy region also seems to connect with something deeper. I draw energy from there, too. What I don't know is whether that deeper universe is a place with free energy we can tap into. Sometimes I think of it that way. Other times I think it's easier to work with the idea that the universe as a whole is also a huge soul and we are connecting to part of it when we draw this universal energy.

The good news is that there is always enough energy somewhere. In the shamanistic traditions we can find the energy in the lower region. I think of this as the Energy region of the soul of the universe. It's a really big place. There may be some limit to the amount of energy there, but humans aren't going to use more than a tiny bit of it. We humans might not be bringing in a whole lot of positive energy right now, but knowing we have souls gives us a reason to work harder at it. I'm not worried that we will run out. There is enough.

The real problem is whether we can access the energy. Hoocha can stop us from reaching the positive energy we need. Traumas damage our connections between soul regions, both within our own soul and between our soul and another soul.

Hoocha and trauma are different because hoocha is confusion that stops us even when the ability to transfer energy is still available. Trauma is damage to the connection itself. Even if we see the trauma and the need for energy clearly, we still need to heal the trauma before we can get the energy we need. Getting energy isn't the only issue. We can also lose it or get negative energy.

Other beings can steal energy from us. They can also fill us full of negative energy, which has an even worse effect.

All of these result in having too little positive energy. We'll look at the situation with hoocha here and the problems with trauma and other beings in Chapter 7.

Imagine that you have a wish to do something. That should be pretty easy because we wish to do something pretty much all the time. Imagine also that your Will agrees to support your wish and your Heart is getting a lot of positive feedback from your friends. And still, you can't find the energy to get started.

Let me give you a personal example. I wish to write this book. My Will and Heart are totally on board with the project. Voice is ready to type. Mind and Info are bringing in and digesting information. But it's really hard to start.

As I look around my room, it's in its usual, kinda messy state. There are things I need to do scattered on my desk. A printer that needs to be recycled is sitting in the corner. There are three or four (or maybe five) piles of folders that need to be filed away. I can also see some boxes that need to be moved to storage. And there are e-mails I haven't gotten around to answering sitting behind my Word window.

There's not much negative here and there's nothing I can't deal with, but it isn't dealt with. It's sitting around like little barriers to writing that say, "Do me first." Focusing on writing this book is really hard with all the competition. And I believe this mess, my leaving things out where they pull me, is one of my personal forms of hoocha.

This hoocha is stopping me from concentrating on gathering the positive energy — and information — I need in each of the soul regions so I can get on with the task of writing. It's like walking on a rocky path at night. The distractions keep getting in the way of what I wish to do.

When I remove the distractions, or the hoocha earthworms help me remove it, I can reach the energy and get on with my work. That's what the energy part of life force is all about. It lets us make the effort to do the things we wish to do.

Information

The information part of life force moves ideas from one place to another. What moves from one place to another through the Voice region is expressed in words. In the Heart region, it's feelings. In the Mind, it's ideas.

As with energy, we get information from many sources. We may get it directly from the universe. We definitely get it from other beings. I think most of the information we get comes through Voice. It may also move directly between Heart regions or Mind regions.

We use the information to decide what directions we want to go to fulfill our wishes. A wish is usually pretty simple. How we accomplish our wishes may take a lot of thought. We may have to try several ways before we find one that works. It's the Mind's job to put together possible solutions from the information we gather.

The information is shared between our soul regions. Mind suggests possibilities to Wish. It can be a fairly complex picture of what will happen. Wish looks at the end result and decides if the result satisfies the wish it has. There can be a lot of compromise because some wishes may not be possible. How this all works out is through negotiation between the regions of your soul.

Sometimes wishes are contradictory. We might wish to lose weight while at the same time we wish to eat because we feel hungry. There really isn't a good solution to the conflict. Hunger wins, most of the time, because it is the more basic wish. When hunger is combined with other basic needs, such as sleep, the hunger gets even harder to control. Sometimes the wishes are so strong and the situation so impossible that the Mind shuts down and we end up bingeing without thought.

Hoocha can make the situation even more difficult. It can cloud the Mind so that possible solutions can't be found. Calling on the hoocha stars can clear out the hoocha and let us look at a wider range of possibilities. The upper region of the world may even be able to inspire us to find truly creative solutions.

Positive and Negative

The energy in life force comes in positive and negative forms. Positive energy is used for making things better. Negative energy makes things worse. It is possible to decide whether something is better or worse by looking at the growth of all the beings in the situation.

Good happens when there is more positive life force. More energy and more information are available for everyone. Most of the beings learn and grow more energetic. When we have good intentions, walking into a place with good energy feels right. If we have bad intentions, a good place feels really uncomfortable.

Bad happens when one of the beings is taking life force from the others. Most of the entities in the place feel drained and unable to act in their best interests. When we have good intentions, walking into a place with bad energy makes us feel uneasy or downright scared. Our thoughts are usually centered on how to get out of there without getting hurt. When we have bad intentions, we like places with bad energy because they support our wish to harm others.

Hoocha builds up like a dark cloud where there is a lot of negative life force so that no one can see what is really happening. Someone from the outside may be able to see what is going on and help. People on the inside are usually so confused that they can't find the information or the energy to do anything.

Being aware of positive and negative life force lets us put up our shields when we are threatened. That way we stay as safe as possible in this dangerous world.

Finding Life Force

Life force is everywhere. It's really not that hard to find. I believe everything we interact with has some kind of soul, and they all need to be powered by life force. If you want to limit souls to "living" things like plants and animals, it still means there is a lot of life force moving around.

One idea that I want to dispel is that life force is a gentle, loving thing. Even if we look only at positive life force, I think gentleness is a myth.

Many practices that use life force start with the assumption that we can live our lives without doing harm to other beings. They believe that we can live in caring relationships with one another and never do anything else any harm. It just isn't so.

When you think about it, physical life is a ferocious thing. Humans, like all animals, destroy life to maintain life. Many animals fight within their own species and most will fight against another animal that wants to harm them. Humans are not alone in that. We may think that we can make choices to do no harm, but we can't. Even humans who choose to not eat other animals still are eating plants, and those plants have souls, too.

For that matter, plants are ferocious in their own way. They grow thorns and irritants that hurt us. They produce substances that kill their predators. They put toxins in the soil that stop other plants from growing. They reach out leaves to block the sun from rivals. They spread out roots to take all the nutrients they can, even if it starves another plant nearby.

Does this mean that the struggle between different beings is powered by negative life force? Is this an act of destruction? I'm pretty sure the answer is no. Let me try to explain why.

In physical reality the rules are clear. Souls are part of every single thing in physical reality. But things in physical reality change all the time. Water forms raindrops and then the drops go into a lake or splash across the ground. Our skin sheds cells and new cells replace them. A rabbit eats a carrot so it has the energy to escape a coyote. We harvest 100 acres of corn to make tamales. It's just how physical reality works. Any soul that wants to experience the physical knows the rules.

So all of this change and growth, living and dying is what we learn by being here. If we are doing it right, we understand that and honor the exchange of life force that comes from the changes. The rabbit honors the carrot it is eating. The soul of the carrot, if it wants to stick around in physical reality, goes to find a seed, so it can start over again physically. Or it might want to try out being a cucumber plant. I think all of these can be positive learning experiences, filled with positive life force.

These lessons aren't as easily available in soul reality. In physical reality we can learn how to be part of the circle of life. Speaking of the "Circle of Life," it's also the name of a song by Elton John, who says:

> Some say eat or be eaten.
> Some say live and let live.
> But all are agreed as they join the stampede,
> You should never take more than you give.

I believe that never take more than you give is the essence of the question when we decide if we are seeing positive or negative life force. Positive life force gives. If we take from one place, we give in another. Negative life force is just taking and not giving back.

Those who want to help the world be a healthier and more loving place, and I hope you are one of them, need to work with positive life force. Here are some things you can do. Start by recognizing that we all have souls — that everything in physical reality has a soul. Honor those souls as best you can.

Life is too complicated to honor every soul every time we interact, but we can honor the larger ones, such as the cucumber soul that oversees all the cells of the cucumber. We can honor the sun and the great systems of weather. We can honor our food and each of the plant and animal beings that have died so we can live. We can honor the plants and animals that are part of our environment. When we take from plants and animals to keep ourselves alive, we need to give that energy back to other plants and animals somehow. We can honor each other as humans with souls and help each other in our individual and mutual growth.

I want to make it clear that this is not some sort of trade where we try to keep everything equal. We will probably never have a day where positive life force that we give to others exactly balances the life force that comes to us. It's not productive to even think that way.

What we need to do instead is live in a dynamic state of balance. Some days we get more than we give and other days we give more than we get. We need enough to clean up our souls and the hoocha that surrounds us. We destroy ourselves when always give more life force than we take in because we can't take care of ourselves that way. But then we give to others what we can. We don't keep life force for ourselves when we have some we can spare.

There are many ways to give life force. One of the first is to give thanks for what we have received. We can sing and dance. We can show loving and caring for others. We can share. Sometimes it's enough to just dream of a better world. Those good thoughts and feelings can become part of soul reality even if you only think the thoughts or feel the feelings. If you share them in person, in a blog, or on any of the other social media, it's even better.

There is a lot more to be said about using and sharing life force. It's one of the largest ethical and moral topics we have. We don't hear questions about life force asked often enough, but it's part of making decisions about just about everything. It might include what foods you choose to eat, how you talk to your family, issues of how we divide resources among all of the beings we are connected to, how we take care of the health of our planet, and what we choose to do about moving out toward the stars.

But that's beyond the scope of this book. What we are trying to do here is to prove we all have souls. Once the world accepts that we all have souls and we all need life force, many of the difficult questions become easier.

Lessons

For the life force exercise, I want to take a quick look at our place in the movement of life force throughout the planet. One point I want to make is that even in the simple things we still use a lot of life force. The other is that we can choose to use life force in ways that minimize what we take from the world. But we can also make different choices that maximize what we can give to the world.

One-Minute Exercise

This is a two-part exercise. For each part use about 30 seconds to write down your answers. The first part is hard enough that I'm going to supply some possibilities. They include creatures that help with the process, but eventually die because that's what happens to all creatures. Use the ones that are appropriate and supply other answers of your own.

Imagine your favorite vegetable. Use a fruit if you don't have a favorite vegetable. If you can hold one in your hands while you do the exercise, it's even better.

- Write down what gave life force in the form of work or even death as part of getting that vegetable into your hands. Some possibilities are dinosaurs to provide gasoline, weeds that were removed to let the plant grow, harmful insects killed by pesticides, insects that pollinated the flowers, the plants that produced the vegetable, earthworms that improved the soil, bacteria that were washed off the vegetable, and all the humans involved in growing, picking, shipping, and selling. The sun and the rain and the soil have a part in this, too.
- Write down how you will use the life force you get from the vegetable to give back to your community.

The first part of the exercise is to show how much impact even our simple need for food has on life force. The second part leads to thinking about how you can do your share. One possibility is to grow your own food to minimize the life force used to create it. Another is to support those who grow food in life-enhancing ways and use the time you save to give life force to the world in other ways. I'm not advocating for either choice, just hoping you will make an informed decision that keeps your interactions with life force balanced.

6. LIFE FORCE AND SOUL

We are the miracle of force and matter
making itself over into imagination and will.
Incredible. The Life Force experimenting with
forms. You for one. Me for another. The
Universe has shouted itself alive. We are one of
the shouts.

— *Ray Bradbury*

In this chapter I want to talk about what soul regions do with life force. In the first part of the chapter we'll look at how a single region handles life force. It changes all the time as the region decides how much life force to hold and how it wants to connect to other regions inside and outside the soul. I think we can predict the changes when we know what is happening to the soul. The soul regions aren't just blobs. Knowing more about them helps us understand ourselves better.

The final part of the chapter looks at how the regions get together with the I-Am to make our whole soul. We'll look at how the regions work together — or not — to reach decisions about what we will do.

If you want to know more about soul connections, you might take a look at my earlier book, *Calculating Soul Connections.* I've learned a lot since then, so some of the details have changed. For example, you won't find anything about the I-Am because I didn't realize how important it is. (It's good to keep learning.) Even with its flaws, the book has many useful insights and details that did not fit in this book.

Region Actions

Each soul region has three things it does to maintain its level of life force. All of the actions try to maintain the level the region prefers.

Energy and information can be stored in a region. The first thing a region does is decide on the amount of life force in wants in the region.

The second kind of action moves life force between regions in the same soul. Life force can come from or go out to other regions in the same soul. The third kind of action moves life force between each soul region and the rest of the world.

How much life force is stored, how and when and where it goes are all determined by the region working with the I-Am. This is not a purely mechanical process. There is a strong component of feedback from anything a region interacts with. The regions change all the time.

Let's look in more detail at the three types of actions.

Life Force Level

The amount of life force in a region depends on how much life force the region has learned to handle and how much life force it wants to have. We can learn how to hold more and decide how much we want. What we want and what we are able to get from outside ourselves are the most important parts in setting the amount of life force in a region.

The central job of each region is to maintain its life force level of both energy and information. Each region has a maximum level it can handle. Each region also has a preferred level of life force. The maximum and preferred levels can move higher or lower based on experiences. The preferred level can also change based on the situation.

For example, if you really wish to do something, all of the regions that are involved will try to bring up their level of life force to fulfill the wish.

At any moment each region has its current level of life force. If things are going well, this will be what it wants to have. For many reasons the available life force may be very different from what the region wants. The region will use its ability to move life force to do the best it can to get to the preferred level. When we're talking about the energy component of the life force, this discussion makes sense.

When we talk about information, it's not as clear what is going on. We need to look at the region's history and what it gets from outside the region. The region can recall history or get information from other regions in the same soul or from outside the soul, just like it brings in more energy. Usually more is better.

Sometimes a region ignores information that might keep the person from fulfilling a wish. This is the kind of thing that happens when Voice and Mind regions choose to not know about a lover's lies because Wish wants the Heart to have someone to love. It is not a healthy thing to do. Fixing the problem requires changing the wish from having someone to love to being with someone we can love and who loves us. Then all the regions can use all the information that is available.

The life force levels in the regions of our souls change continuously. Some levels are better than others. The good news is that we can learn to be aware of the levels and use intention to make the balance between regions healthier.

Connections inside the Soul

Connections inside our souls let life force move between regions. Being in a physical body makes it hard to feel life force moving between the regions, but it is possible. When we understand our souls better, we make better connections.

Many things, especially trauma, can damage these connections. Trauma usually restricts the flow of life force. But sometimes it opens the pathway too wide so too much life force goes through. Repairing the damage lets life force flow at its best level again. Life force can also be restricted when some skill is not developed. One example would be a child that doesn't connect well with his or her parents. I believe children learn how to connect their regions by looking at how their parents do it. If the child-parent connections are weak, the child's soul regions will not be connected well.

Many disciplines have detailed models of paths for the flow of life force. Sometimes the details are helpful. However, I usually prefer a very simple model. I suggest looking at the life force flow between each of the regions without worrying about the paths. That way we only have to think about how much life force flows in both directions for each pair of regions. We have one description of how life force flows between the Mind and the Heart. Then we describe how it flows between the Mind and the Will. And so on, until we look at the flows between all 21 pairs.

An important part of the flow is that each region can handle a different amount of energy and information. The Mind can handle a lot of information but not much energy. The Wish region can handle a lot of energy but not much information. It's not easy to transfer a lot of life force between these two regions because they work with different parts of it. When we try to move life force in either direction, a lot is lost.

Here is an example. Imagine you are taking care of a cranky baby. The baby knows it wants something. It might be food or a clean diaper or a nap or the shiny toy over there. As a caretaker, it's your job to figure out what the baby's wish is. The time-tested method is to go through the usual list of wishes until you find the solution that satisfies the baby. Problems occur when you need to figure out something that is not on the usual list. You have to keep looking for other possibilities. It can be a real challenge.

The Wish region in our soul is like the baby. It knows it wants something. It may have the energy to act, but finding a set of actions that fulfills the wish is beyond its capacity.

Here's what happens between the Wish region and the Mind region when the Wish region wants something. To get what it wants, the Wish region sends a message to the Mind. Unfortunately the information sent is very simple and may not lead to a clear set of actions. It may be so primitive that the Mind region struggles to find a way to understand and satisfy the wish. A negotiation needs to take place.

Doing the best it can, the Mind region sends sets of actions and results to the Wish region. The Wish region decides whether they work. The negotiation, which includes translating information every time, goes on until the wish is resolved. Other regions are part of this if they need to be.

People often say that decisions aren't made rationally with our Minds. They say we make the decision and then use our Mind to explain it. That's almost right, but I think it's more complicated. It's true that the final decision comes from other regions, but the Mind plays a major part in giving the other regions possible answers before the decision is made.

We need to understand how soul regions connect if we want to understand how to have our whole soul work together. It's not good for us to have regions in our soul that disagree with one another. That just leads to being unhappy and not getting what we want.

As we learn more and heal ourselves, the pathways between the regions clear up so we can move life force between regions easily. The goal of the soul is to have the right amount of energy and information in each of the regions to fulfill our wishes. Clear connections inside the soul make this possible.

Connections outside the Soul

Connecting between our soul regions and the soul regions of another being is the third kind of thing soul regions do. The I-Am and each region decide how much life force to bring in — or allow in — from the outside. The region and the I-Am can also decide where to get the life force. There are often many sources and some are better than others.

Receiving Life Force

The inward flow of life force depends on three things: How much does the region want to change its life force level? How much life force is available in the outside world? How good is the region at bringing in life force from the outside world? Life force can come from a person, animal, plant, creative work, or anything else that has life force.

Life force in a region can be either positive or negative. It is possible for a region to absorb the kind of life force that is in the thing it is connected with. If a region brings in negative life force, the life force in the region will get more negative. It may move from positive to negative. Life force from a positive source reduces negative life force and increases positive life force. This agrees with the folk wisdom that we should surround ourselves with positive people to make our lives better.

For example, if you are wishing for a lot more love in your life, you'll be trying to bring in life force related to love. When the Heart and I-Am let love in, you have a chance to find someone who can give you the love you are looking for. On the other hand, if the Heart or the I-Am blocks love from coming in, you will never be able to receive love. You will never fulfill your wish for this kind of interaction with others.

Often we think about the energy part of life force instead of the information part. (Love has both parts.) But, the right amount of information is also important. It may seem like we want all the information we can get, but there can be "too much information." Being flooded with all the memories of a past trauma is one example. But even when nothing bad has happened, we may still want to limit the flow of information so we can process some of it before we get more. Eventually, sometimes after healing, we can take it all in.

Because souls usually choose to be separate from one another, at least part of the time, we want to be able to block life force from other souls. This is especially true when our soul is blocking negative life force. How well we are able to choose to accept or reject life force is an important part of staying healthy.

We also need to consider how a soul connects to free life force. Free energy is taken in through the Energy region. Free information comes in through the Info region. Each region has the ability to sense whether the life force component is positive or negative and decide whether to bring it into the soul. As I said earlier, the soul doesn't completely control these regions. An overwhelming amount of energy or information may break through the soul's desire to keep it out. Even if the life force that breaks through is positive, it can cause harm. Negative life force breaking through is never a good thing.

Trauma affects the ability to receive life force. It may make it hard to receive positive life force. Trauma may also make it harder to block negative life force. The effect is biggest when the situation is like the one that caused the trauma. Sometimes the trauma is bad enough that it affects parts of the person's life that don't seem related to the trauma. Healing the trauma restores the ability to receive only the kind of life force that is desired.

Sending Life Force

Each region also decides how much life force to send out. If the outside being or object seems to need a change in the level of life force it has, our regions may try to change the other level by sending life force to it. The outward flow is a mirror image of the inward flow. Life force flowing out of the soul can go to every place in the world.

What is outside can be another person, an animal, a plant, or something like a work of art. The kind of information that can be transferred as part of the life force depends on which region is sending the information and the capabilities of the receiver. Writing this book involves a transfer of life force from inside me to the keyboard. Then it goes into the document and finally out to you as you read it. Once I put the life force in the book, I believe the book part is finished. The book has its own soul. Now the life force is in the book and you work with the book's soul to bring in what you want. When you want to send life force back to me or get more life force from me, we'll need to make another connection, such as via WeAllHaveSouls.com.

The outward flow of life force will depend on four things. The region will send out the amount of life force that it thinks the outside world needs, but not more. The region can't send out more life force than it has plus the amount it can channel from other sources. The region and the I-Am may be limited in their abilities to send life force to the outside world because of trauma. The place the life force is being sent needs to be willing to accept it. If there are limits on the ability to send, the same amount of life force can be sent. It will just take longer.

A region can send life force even if the outside world has plenty. When we want to get something done, we can drain our life force down to nothing. But doing that is probably not the wisest choice.

As with receiving life force, trauma affects the ability to send life force. The effect is biggest in similar situations, but it may affect other parts of the person's life, too. Healing the trauma restores the ability to send life force.

Changing Soul Regions

Experience affects a soul region's life force level and connections. The basic process is pretty simple. The region looks at the results of an action. If the results are what the region was trying to do, the preferred life force levels and connections will become more like the current levels and connections. Or the results may not be what the region wanted. Then the preferred levels and connections will move in the other direction.

There are small changes all the time. And there are also long-term preferences that don't change as fast. For example, for a close friend the preferences will be set with the values we prefer. We've learned this set of values throughout our whole experience with this friend. There may be small, short-lived changes based on the current interaction, but the changes will not be far from the basic set points.

As we continue to live in the world, our soul slowly changes. Important events, both positive and negative, can cause much faster change.

Each person and place has its own set of levels and connections. Our soul regions shift their life force and connections to handle where we are and who we are with. I'm not sure how it is done, but the regions usually seem to find levels that work. Sometime, though, we can feel our souls' confusion. One example might be a teacher. We are used to seeing her at school, but meeting her in a grocery store can be really confusing. We connect differently with a teacher at school and a person in a grocery store. A teacher at school is an authority, which means we interact with Will and Mind. We interact with a fellow shopper in a store with our Heart. When we meet a teacher in the store, our souls often have a problem choosing how to connect. But we sort it out and use the location to help us decide how to interact. These ongoing changes help us find our place in the world.

Coordination inside the Soul

Regions are like pieces of the puzzle when we study them separately. Putting the regions together gives us a complete picture of a soul. Info is at the top. Energy is at the bottom. The I-Am contains the middle five regions and sometimes contains the top and bottom.

When the actions of the regions are combined, we see how souls act in the world. In every moment, in every situation, each region has its own level of life force. At the same time it sends life force to other regions in your soul.

A fascinating question is just how closely are these regions integrated? Do they all hum along in harmony? Are they all well coordinated to reach the goals of the soul? And just who or what is in charge, anyway? Throughout history, people who have asked these questions have often decided that we are not unified, single-purpose beings. We have separate parts and the parts don't always get along.

Sigmund Freud's id, ego, and superego are a classic Western division, but there are many others.

The best case is when all our parts work together for a common goal. Too bad we don't all work that way. Some of us fight battles between being in a loving family (Heart) and gambling or drugs (Energy or Wish). Teens and parents struggle with Will and Heart until the teens strike a new balance as adults. Info and Mind may pull us toward different solutions as we face problems in our lives. Sexual harassment at work tangles the Will region and dark side of the Wish region. Then they battle with society's feelings (Heart) about appropriate connections.

So, how do regions work together to decide what to do? When we looked at the way regions share life force with other regions, we talked about how regions interact. Let's combine that with a region's experience. That should give us enough to explain most of the decision-making process. The I-Am helps the regions coordinate, but I don't think it controls the process.

Here's how I think it works. We are in a particular situation. Each region has information about what it did in the past and what it intends to do in the present. The past may or may not be directly related to the current situation. The region will use the similarity to look at what it did before and how well it worked for the soul as a whole. The possible wishes and solutions are shared among the regions. The past also suggests the best life force levels for each of the regions. Regions that have found a good solution in the past will have a lot of life force. They will be asking the other regions to help with the proposed solution and to contribute their kind of life force.

Once the desired life force levels are set, the regions share their life force as best they can. The region (or regions) with the most life force control the situation. If the solutions the regions come up with agree, all of the regions will work together. If different regions have actions that don't match up, we will see a less effective response. The common phrase, "being of two minds," gets translated in this model to "having a divided soul."

We act quickly and decisively when all the regions agree on a solution. Some people focus their life force in one region. Heart and Mind are the most common. These people will also be more decisive than people who have high life force levels in more than one region.

The I-Am holds all the regions together. What moves through the I-Am to other souls is decided by the regions. The I-Am usually changes more slowly than the regions. That's why we usually appear to have a consistent personality.

7. Connections

We are the living links in a life force that
moves and plays around and through us, binding
the deepest soils with the farthest stars.
— *Alan Chadwick*

So far we looked at what happens inside one soul. Now let's look at how souls connect with one another. Later on we'll look at what these connections can do for us and how they explain the evidence that we all have souls.

One of the most important aspects of connections between souls in soul reality is that they are not like connections in physical reality. Physical reality is concerned with space and time. Soul reality is not. When we are talking about souls, I think size in the sense of tall or wide or long does not apply. Time does not flow the same way.

As I described in Chapter 2, I think that souls exist in no dimensions and no time. Luckily we don't have to agree on this question to show that we all have souls. For this chapter we just need to look at how we connect with one another. Some are based on our interactions. And, because we have physical bodies, other soul connections are affected by our physical connections.

Basic Abilities

Each of us is able to send and receive life force through our connections with others. I think we each have different levels of ability when we are born. They probably are similar to our abilities in our previous life. As we grow up, we each have different chances to practice working with life force. Some families encourage it, but in the Western world most focus on physical reality instead.

Sending and receiving life force are skills that need practice. For those who do not have support from their families, some of the skills may be hard to find. Everyone can get better at working with life force if they practice, but some will find it harder than others.

As far as I can tell, the ability to send life force is not connected to the ability to receive it. Some people are very powerful senders, for example, successful performers, politicians, and sales people. Others are good receivers. They are less visible because there is nothing about receiving that attracts our attention. You can recognize them because they are people you like to talk with. They seem to know what you are saying.

Some people are powerful at both sending and receiving. They understand what people are feeling. And they have the ability to make changes when they are needed.

These people often come from cultures that provide life force training for people with strong natural talent. Those who have the training look after the life force of their communities. They may be called medicine people, shamans, kahunas, curanderos, altomesayoqs, and many other names. They have a special place in the society because what they do is very hard.

There are other ways to train to use life force. Some are found in cultures that don't usually do much with life force. The trainings include martial arts groups, meditation practices, Wicca, Reiki, and dozens of other traditions that enhance our abilities to use the life force.

There is an evil side to this, too. People can also be trained to steal life force from others and do them harm. They go by names like brujos, sorcerers, and devil worshipers.

There is nothing in the skills that is tied to good or evil. A person who is skilled at using life force may use it to make the world better or make it worse. If you choose to follow a person because he or she seems powerful, you have to be careful. The person is certainly trying to make his or her life better. But how do the lives of the followers change and how much harm or hoocha happens for non-followers? We'll answer that question later in this chapter.

First we'll look at ways to measure basic abilities. When we look at sending and receiving, it helps to divide the life force into its parts. For the information part we can look at ESP experiments and knowing what happened to a loved one. These connections go through the Mind and Voice regions. For energy we have things like the healing force of Reiki and forces in martial arts that go through the Heart and Will regions. The Wish region also has powerful forces that we are sensitive to.

Ability to Receive

Several things affect our ability to receive life force from a particular source. I think it's a lot like trying to talk with someone in a crowded room. The basic part is how well ears hear, nerves work to send the information, and brains process the signal they get.

Beyond that there are other issues that go into understanding someone. It makes a lot of difference how far away they are. Hearing someone across the room can be very hard. We need to have a common language. We need to want to hear what the person is saying. We don't understand if we don't try. There are a lot of distractions that try to pull our awareness away. We need to focus on the person we want to hear. Even if we are able to focus on one thing, there is still a lot of competing noise. We need to filter out the noise that makes the person hard to understand.

I think receiving life force is similar except for the physical part of hearing. For hearing we need physical equipment and intention. For the soul, we have only intention.

We need to be close to the person — well connected — on a soul level. That's like distance apart in the room. I'll talk more about that in the next section. We need to speak the same language. We need to want life force from the other person. We need to avoid all the other distractions of life. Finally, we need to filter out life force that is coming at us that we don't want and select life force we do want.

When we look at the soul as a whole, there is one more vital part of receiving life force. The regions of the soul and the I-Am have to work together. We've talked about how the soul makes decisions. Receiving life force is one of those decisions. The I-Am and the regions need to have the intention of receiving the life force that is being sent to them. To enhance what all the regions receive, each region has to share what it received with the other regions. Energy that gets to the Will helps the Mind process the information it receives. Information from the Mind lets the Heart and Will know that there is energy available. If one region doesn't want life force from a source, it's much harder for the other regions to focus on it.

The most important part of receiving life force is that we intend to receive it. Caring about someone increases our intention and practice increases our ability.

Ability to Send

Let's continue the idea that sending life force is like talking in a noisy room. Then the ability to send life force is the same as how loudly the talker can speak. Some whisper and can't be heard. Others shout loudly enough that the whole room turns to pay attention.

We've probably all been in a place when the whole feeling of the room changed when someone walked in. It may have lit up in a blaze of good feelings. It may have gotten cold as ice. Either way, we felt a change in the life force of the room that was caused by a powerful sender. The new person added his or her life force to what was already there.

The life force we send out may come from any of the regions of the soul. Each region has its particular feel. If we are aware of our souls, we can tell what kind of life force is being sent. Being aware also lets us react to the life force more effectively. Let's look at some examples of people who are good at sending life force. We'll also see some of the training we use in Western culture to teach people how to use life force, even if it isn't called that.

Singers are taught to use the diaphragm and other areas for breathing. Breath is closely tied to the life force. Reaching the regions of Heart, Will, and Wish adds to the connection with the audience and makes the singing powerful and sensual.

Actors and actresses learn to create a character by connecting on many levels. One of the most important is the performer's ability to send life force that makes sense for the character they are portraying. In Western terms, this is described as personality.

In the world of business we see people rising to the top of their profession. There seem to be two ways this happens. Dale Carnegie talks about winning friends and influencing people by using positive energy from the Heart. Other equally successful businessmen are as friendly as a shark and still have people following them. They are more likely to be using Will. If business-training programs are to be believed, both can be learned.

Politics is similar to business, though there is more emphasis on fooling people. Politicians pretend they want to give power to their constituents, but they really want the power for themselves. When politicians learn to control their image, they become successful. A successful politician uses his Voice and Will to show the side of himself or herself that looks best to each donor or voter. The best can convince a voter to believe something that goes against all the available evidence. That happens when they overpower the voter's Wish region.

Athletes also train to use life force. In physical reality we talk about drive, desire, and focus. In soul reality these concepts are part of Will. We know that the most physically talented athlete is not always the winner of a contest. Will is as important in sports as physical abilities and often decides the outcome.

We can also use life force in ways that are bad for us. Criminals who attack people on the streets look for the weak to prey on. Lacking life force is the problem for the victims. Self-defense experts tell us to appear confident and prepared. I think that sending out life force is how we do that.

Different types of people use different soul regions and get different reactions when they send life force. We are used to physical-reality terms like drive and desire. But I think we can understand what is going on better and learn to be better senders when we use the concepts of soul reality.

Measuring Abilities

It seems as if life force is sent between two people in two different modes. One is the emergency mode where a person knows that something really important has happened to someone they care about. Those are the strongest connections. But we're not going to test how well a person senses life force by endangering friends, family, or pets.

The other mode is what we do on a daily basis with a mix of people we know and don't know. A way to measure that comes from Rupert Sheldrake's Sense of Being Stared At. I call the version that uses this model of souls the Sense of Connection. It is about as simple as things get. It also taps into very primitive sensing. Whether you're in the concrete jungle or a wolf-infested forest, knowing when someone or something is looking at you is a key to survival.

Turning the Sense of Connection into a standard measurement is similar to what we do with any test, such as an IQ test. We run lots of trials to find out how well people can sense life force. With an IQ test you can find standard questions. Ask the questions and add up the score to find the IQ. With the Sense of Connection, you need to find standard people. Have those people send to and receive from the person being tested to find the person's ability.

Abilities vary throughout a person's life and as a result of physical health, emotional state, whatever. Results will vary because some pairs work together better than other pairs.

Nothing that has to do with people is consistent. Not IQ. Not the ability to solve problems or ride a bicycle. Not the ability to create a tasty and nutritious meal when there are two soccer games and a band concert starting in 20 minutes. We're looking for a rough estimate of a person's skills and a way to measure changes. The Sense of Connection is a place to start.

Lessons

The first step toward working with life force is being aware of it. Here is an exercise David Spangler created for his work in Incarnational Spirituality. It can be done in a minute, although you will probably want to spend more time because it feels so good.

One-Minute Exercise

The object of the exercise is to connect with other things in the world, nothing more. You're not trying to send or receive life force. It may happen, but it's not what this exercise is about. You just want to stand (or sit) in connectedness with what's around you.

- Find a place to practice. It could be indoors or it could be outdoors. You can stand or sit, but whatever you do, you want to be comfortable and at ease.
- Make a mental survey of where you are, noting what is around you. You are paying attention to your environment in the moment.
- Feel your body in this place. Feel what is beneath your feet. Feel what you are sitting on, if you are sitting, or standing near, if you are standing. Feel the air around you. Feel the presence of light. If it is sunlight, feel its warmth. In other words, feel your physical presence in this place. Relax into this presence, into this place.

- Now let your awareness drop into your torso, out of your head, into your heart. Feel your lungs breathing. Feel your heart beating. Be present in your torso.
- Feel your breath expanding out from you as you breathe. Feel the sound and life of your heartbeat radiating out from you. Let your presence fill the space around you, making connection with what is around you. Relax into this connected space.
- Stay in this connected space as long as it feels comfortable. Pay attention to the felt sense in your body of being part of this space, part of the environment, connected to what is around you.
- When you feel finished, bring your attention back to your breathing, then back up into your head. Look around, mentally giving thanks for everything you see around you. Give thanks for yourself as well. Take a moment to stand in your sovereignty, then go about your daily business.

Building Connections

I think the next question to look at is how our soul connects to another person. The same question can be asked about how we connect to non-human souls, too. There seem to be four ways to build connections: family connections, shared experiences, intentional connections, and Wish connections.

What we will find is that we build connections when we share life force with another being. Sharing life force is a connection. If the sharing gives us results we like, we will work to increase the sharing and the connection.

Family Connections

Folklore suggests two souls are closer to one another just because they are from the same family. Identical twins seem to be the most connected. One possibility is that there is a connection based on similar

DNA. In Chapter 3 all of the evidence of sensing at a distance came from people with similar DNA.

More evidence comes from Thomas Bouchard.[58] He looked at twins who were separated at birth and raised in different families. He measured the personality, interests, and attitudes of the twins. What he found was that it didn't matter where the twins were raised. An identical twin raised away from the co-twin seemed to be as similar as a co-twin raised with his or her co-twin. DNA seems to matter here, too.

Orion Foxwood[59] says that our bloodlines are important because we can get special wisdom from our ancestors. His work seems to say that our DNA is important for our connections with others. It would take too long to explain his ideas, but you can read his books. Two are listed in this book's Reference section. They will help you if you decide to study more about how to heal and strengthen your soul.

I trust the evidence that people in the same family are more closely connected. It may be because the people share DNA. But I'm not sure DNA is the only way to explain the connections. I can think of two other possibilities that we might consider.

One is that similarity between twins (or other relatives, for that matter) can be explained by having the same experiences, as I describe in the next section. Arguing against that is Bouchard's work, which shows that twins connect more even if they do not grow up together.

The other possibility is that souls are strongly connected before coming into bodies. Some people believe that we reincarnate with the same set of people through many lifetimes. If that is true, we are connected because we have shared many experiences in past lives. DNA may not matter at all.

This is one of the places I really don't know what is going on. It doesn't really matter for this book. We just have to remember that families have closely connected souls.

Shared Experiences

Sharing an experience involves life force moving between people. It happens a lot in families. That's why it's hard to be sure about the genetic part of connection. Sharing also happens outside the family. We share experiences with other people. We may also share experiences with other beings and increase our connection with them. People who practice shamanism work with spirit helpers. Others meet with nature spirits, the Sidhe, and other beings in soul reality as part of what they do.

One thing I've learned is that it takes time to develop these relationships. There are no shortcuts to make these connections grow quickly. It doesn't matter if they are with humans or other beings. Of course, time by itself isn't enough. Life force must also be shared.

Just working together in the same office for years is not as important as sharing the birth of a child. Love involves a lot of sharing. You can also find intense sharing in climbing a mountain or helping retrieve parts of someone's soul. The more life force moves during each experience, the more connection the souls will have in the future.

An interesting question is if it matters whether the sharing is positive or negative. Does a child who is being abused by his or her mother form more connections because of the abuse? I have friends who dearly hope that they did not. Sadly I believe that they did form close but negative connections that lasted until they worked to cut them.

Elizabeth Lloyd Mayer[60] talks about another example. She describes a woman who had a connection with her abusive father. The woman said

"During the late afternoons, I'd start listening for him. It was a kind of listening. It was like listening with my whole body, not my ears. I don't know how to describe it except to say I was tuned in, vigilant with every part of me. Suddenly I'd *know* — know he was fifteen minutes away and driving home drunk. Then I'd hustle me and my sister into the closet. I couldn't afford to wait and hear him at the door. He'd crash in and grab whoever was in sight, then hit...."

"My dad didn't drink all the time. So there was no predicting. I had to stay tuned in every day, be ready and never trust any pattern. We'd go for weeks and be safe. But I couldn't get lulled into thinking that's how it would stay because suddenly he'd drink again and we'd have to hide again. I'd have to know way before he pulled up at the house...."

The girls learned to be physically hypervigilant, but there is more to this. The element of sensing danger before the father gets home requires something beyond physical reality. "Listening with my whole body" sounds a lot like a soul connection to me. These negative interactions take a huge toll. PTSD will almost always be present. Beyond that, people who have soul connections with their abusers often feel terrified or shamed because they have them.

People who know what their loved ones are doing through positive sharing don't feel the same sort of stress. They are much less likely to take their stories to a counselor. In fact, they probably enjoy knowing.

We also need to look at times when two people meet and feel an instant connection. It probably means that they spent time together in a past life. Why do we remember past lives with some people and not with others? I think the most important part is the strength of the connection we had before. The connection may be reduced by what happens between lives. It seems to be different for different pairs of people.

There is another part to shared experiences that shows some of the complications. Sometimes we meet a person we knew a few years ago and all the connections are just the same as before. Other times it's more like, "Now what was your name again?"

I think that more intense connections help us remember more, but that's not the whole story. The first person may remember the second person well, while the second person has fewer memories. Different people form different amounts of connection.

Maybe the first person stored connections in the Mind. The second stored them in the Will region. The first person will remember quickly. The second person may take some time for the memories to get from

Will to Mind. Another possibility is that the current focus of each person's life may make it easier or harder to focus on the connections. It's not as simple as adding up what has happened in the past.

How many friends we have may also be part of shared experiences. It's not clear how the number of friends affects the strength of each relationship. If a person has many friends, is each connection weaker? Or does having many friends make us more connected to each of them? I think the answer is that we need to have enough friends to build up the skills to connect. But it's still the amount of life force shared, not the number of friends. We can connect strongly with many people if we choose.

Most of these examples have been with two humans. The same effects of sharing life force apply when we look at how we share with non-human beings. The more we share, the better we connect. With all beings, I think our connections are stronger when we share from all the regions of our soul.

Intentional Changes

We can change our connections with another being simply because we intend to. We can make the connections stronger or weaker. We can start a relationship with a new person or cut the connections with an old relationship. Let's take look at how that happens.

I want to start with making connections stronger. I can do that by spending more time and having more experiences with the other person. We covered that aspect in the discussion on mutual experiences. But remember that it is more than just the time involved. It's also more than the kinds of experiences.

How our connections change also depends on whether we intend to make the connection stronger. We can go through something difficult and hope we never see the person again. That would be an intention to avoid negative connections. We can go through the same experience and use it as a springboard for a closer relationship. That intention makes the positive connection stronger.

Intentions come from all the regions of the soul. Our Mind might envision our life being better with the person around. Our Heart might love the person. Our Will might feel more able to accomplish great things. Any of those will increase the intention of all of the regions to strengthen connections. And they will change the I-Am to allow more life force from the person through.

These possibilities happen when we are with another person. Next I want to look at whether intention can increase connection without shared experiences. I think the answer is maybe and there are hazards.

In fifth grade I wrote Mary Lee's name over and over. I certainly didn't understand the concept of trying to increase that connection, but I think that is what I was trying to do. When we think about somebody, when we care about somebody, when we wonder what they are doing, when we try to know what they are thinking — these all intend to have more connection.

The danger of trying to increase connection when the person isn't there is that it can lead to obsession. The bond may seem like a connection, but it is with an image we have in our head, not to the real person. Real people keep their sovereignty. They don't change just because we want them to. I know I had a lot more success making a connection with Mary Lee when I talked with her. To strengthen a bond, we need to spend time interacting in real life. Here's a quote that says it all in six words:

> Absence sharpens love, presence strengthens it.
>
> — Benjamin Franklin

For those who prefer the more poetic, I offer:

> But let there be spaces in your togetherness and let the winds of the heavens dance between you. Love one another but make not a bond of love: let it rather be a moving sea between the shores of your souls.
>
> — Kahlil Gibran

It's easy to make a connection stronger when you are with a person. That's your choice. It's hard to connect more when the other person isn't part of the interaction.

The feeling we have when we are connected to another person is important for another reason. When we work with beings in soul reality, we may wonder if they are real or something we are making up. The best answer I know is that they are real if it feels like you are with another person. In those encounters connections change with mutual sovereignty.

The next question is whether you can make your connections weaker or cut them completely using your intention. I believe the answer is a strong yes. And it's often something that you really want to do.

The most important time to cut connections is when the person is harming your body or one or more of the regions of your soul. Being uncomfortable with someone is a reason to reduce the connection. Actual harm is a reason to disconnect completely.

Anyone who has escaped a relationship with a bad person knows that one of the vital parts of healing is separation. The first task is to cut the connections with the other person. Hopefully this won't shut down all the good connections with other people at the same time. We need to keep those to have enough life force to balance the negative life force we have been receiving. The second part is to dump all the negative life force that came from the other person and remove the hoocha that resulted. Both can be done if we intend to. Sometimes we need help from others to strengthen our Will to do the work.

The idea that we can get help from others brings up one last point about using intention to change our connections. We are not helpless souls floating through our lives. We usually know what is good for us and what is not. Our I-Ams encircle our souls and keep life force from getting to us without protection. We can intend to do things that make our lives better, such as connecting with healthier friends. We all have challenges from this life or previous lives, but being here on earth gives us the chance to change.

Wish Connections

Intentional connections form between two people who know one another. They connect the people through any of the soul regions. In this section we will look at another kind of connection. These are open-ended connections based on purposes you bring into this life or discover while you are here. These are held in the Wish region. You want to connect with someone or something based on a wish, but you don't know exactly who or what.

Popular examples come from the concept of the law of attraction. Rhonda Byrne wrote two books, *The Secret* and *The Power*, describing how to use this law. Byrne says that by using something that sounds very much like life force everyone can have everything they desire. It's a wonderful hope, but let's look at the concept of fulfilling desires and how it can change our connections to others.

I believe that one part of Byrne's claim is true. When we send out open-ended life force through the Wish region, it can find a compatible target. We can bring things into our lives by wishing for them. Unfortunately, the well-known saying, "Be careful what you wish for; it might come true," applies here. Sometimes what we wish for has more negative life force attached to it than we realize. It may bring negative things into our life along with the positive.

Another part of the claim is not true. Byrne says that everyone can get everything they want. The problem is that sometimes people have incompatible wishes. For limited resources or conflicting wishes, the stronger ones get their desire and the weaker ones don't. In some situations, no one gets their desire. The universe is filled with many beings. Some are much more powerful than we are. The chaotic nature of all realities means that we can't control everything that happens. This is especially true of our physical reality.

A third point is that having desires can be a serious problem in itself. For Buddhists, desires are the root of unhappiness. Just to want fancy clothes or a new car means that the person is already on the wrong path for a good life.

The fourth point is that we need to allow for promises we made in earlier lives. There are at least two forms for this promise: The first is an agreement we make before we are born that we will spend part the next lifetime with a person. The second is a vow to get even with a person for something that was done to us. In either of those cases, if we are born apart from the other person, it is the Wish connection that brings us together.

We all have wishes. There is nothing good or bad about that. But we need to look at how Wish affects our interactions with others and shapes the direction of our lives. We find people who share our wishes. We may have known them in a previous life or we may be meeting them for the first time. We are more connected to others through love or working friendships when our wishes match up. Wish strengthens our connections most when being together will get us both what we wish for.

Lessons

Knowing how we are connected to others helps us to know who we are. We could write down all the experiences we've had with another person in this life. We could add up the life force shared to make a guess about our connection. But that's really hard to do. And, as we've seen, it probably doesn't give accurate answers anyway. Let's look at another possibility.

An easier way to find the connection is to look at what is going on right now. Marriage, family, and intense friendships all have a common theme: We share a lot of intense time with another person. Here is a set of questions to find out how well we connect.

One-Minute Exercise

We are looking at how well you connect with another person. Think about someone you see almost every day. There are eight pairs of statements. Each pair describes the extreme ends of the connection range for one of the soul regions or the I-Am. Write down where you are in the range between these pairs of statements using a number from 1 to 5. Use 1 if you agree with the first statement. Use 5 if you agree with the second statement. If you are between, use 2 for agreeing more with the first, 3 having no preference, and 4 for agreeing more with the second.

1. "We drain each other's energy."
    "We energize each other."

2. "What we wish for is so totally different."
    "We have the same dreams."

3. "I don't know what he or she is doing even when I'm right there."
    "I know what he or she is doing even when we are apart."

4. "We feel differently about everything."
    "We feel the same thing all the time."

5. "We don't even talk to the same people."
    "We always finish each other's sentences."

6. "I never know what he or she is thinking."
    "I can almost read his or her mind."

7. "We look on the world completely differently."
    "We have the same views of what the world should be."

8. "We are not close at all."
    "We are very close."

Add up the scores. The total will be between 8 and 40. The higher the score, the stronger the connection. There aren't any right or wrong answers, but looking at your connections with other people might help you understand your life better.

You can use this as a way to keep track of changes in your relationships. Because there is one question from each soul region from Energy to Info, plus one from the I-Am, the exercise will also help you see how each soul region is connected with this person.

Physical Reality Effects

So far we have looked at connections in soul reality. But we are physical beings. Because of that, the strength of our soul connections is affected by what we are doing in physical reality. The biggest effect comes from the physical distance between the two beings that are interacting. In this section we will look at how physical reality and soul reality interact.

How connected souls are does not seem to be directly related to physical distance. Connection doesn't seem to get a little bit weaker if we are a little bit farther away. I think the soul experiences physical distances more like zones. If we are a long way apart, a certain kind of connection is possible. The closer a person gets physically, the more kinds of connections the soul can have. Touching gives us the strongest connection. Let's start with the distant connection and move closer to explore the effects of physical distance.

Soul-Reality Connection (Far Distance)

When we are physically too far away to see or hear each other, souls have only a long-distance style of connection. I'm calling this the soul-reality connection, meaning we only connect through soul reality. I think the situation is different when we are connected by something physical, like a phone or text messaging. In those situations we can use our physical senses to connect. We'll talk about those connections in the next section about sense connections.

The soul-reality connection is beyond what we can physically sense. Even so, it lets a mother sense that her son has been in an accident. We called it perception at a distance in the evidence in Chapter 3. It's the one connection that is always there.

I believe that physical distance has no effect on this type of connection. If the mother can sense the son's accident next door, she can sense the accident just as well on the other side of the world. The connection strength comes from the concepts we talked about in the previous section: family, shared experiences, intention, and wishes.

This type of connection very rarely gets a message through. The ones that do get through have a lot of life force coming from an important event. Even then, the people must be closely connected. Most of the time there is so much going on in our daily lives that the signal isn't strong enough to be sensed.

We can actually do experiments to show this kind of connection. One set of demonstrations was done by Guy Lyon Playfair.[61] For a television show he had twins Richard and Damien Powles working together. Richard was in a soundproof booth in another studio, some distance away. He was hooked up to a polygraph that measured respiration, muscle, and skin response. Damien did some things that caused a relatively strong physical reaction. One was to plunge his hand into ice water. The other was to open a box expecting a nice surprise. Instead a snake popped out. In both cases there was a reaction on Richard's polygraph readings at the same moment.

As Playfair pointed out, these experiments were not conducted with strict scientific protocols. However, they do show that there are connections outside of physical reality.

In her book *Extraordinary Knowing* Elizabeth Lloyd Mayer talked about a more structured experiment.[62] She described the work of Dean Radin[63] who tested a pair of people who knew one another. Both were wired up to detect physiological signs, including an electroencephalo-gram (EEG) to measure brain waves. One of the pair was told to try to mentally calm or arouse the other person. The two people were in separate rooms with no physical way to communicate.

Radin found that the receiving person reacted to what was sent. The receiver also guessed what feelings were being sent. The guesses were correct more often than not. But they were not as accurate as the reactions of the body. In my terms, Radin showed that we can connect with the Mind region and other regions connect more strongly.

We can use Radin's experiment to find the connection between people. By varying the situation we can find what makes connection easier or harder. This kind of work shows that we are connected to one another outside of physical reality. It also lets us study more about how the connections work.

Effect and Sense Connection (Middle Distance)

Now let's look at what happens at closer physical distances.

As we move closer together, other connections can happen. Let's look first at the three senses that work outside of touching distance: vision, hearing, and smell. When we can sense one another through these physical senses, our connections change.

As Gichin Funakoshi, founder of Shotokan Karate, says[64]

> The eyes do not miss even the slightest change.
> The ears listen well in all directions.

He doesn't mention smell, probably because it is not a precise sense during combat.

We talked about this Sense of Connection as part of the evidence in Chapter 3. One example was Caylor Adkins' story about stalking and standing sentry. Another was Rupert Sheldrake's Sense of Being Stared At. In each of these the distance is about 20 feet.

Physical distance is not what counts here. Think of a sniper who is capable of shooting several hundred yards. When a sniper sees a target, the person he is looking at should sense the threat as strongly as a knife at 20 feet.

When the sniper aims his rifle, the threat should feel as strong as a knife moving toward the sentry's neck. This moves the interaction into the Touch Connection distance described next. What counts is that the bodies connected to the souls in the interaction can affect one another. It doesn't matter that they are not in direct physical contact. When the interaction may be harmful to one of the souls, the level of connection (because of the attention and intention) goes up.

How strong the connection is depends on how much impact it will have on a person. Stalkers and sentries have a strong connection. A hundred disinterested people in the same subway car really don't matter.

But if one person in the subway is staring at you with malice, you will be much more likely to connect.

There are three aspects to the malicious stare. It is strong. It is focused on you. The intent behind the interaction could potentially have a large effect on you. Stronger focus and larger intended effects make the connection stronger. More complete plans will also send more life force to the receiver. Note that the strength of the connection probably doesn't depend on whether the effect will be good or bad. Either way a strong effect will lead to a strong connection. This effect may be what caused people to be more sensitive to strangers in some of the Sense of Being Stared At experiments.

Note that so far the person being stared at has not seen the starer. When both people look at each other, they add a physical connection. Seeing someone increases the connection strength for positive interactions, too. For example, the song "Some Enchanted Evening" from *South Pacific* describes someone who sees a stranger across a crowded room. Through this love at first sight, the person knows the stranger will be important for the rest of his life.

For most people the physical part will be stronger than the nonphysical part because most of us rely more on the physical. With this complete connection each person can affect the other.

What we have now is a connection in the middle distance with a feedback loop. If it is a threatening stare and your reaction is to be scared, the intensity and connection will increase. The person staring at you can see the fear reaction. If your reaction is to make it clear that you are not afraid, the intensity and connection will decrease.

The unafraid reaction has at least two possible modes of operation. You may be indifferent to the threat because you know it is not really a threat to you. In that case you have blocked or denied the connection. The other possibility is that you send threatening feelings back at the person who is staring at you. That should have the effect of causing the other person to lose strength and focus.

If you're in a bar and see someone looking at you in a friendly way, the situation is reversed. Being scared or acting indifferent makes the connection weaker. Acting interested increases the connection.

Studying connections in the middle distance is not too hard. It's not likely that we will be able to run reproducible tests with snipers. Having someone meet the love of his or her life for the first time is even more unlikely. Luckily the Sense of Connection experiment can be used to test different distances between single sender-receiver pairs to see if distance in the middle distance matters.

We can also study the effect of far distance and middle distance. In the middle distance the starer looks either at the person or at something else. For the far distance the starer might look at a picture of the person instead of the real person. I would expect that staring at the real person would have more effect.

We can also study how well life force is sent when both sides become aware of the other's gaze. This one is trickier, but it comes out of the idea that we usually know someone's intent better when we look in their eyes.

Touch Connection (Close Distance)

The next distance is where the two souls are close enough so their bodies can touch one another. This is a distance people seldom study for connections between souls.

The classic research is done beyond arms' length. For example, card guessing experiments usually have physical barriers between the participants. Often the tests are done with people in different rooms. The purpose for that is clear, of course. The experimenters want to be sure that there is no way for the person guessing the cards to see a card or get non-psychic signals from the sender. Other experiments with dreaming or looking at pictures have participants in separate rooms. Sometimes they are done with participants in separate cities.

Sheldrake's recent experiments have non-touching restrictions. They take great care to avoid any kind of physical communication in the Sense of Being Stared At experiments. Closed circuit television is used successfully. The starer doesn't have to be in the same room as the person being stared at. The telephone and email experiments are done with people far apart. The dogs that know when their owners are coming home are on video when no one is in the house. If there is a trend, it is to move the participants farther and farther apart. They want to be sure that the information is not being passed through one of the five physical senses.

Luckily, we are not trying to design an experiment right now. We are trying to figure out how souls communicate. Let's take a look at that.

It used to be magical (and terrifying) to sit in a movie theater and wonder if it is all right to put an arm around your date for the first time. I wonder if that is still an issue today. Holding hands across the table at a restaurant used to have the same kind of tension.

Tension is a really good term to use here. The feeling is somewhat similar to the surface tension of water. We have our personal space, which is established by the I-Am. Some people are invited inside that space, but we want most of the world to stay outside it. There is often a conscious decision to change a relationship. We go from a nod to a handshake or from a handshake to a hug. For those living outside of the United States, let me suggest that air kisses are roughly the same as handshakes. Both are culturally accepted methods of greeting that show it is possible to keep barriers up even when we are in physical contact.

The question we are trying to answer is how much the connection between souls is changed when bodies are touching and which regions are affected the most. The first aspect to consider is how compatible the two people are. Some people welcome a touch. To others touch feels creepy. When we are talking about the connection, it becomes stronger when the touch is welcome. The connection is probably reduced when someone's touch feels creepy.

My martial arts instructor once told us that if we were touching our wives or girlfriends, we would know if they were telling the truth. (He forgot to mention that the wives or girlfriends can also tell if we are telling the truth.) What he was saying is that our souls connect better when we are in physical contact. This is another channel that can transmit information.

One important point about touch connection is that connections between souls and bodies go on at the same time. It isn't a case of one or the other. The physical contact makes the soul contact stronger and vice versa. The physical sensations may be strong, but the soul connections are strong, too, when physical contact is made. Some of us just don't notice them as much.

I think touch contact can enhance connections between any of the soul regions. Note that these examples are all about positive connection. That's important because we are looking at whether touch makes them stronger. Heart is the region that seems to be talked about the most. Think of a lover's touch or a kiss. Slapping someone on the back seems to help the Will. Think about athletes' behavior after a score. I find it easier to talk with someone when we are together in the same place. Voice is enhanced by close contact. Wish also seems easier to share when there is contact. And being touched by the hand of God is one of the most powerful experiences in the Info region. Mind is the only one I'm not sure about. Sometimes touch can distract from thought. It depends on the topic.

It doesn't always have to be bodies that are touching. When a real thing, such as a care package, arrives, it means that the connection has moved into a closer distance. The contents are things that can be touched. The more personal the things are, the more efficiently they will transfer life force from the sender to the receiver.

We need to look at close-distance connections to understand all the ways two souls can connect. How far we are from someone makes a difference in what we sense.

Lessons

Let's take a look at how different distances affect our connections. We'll do the best we can to create the three distances and see how our interactions change when we move from one distance to the next.

One-Minute Exercise

You'll need a partner for this exercise. The exercise is to let your soul feel the difference between the three different physical distances. Find a place where you can sit or stand comfortably. You need a location where you can't see your partner's starting place. Through a doorway in another room is one possibility. You should be five to ten feet from where your partner will first see you.

There are three parts to the exercise.

- Breathe a few times with the intention of filling the space between you and your partner with something that lets you feel his or her movements. Let your partner know you are ready to start. You partner should start thinking about you and keep thinking about you for the whole exercise. You quickly write down a thought or two about the current connection.
- Face where your partner will be coming from. Close your eyes. Tell your partner it's time to start moving. Some time in the next 20 seconds your partner will move to a place he or she can see you. Your partner counts off five seconds and says, "I'm in here now." You open your eyes and write down your change in connection when your partner saw you. You know it was about five seconds ago. If you felt it when it happened, write that, too.
- Close your eyes again. As quietly as possible your partner moves toward you. Just inside touching distance, your partner slowly reaches toward you and touches you on the shoulder. Open your eyes and write down your change in feelings during the walk and the reach.

You will probably want to trade roles with your partner. Note how your feelings are the same and how they are different. It will help you find out more about yourselves.

This is not something that only works the first time. In fact you will probably get better with practice and often find new ways the distances feel different when you try the exercise more times. One place to explore is which soul regions are affected the most by the change in distance. It will not be the same for everyone.

Some of these parts might seem too fast. Slow them down if you want. The one-minute time limit is so you will feel like it takes almost no time to try these exercises. Learning more by doing the fun ones again is what you do for yourself.

Soul Interactions

There are several ways to look at soul interactions. One is to consider the total connection between two people. This is also a great time to look at how soul interactions affect us in our lives. We can also look at how soul interactions explain some of the evidence we talked about earlier. A final topic is whether soul interactions are healthy or unhealthy. Let's take a look at some of these interactions.

Total Connection

We find the total connection between two people by adding up the connections from all the distances. If the people are too far apart to sense each other, we use only the soul connection. Remember that is made up of family, shared experiences, intention, and wishes.

If they are able to physically sense one another, we use both the soul connection and the sense connection. If the two people are touching, we also include the touch connection.

The soul connection is relatively stable. It doesn't change much during a short encounter. The other connections can change a lot from one moment to the next, depending on what is happening.

When we add up the connections, we find how much life force can move from the sender to the receiver. How much actually moves also depends on other factors. How much life force does the sender have? How much life force is the sender trying to send? How fast can the sender send life force? How much life force can the receiver take in? How much life force is the receiver willing to receive?

The connection changes as the situation changes. The amount of life force going in one direction is not the same as the amount of life force going in the other direction. We always need to keep track of both directions. Each region connects to each region in the other soul, so the connection for the whole soul is the combination of the values for each region.

There are three important aspects of life force flowing between two souls. The best relationships have a lot of life force moving between the two people. It's best if most of the life force is positive. The total life force should be about the same in both directions, but each person can send life force to the other from different regions. The conclusion seems somewhat obvious — balanced and strong is best. But looking at what each region is doing lets us find ways to make relationships healthier and better connected.

Effects on Life

We can't look at everything, but we can make all this talk about souls more real. We can start by looking at how connections make a difference in our lives.

Let's start with what happens when we hang around with a group of friends. I like to be with friends who usually have positive life force. Let's start with that case.

We are friends and we like each other, so we can expect to receive a lot of life force in the Heart region. But it will not be the same from each person. Some friends are powerful sources of life force. We can soak up the life force from them and get as much as we need. Other friends might send less life force out, so we can take less in. Usually there is more than the normal level of life force when we are with close friends. It's likely all of us will be sending out and taking in a lot. Sharing life force feels good. By the end of the evening there is usually more Heart life force than there was at the beginning. We either generate the life force as we interact or it flows to us from some reservoir in the universe.

If a friend who is usually there is missing, some of the life force will flow to him or her, even though the person isn't there. If there is concern about the person, a lot of life force can be flowing.

Now let's add friends to the mix who need exceptional amounts of Heart energy. Maybe they are just breaking up with a partner or they have suffered some other kind of loss. In the group setting they will usually need more love energy than they have to give back. Friends are good sources of this kind of life force, so each will share more with the friend than they get back, but no one will be especially drained. Given that the situation usually generates life force, there may still be enough Heart energy to increase it for everyone. But there probably is not as much as there would be if everyone was happy.

It's a different situation if one friend always needs love energy and pulls life force out of the group. At some point people in the group may get tired of the support they are giving and just not give as much to that person. Less life force flows in the direction of the person who is seen as too needy. Life force can still flow to other members of the group because we can decide who we share life force with. Pay attention to your feelings in this kind of situation. See if you feel yourself shut down when a life-force-draining person comes into the room. Check if you shut down for everyone or just the person who is too needy.

Sometime you can't shut down. It happens when a life-force-draining person overcomes your ability to block your life force from flowing out. In that case your life force flows out whether you want it to or not. It's usually a good idea to stay away from this kind of energy vampire.

Another thing to notice is that we connect differently with different members of a group. With one there might be an intense physical attraction. With another we enjoy good conversation. Some are good friends and others are not.

Let's look next at what happens with a friend who is in a bad situation and is radiating negative life force. You want none of it. In that case you try to block the life force coming from the friend. If things work well, the friend will receive enough positive life force from you and the others in the group to balance out the negative life force. If things work out badly, the friend's negative life force will bring the whole group's life force down. It all depends on the ability of members of the group to block negative life force coming toward them. They need to be better at blocking than the friend is at sending out negative life force. For real healing, the group also needs to help their friend remove the cause of the negative life force. That would involve positive life force directed toward the friend.

The connections with a friend are relatively stable over time. A blip, maybe from a misunderstanding, may cause a change. Usually they go back to the normal values pretty quickly. Friendships can change, but this usually takes more time and happens because of many experiences.

An important point to get from these examples is that we can decide how much life force to send and receive from each person. We have a normal way of interacting. Around that average we may vary a great deal depending on the exact situation we are in. Our intention causes the changes. When we are sovereign, we can accept life force we want and block life force we don't want. If you have problems with sovereignty, it's good to know that you can work on becoming stronger.

What happens when we interact with someone who is not a friend can be very different. Think about dealing with a policeman giving you a traffic ticket. I, and probably you, connect differently with the policeman. I use different regions of my soul and different amounts of life force.

There is one more case that I find interesting. Folk wisdom suggests that people who appear to be the most generous with their life force are often the worst at handling negative situations. They become the neediest. What people sometimes think is that they were just pretending to be happy.

But this really isn't the case. When we look at the details of the connections, we can predict a faster collapse. The person is used to sending a lot of positive life force. Even when something negative happens, the person still wants to send out a lot of positive. So all the positive life force the person has flows out and there is nothing to replace it. This leads to a total collapse much faster than in someone who sends out less life force. The generous person has more difficulty getting back to the preferred life force level.

In Chapter 8 on proof I'll look at the power of being able to predict what will happen in specific cases. Being able to do this goes a long way toward proving that we all have souls.

Healthy and Unhealthy

It would be nice if people were simple. Two people could fall in love and share all that wonderful Heart life force back and forth. They could fall in lust and share life force between Wish regions. Or they could do both. Why even bother with the other regions when all that is going on? Life would be simple.

Unfortunately, that's not how the world works. We are here to learn to be individuals. Being dominated by someone else stops that from happening. It's also not good for the person doing the controlling. It takes a lot of negative life force to control someone else. Souls that carry that much negative life force are not healthy.

Some bosses coerce their workers into sex. The boss uses the Will region to force the worker. That also lets the boss release unwanted (probably negative) Wish life force in the worker's direction. In this kind of coercive situation, there will be a lot of negative Heart life force flowing both ways. The boss uses Mind and Voice life force trying to not get caught while the worker tries to find enough Will to get the boss busted.

A parent who tries to force a child to love her is similar. So is a relationship where a person is talked into a friendship that isn't in the person's best interest. I believe that, for the most part, relationships based on non-matching soul regions are unhealthy. Too often a person uses negative life force to get positive life force in return. That lack of balance just doesn't work for the highest and best good.

One exception to the control situation happens between parents and children. Parents should use Heart and Will to guide their children. It's important that Heart connects to Heart and Will connects to Will. If children do not experience control, they will never learn to control themselves as adults. Poor self-control leads to all sorts of hoocha in the person's life.

Interactions between regions let us ask whether one person can force another person to give up or take life force. For example, can one person steal someone else's Will? I believe the answer is no when only one region is involved. Usually more than one region has to be involved before a person can be forced to give up positive life force or accept negative life force.

Trauma may change that. It can damage connections between soul regions within our own soul, which makes us less safe from negative life force. Others can steal life force from us when we don't have all of the parts of our souls working together. It's one of the reasons why healing traumas is one of the first steps in working to heal and strengthen our souls.

Healthy relationships send most of the life force between the same regions. When matching regions connect, each region understands both parts of the life force being sent. A region is best at handling life force coming from the same kind of region so it will not be overwhelmed by life force it can't handle. When our souls are healthy and strong, they know how to accept life force from the same regions in other souls. They also can block others who try to send negative life force between different regions.

Explaining the Evidence

Soul interactions explain some of what we looked at in the evidence in Chapter 3. Notice that it's easy to explain what is going on in soul terms. Explanations that don't use soul interactions can be far more complex. Let's take a look at the evidence and what is happening from a soul viewpoint.

Sense of connection. The basic experiment measured how well we can tell that someone is staring at us. It found that, when you average everyone, we can tell a little bit. People who are more sensitive can tell more accurately. These results are expected from pairs of souls that connect to one another with different strengths. We can sense connections between us. We also looked at training to better sense others around us. As expected, more training led to more ability to sense others. When souls learn about interactions, they get better at sensing other souls.

Extrasensory perception (ESP). We looked at people who knew when a loved one was in danger or was shocked. Loved ones have strong connections with one another. When the message is important enough, it can get through. The evidence suggests that people who are emotionally close sense more of the events. Our soul model explains that with Heart connections and its description of closeness. We also looked at knowing the future. The soul model covers that by saying that souls exist outside distance and time. Sometimes we can avoid the constraints of time even when we are in bodies.

Ghosts and human spirits. People see ghosts. Souls continue after death. With a soul model we can continue to connect with the bodiless souls we call ghosts. We also talked about places that hold a memory. This is explained by a soul model that says everything has a soul. The soul of the place or object can hold a memory, too.

Near-death experiences (NDEs). Most NDEs involve meeting loved ones who have already died. In a soul model, the souls of loved ones continue. We can meet them any time, but it's easier when our soul is apart from our body in an NDE experience. Naturally we see our loved ones because those are the souls we are connected to.

Inspiration. We looked at ideas seemingly coming to us from outside our own minds. Sometimes we get to levels of understanding that we really can't explain. This is easy to explain using a soul model that includes other beings with more understanding than we have. Through the Info region they tell us what we wish to know. Sometimes inspirations come through very specific and reproducible interactions with soul regions.

Other beings. We looked at other beings that we may interact with. Our soul model predicts that there will be a wide range of beings who are souls without bodies. It's no surprise that we sometimes sense them in their many forms.

Human magic workers. We talked about humans who can use the life force for many purposes. Since we have souls that can use life force, we expect to see humans using it.

We'll look at more evidence and how a soul model explains it in the next section.

Body and Soul Connections

We are a soul and we are a body. The soul operates using life energy and the body operates using electromagnetic energy. I'm pretty sure I understand why souls like to be in bodies. I'm not as clear on how it is done. Let's start by looking at the why.

Then I want to take an in-depth look at the topic of memory. There is information there that helps us understand how bodies and souls connect. We can look at how souls and bodies interact and what it means for a soul to be self-aware. At the end of the section we'll look at how body and soul connections help explain more evidence that we all have souls.

Purpose of Bodies

Souls have spent billions of years creating physical reality and bodies that can act in it. The problem the souls solved is that life force is not strongly coupled with physical matter. It seems to take a whole lot of life force to move even an atom or two.

When you want to move something, you need to push against something else. A physicist would say that you are conserving momentum. I think that the need to push against something applies to the life force, too. We can physically throw a ball by pushing against the earth. The earth hardly notices. But what can a soul push against if it wants to throw something?

Souls are clever. They figured out that they needed to increase their influence on physical reality. Souls needed something that could, for example, make a small change in an electromagnetic field to produce a large effect in physical reality. Single-celled creatures were a start. Dinosaurs were a pretty good step. But jumbo jets and trips to the moon are even better. Souls influence the brain and probably other groups of nerve cells. The brain moves the body and the body moves whatever tool it controls. Now we are looking at two-stage amplification of the life force. A little life force can produce a big effect.

So one reason we added a body to our souls was to make it easier to explore and change physical reality.

A second reason for bodies is that bodies are fun. Some folks who believe in reincarnation don't think people who come back lifetime after lifetime for the current equivalent of sex, drugs, and rock and roll are on the right path. One group thinks our purpose on earth must be greater than that. The other group just wants to *PARTY!*

I believe that we really do have a greater purpose here, but that doesn't mean that a good party is a bad idea. As long as there is lots of positive life force running around, it can be a good thing. The negative side of sex, drugs, and rock and roll is the problem.

There are downsides to having bodies, but overall the good seems to outweigh the bad for many people. If it didn't, why would so many souls choose to come back into bodies?

A third reason for bodies is that the physical brain helps us think and create. The human brain was developed to reason and use symbols. The whole history of humans seems to point that way. Early humans drew pictures on cave walls. We invented words to remember and share our stories. We are fascinated with building computers that match and sometimes exceed our abilities. Then we use them to amplify our thinking just like we use machines to amplify our strength.

Many humans see themselves as the top of the list in thinking, but I believe other animals are pretty good at thinking, too. Whale songs come to mind. Crows use tools and have memories that last a lifetime. And we also have to consider the mockingbirds who sang outside my window as I was growing up in Southern California. They composed their songs all night and I never caught them repeating. There seem to be many ways brains work with Mind.

A fourth reason for having bodies is that we can gather energy to send into soul reality. I got this idea from David Spangler of the Lorian Association. He and I agree that we need to work to increase the positive life force everywhere. Physical reality is one place we can do that. David calls his point of view Incarnational Spirituality.

He says that each of us come into this world as a unique mix of "energy and intentionality of the soul, the energies of the world and of nature (which collectively I think of as the World Soul), the energies of spirit and the non-physical realms, and the energy of sacredness." We are born with the spark of the Creator, a radiant, spiritual force, which is like a self-light that "comes on" when we incarnate. This light has the potential to develop and grow throughout our lives.

David believes that this incarnational light is a vital part of the world. It is a gift to the cosmos. We are spiritual energy sources in the world and not just energy recipients or energy consumers. He says that we produce this spiritual energy because we are in bodies. It's all part of the process of being on earth.

Shamanistic practice has a related idea. The upper and lower regions are separated by our middle region. I think we may also be able to move life force between the upper region and the lower region. When I do that, it seems to be appreciated. If an energy transfer goes from humans to entities in soul reality, it is another reason for having bodies.

It seems clear that we have developed bodies for many different reasons. It's taken some time, but we seem to be in a place and time where we can benefit from all of the hard work. Having fun while making our realities better seems like such a good idea. It makes me wonder why there is all this hoocha keeping us from doing that. We'll talk about possibilities later in this section.

Memory

One of the great problems of modern science is how brains store and access memories. In fact, it's been an unsolved problem since the early 1800s when people first realized that there was a problem. The biggest problem is that no one has found a way for the physical brain to keep all that we are able to store.

It is important to note that there are two kinds of memory: short-term and long-term. Short-term memory holds about seven items. As a new item comes into our attention, another item drops out. We use the items in our short-term memory to solve problems. I think the structures we see in the physical brain can explain short-term memory and some of the ways we solve problems.

So for the Mind region, we can use models of short-term memory to look at one of the things the Mind region does. Other regions may be similar. For example, in the Will region we talk about a gut feeling. It's simpler than our Mind's decision-making process. But that's just what we would expect from a region that contains less complex information.

Long-term memory is different. Physical-reality science says that a memory is saved when it is important enough. I'm not sure what important means here. A lot of things that don't make much difference are also stuffed into long-term memory.

There have been many suggestions for how the memory process occurs. Here are some: Brain cells each encode a memory. Memories are stored by changes in how neurons connect. The brain is a complex hologram. Memories are stored in proteins. Memories associate with similar memories. The amygdala and the hippocampus, both small parts of the brain, are vital to storing memories. These days the belief is that a memory is saved when it is rehearsed — when it is considered enough times to set up a pattern in the brain. The pattern is the memory and can be recalled as a whole when parts of it occur again.

Unfortunately, none of these ideas provide details for how the cells in the brain store or recall the memory. Small structures of the brain like the amygdala and hippocampus simply can't store enough to hold and sort through memories.

Perhaps the best summary of the situation is Dubuc's[65], "... the anatomical substrate of working memory is far from being understood in detail. Moreover, the phenomenon of working memory is made all the more complex by the fact that it takes place over time." He says we really don't know what is going on. It's even worse than that because understanding time makes it even harder.

I'm not saying the brain doesn't help process memories. It does. We need to include the brain in anything that is proposed as a way memories are stored and accessed. We also need to include the Mind. Perhaps the best way to move forward is to look at some of the things we need to explain about memory. Here's a list of the ones I think are most important.

- Memories have a time structure. We remember in a time sequence. Usually we are more or less correct. Associations do not have a time structure.
- The number of things we remember is very large.
- Some people with eidetic (photographic) memory can recall the exact words of many books and reconstruct events as well as a photograph or movie.
- The effect a memory has on us can change with time. Often remembering a trauma that caused PTSD will cause us to have a PTSD reaction again. We can work on the memory so we can access it in a way that does not cause a PTSD reaction.
- Sometimes an event is so bad that we can't even remember it. Yet we are still afraid in similar situations. The associations are very strong. The memory is very significant. But the associations are not enough to make us conscious of the memory.
- We need to explain both verbal and non-verbal memories.

- We store many kinds of memories: facts, words and stories, pictures, tastes and smells, touch, feelings, societal structures, and physical skills.
- Birth memories are quite common, often all the way back into the womb. We need to explain why some people have very early memories and why most people don't have them. This quote from a fellow named Mark provides an example of one memory:

  I remember being born. I tried for a moment to tell the people who were around me that WE FORGET! This is because the moment I was born, I watched the memory of where I had been before birth leave me.[66]

- A few young children have memories of previous lives. Ian Stevenson[67] spent half his life researching this. We need a mechanism that allows this to happen but prevents it from happening most of the time. Mark's remark in the previous item says he experienced this but didn't explain why.

Let's move away from humans to look at memory in other creatures and the kinds of things we need to explain with them.

Many of the explanations of memory say structures in the cortex of the brain store the actual memory. However, humans are not the only creatures with memories. Some of the others don't have cortexes and still have memories. We need to account for that.

- Some migrating birds remember where they made their nests the previous year so they can return to them.
- Bees remember where flowers are and perform dances to let other bees know how to find the flowers, too. The other bees have to remember the dance as they go to look for the flowers.
- Bees can count the number of objects in a picture. Then they can make a choice later based on the number of objects they saw.[68]
- In the discussion on the Mind region in Chapter 4 we looked at how a caterpillar learned to react to an odor and still remembered it when

it became a butterfly. For part of the time there were no nerve cells. We need to have a model that allows this to happen, too.

All of the items on the list can be explained if soul regions have memories. The Mind has the kind of memories we usually mean when we talk about remembering. The brain accesses the Mind's memories when it needs to solve a problem or remember something that happened. In the soul discussion on the akashic records in Chapter 4, I said "memory" is likely to be a soul connection to another time in physical reality. Brain and Mind work together to find the connection. The other regions bring in their non-verbal memories, too.

Birth memories and reincarnation memories deserve some thought. Rionagh na Ard[69] wrote about being a Sidhe who moved into a human body. She was overwhelmed by the physical body. All her memories of what she had been before were lost. Mark said the same kind of thing in his birth memory. It seems to happen to almost everyone. I think that is explained because working with the trillions of cells in a body takes just about everything a soul has. Weaker connections from the past can't be found when there are trillions of connections in the present.

In Ian Stephenson's work on reincarnation there are two important points. One is that the child doesn't remember a time between lives. He or she remembers being in a body just a little while ago. The second is that almost every child in the studies had a great wish to finish something from the life before. When we have strong wishes, I think we can hold on to connections for some of our memories. So reincarnation is not a problem either.

There is one observation, though, that is a problem. Sometimes memories aren't formed. Sometimes they can't be found. We know that stopping a chemical process in the brain stops us from storing memories. We need a model that explains that. We also need a model that explains why damage to the brain, for example from Alzheimer's disease, can stop us from either storing or accessing a memory. I really don't know why either of these things happens from a soul point of view. The best I can offer is that a body and soul need to work together and it looks like a healthy body is required for that to happen. This aspect of memory is an important topic for future research.

Body and Soul Interactions

Looking at how bodies and souls interact with one another takes us deep into the mystery of life. People offer many simple explanations, but they just don't answer all of the questions. We need to look for answers that are as complex as the problem.

One simple idea that many people have is that the soul is divided into chakras. Each chakra is attached to a specific part of the body. I think this is too simple. It tries to make the soul part of physical reality, which it is not. Goswami[70] and others who have spent lifetimes in study agree that chakras are not part of the physical body.

Physical reality also gives us hints about how the soul interacts with the body as a whole. Rupert Sheldrake and others have done enough research to convince me that there is not enough information in the DNA of the fertilized egg cell to create a body. These researchers all say there is something outside of physical reality. I believe the soul surrounds the body and guides its growth. The same thing usually continues after we are born. In healthy people the I-Am reaches out beyond the body to connect to the world.

Souls Coming into Bodies

There is a belief among many people who study souls that only a small piece of our soul comes into the world to connect with our body. The rest stays with our soul group somewhere else. I don't like that model, so here are other possibilities.

As Rionagh na Ard tells us, it is traumatic to incarnate. One possibility is that a piece of our soul breaks off when we move into our body in the same way we lose soul pieces because of other traumas. That piece may be looking for a way to reconnect with the rest of our soul. That might feel like a connection to somewhere else.

I just don't see human souls as powerful enough to divide themselves up and choose to be in more than one place. We seem to be pretty near the limits of our soul power when we try to survive in physical reality. When we are in our bodies, our soul needs to connect with the souls of trillions of our cells. Between lives might actually be easier.

We'll talk more about this in Chapter 10 when we look at next steps. The issue doesn't take away from this book's central theme that we all have souls. It's just another aspect of souls that we still need to study.

Body and Soul Regions

We need to explain the interactions of soul regions and areas of the body. The regions don't match up exactly. When I practice karate, it feels like the energy and connections are centered in the belly and Will region. In a serious confrontation, it's better if the Mind and brain are not involved. What we need to explain is how my Will can use my arms to make movements in practice and my Voice and Mind regions can use them at different times to write this book.

I think that the body follows the most active soul regions. It also makes sense that the body follows more strongly when all the regions agree on what should be happening. When athletes speak of being in the zone, it probably means that all the parts are working together well.

Without suggesting a complete answer, let's look at the pieces that we have.

First we can look at actions. High soul energy in a region brings higher physical energy along with it. The arms and legs can follow nearby regions well and more distant regions to some extent. When the regions lack a unified intention, the body cannot act effectively.

Next we can look at perception. In sensing what is happening in the outside world, Mind and Voice need to reach out to effectively take in information. It's easy to miss something if we are not fully tuned in. We sense by receiving both life force and electromagnetically based forces.

Finally we can consider existence. We maintain our health, well-being, and emotional stability more effectively when we have positive energy in all of our regions.

The nice thing about these suggestions is that each is testable once we agree on a measure for the amount of energy in a region. We can see how much influence regions have on actions, perceptions, and health. Armed with that information we can make better models of the connections between soul and body.

Other Questions

There are many more questions about how souls and bodies interact. Here is one important one where I don't even know how to start looking for the answer.

We know that bodies work with electromagnetic forces. Souls work with life force. Electromagnetism and life force need to interact. This is not much different from the way that physical forces like electromagnetism and gravity interact. Light bends in a gravitational field. In a similar way life force needs to affect processes in the cells of the body and the cells need to affect life force, too.

Self-Aware Souls

One of the biggest differences between life force in soul reality and energy in physical reality is that souls are aware of themselves. They can do things to change their life force levels.

I am not suggesting anything like total awareness or the ability to make changes easily, accurately, or all the time. We all know better than that. But usually we know when something is wrong in our lives. We try as best we can to fix what makes us uncomfortable. One way to think about our changes is to look at how we are changing the life force in our soul.

The life force in a region is affected by four things. Life force goes out to other regions in our soul. Life force comes in from other regions in our soul. We get outside life force through the Info and Energy regions. We get life force from other beings through the regions inside the I-Am.

Self-awareness arises because we realize that we can make decisions in the future when we face situations similar to ones we faced in our past. We know how to study what has happened in the past to make better choices the next time.

I believe this ability to study the past and predict the future is partly because of our Mind. But even more than that, I think it's because of our physical brain. We spent a lot of evolutionary energy to develop a brain. This seems to be one of its purposes.

I believe the brain allows us to imagine future scenarios. The imagination produced by the brain is powerful enough to allow the soul regions to react to it. When the regions react, they store the thought experiences. That resets their life force levels and prepares them to handle things better in the future.

We know this works. Athletes and performers improve their abilities by imagining themselves making exact movements. Most of us rehearse what we are going to say in difficult situations. We also think about what we should have said. We relive our bad experiences until we can detach from them by having better ways to cope with what happened.

This model also explains some of the things that happen during dreams. Most of our waking thoughts use Mind and Voice memories. In dreams the other regions can access the Mind to find answers to their questions. Dream images are interpretations the Mind makes of the situations found in other regions. In a dream state all the regions are freer to interact with the Mind to solve their problems. This is an effective way of planning future actions, especially actions that are not directly related to Mind.

Many animals also dream. So we can guess that they are also adjusting reactions to past events. To the extent that they are making plans for the future, they are also self-aware.

The purpose of sleep and dreams becomes clearer. It happens in a relatively safe environment. With the body shut down, the soul lets all the regions interact to figure out better ways to deal with the world. Self-awareness and the way the soul adjusts its parts in dreams is how our souls hold each of us together.

Explaining the Evidence

Soul and body connections explain some of the evidence we looked at in Chapter 3. Let's take a look at how these connections explain what we see.

Martial arts. We looked at aspects of life force — ki or chi. Life force explains why the winner of a fight is not always the person with a physical advantage. When we train our souls to handle life force well, we can use it to affect other people in ways that make us more effective. Souls that are trained make bodies more effective. Having souls explains how this works.

Energy healing. Our bodies can be healed in non-physical ways. A soul model lets us see how life force moves between the healer and the healed. The healing can be understood when we think about life force moving between both the souls and the bodies. Healing either the body or the soul helps to heal the other.

Reincarnation. Souls and bodies working together is what reincarnation is all about. One of the ways we know that souls continue after death is that we see them again in a new body. The model talks about how this happens.

Superpowers. We find extra strength in times of extreme stress. Our bodies can't put out that much effort. An energized soul explains why we can do these things. To levitate we need a soul to change how gravity affects the body. We don't see the other superpowers very often. But they need a soul along with the body to explain how they can happen.

8. PROOF

When shamans enter nonordinary reality, the rules of the outer world are suspended.

— *Sandra Ingerman*

Now we come to the question that is at the heart of the book: Have we proven that we all have souls? It turns out that the question is not as simple as it looks. That's why we have this chapter on proof. Let's look at the issues we will consider.

At the beginning of the book, I asked you to join me to bring caring about souls back into Western culture. I hope you have decided we can work together on this. If you have, the first part of this chapter helps explain the environment we will be working in.

It's important to consider who needs the proof. For some people there is no need because they are sure they have a soul. We ask them to join the group and work with us to find more effective ways to let other people know. Others have doubts that souls exist. We need to figure out how to connect with them in ways they can understand. Many people flatly deny that souls exist. To reach them we need to understand the proofs they have and the proofs that will help them change their minds.

The second part of this chapter looks at the kinds of proof that are available. Each is a tool for explaining that souls exist. We need to understand the tools so we can use them effectively in talking about souls.

In the third part of this chapter we'll look at the evidence and I'll give you my thoughts on what it proved and how. These are the things we can share with others.

And now let's consider the question: Have we proven that we all have souls? The answer depends on who you ask.

I'm convinced some of us have souls. As we'll see in the discussion on proofs, it's much harder to prove we *all* have souls. But I believe we have enough proof to say that we all do.

I hope you are convinced. It's great if you are! But if you aren't convinced yet, you have lots of company. Maybe this chapter on proof will help by summing up what I have discussed. Maybe not. Whether we have proved to *you* that we all have souls is something each of you gets to decide for yourself.

Some people who read through earlier versions of this book said that they got bogged down in this chapter. And they also said that the next two chapters are the best in the book. I happen to agree with them. This is a dense chapter. The instant that you feel like you don't want to read another word about proof, move on to Chapter 9. It's much more inspiring. With that said, let's start this chapter with a discussion of why we need proof.

Why We Need Proof

In Western culture we have a tremendous bias against souls. To even say you believe you have a soul can be an act of defiance. I seldom hear it said as a simple, "Of course I have a soul. Everything does." People who make that kind of statement have spent years looking at the question and are confident about their position. They also have the support of friends who agree with them.

For others, there are several reasons that saying they have a soul is difficult. And I'm not sure which of these is most important, so no order is intended.

One reason it's hard to say you have a soul is that you are afraid the other person will make fun of you. Western culture has a strong belief that the only reality is the physical one. People in this culture fight hard to keep others from suggesting there might be more to reality than that. The term usually used for a defender of the physical-only view is skeptic.

It goes beyond disbelief. Even when people believe in soul concepts, they work very hard to tie that belief to something physical. One example is quantum entanglement. In the quantum mechanics branch of physics, quantum entanglement describes how two atomic particles that are created at the same time affect one another after they are separated. People suggest that this might explain how we know something is happening far away from us. It's too much to go into in this book, but there are many reasons why it won't work to explain information sent between brains. Nothing in physics, including quantum mechanics, lets us do what we can do in soul reality.

I think the defenders of physical reality are scared. Physical reality can be controlled. Soul reality is wild. When you get deeper into it, it's much wilder than what I talk about in this book, so it can be scary. Many of the defenders of physical reality are afraid that the control they think they need will be lost. They often express that by saying belief in souls and the things souls can do will take us into a new Dark Ages.

I have two thoughts about that. One is that belief in souls will take us out of our current Dark Ages. The other is that we don't have to lose anything that science has discovered. Physical reality stays as it is, and gets even better. We don't have to choose one or the other. We can choose both.

Some of us will be uncomfortable living in both realities. Some of us are uncomfortable living in only physical reality right now. There are no promises, but I believe most of us will be better off when we find the part of us that is soul.

A second reason that it is hard to say that you have a soul is that it might start a long and uncomfortable conversation about religion. I usually don't mind this, but sometimes it can be really unpleasant.

Belief in a soul does not give others the right to tell you what you must do with it. As with the skeptics in the first reason, this seems to be about fear and control. There are many beings in soul reality. We get to choose which ones we want to co-create with and how we want to do it. This is not permission to be evil. There are consequences in both realities for harming others whether we believe in souls or not.

A third reason it is hard to say we have souls is that we forget. Many people find it hard to remember the experiences they have in soul reality. Before I started to write my experiences down, I forgot most of them. I still forget a lot.

The fact that the culture doesn't honor the experiences isn't all of it. The other part is that we have chosen to be deeply physical. All by itself, being physical is so hard that keeping track of our soul experiences can get lost. In Chapter 7 I talked about Rionagh na Ard moving into a human body. Robert Moss[71], another researcher of soul reality, talks about remembering soul-related dreams. Even if we have had soul experiences, if we don't remember them, how can we say we have a soul? As more and more people talk about soul reality, it will be easier for us to share our memories and keep them alive with our friends and co-creators.

A final reason for not saying we have souls is that having a soul makes us feel different. And who wants to feel different? It's a lot more comfortable to fit in. In the past I would approach the topic very carefully and back off right away if the other person seemed uncomfortable. I still avoid talking about souls in most situations. But I have often been surprised at the support I get from others when the topic of souls comes up. Unexpected people have said to me that they believe in souls, too.

In a Gallup poll[72] taken in 2005, 73% of Americans said they believed in one or more parts of soul reality. The poll used the term paranormal. But all of these things require something besides physical reality. Here is the list and the percentage of people who believed in the phenomenon:

- Extrasensory perception, or ESP: 41%
- That houses can be haunted: 37%
- Ghosts/that spirits of dead people can come back in certain places/situations: 32%
- Telepathy/communication between minds without using traditional senses: 31%
- Clairvoyance/the power of the mind to know the past and predict the future: 26%
- Astrology, or that the position of the stars and planets can affect people's lives: 25%
- That people can communicate mentally with someone who has died: 21%
- Witches: 21%
- Reincarnation, that is, the rebirth of the soul in a new body after death: 20%
- Channeling/allowing a "spirit-being" to temporarily assume control of body: 9%

Adding to the number of people who believe in soul reality is a poll by Baylor University[73] that found that 55% of Americans believe that they are protected by a guardian angel. Of all the parts of soul reality, angels are the most accepted.

When I see results like this, I am amazed that Western culture still seems so set against soul reality. Many of the people who have these beliefs talk about their experiences. I hope that bringing all these experiences together in this book will help.

The difficulties we have in saying we all have souls are why we need proof they exist. Looking at all the ways we know about soul reality will make it easier to talk about it, learn more about it, and live in it.

Types of Proof

There are many definitions of proof. We've taken a look at some of the best evidence for souls. We've put together a model of what a soul looks like. We've shown how souls are connected together. So which definitions of proof have we satisfied?

We'll look at eight ideas about proof. I'm pleased to say that we meet the standards of proof for most of them. Where we don't meet the standards, it's because the standard requires something from physical reality that our soul model says can't be found. It's more of a problem with the standard of proof than with the evidence.

Problems with evidence may show up in all of the proofs. It's always possible to say the proof is wrong because the evidence is no good. The order of the proofs in this chapter goes from those with less certain evidence to ones where the evidence is more reliable. When people say all the evidence is bad, it's time to look at how they are proving what they say. We'll look at that first.

Proof by Authority

Before we look at proofs I think are valuable, let's look at proof by authority. That's where someone who claims to be an expert tells us what must be true. It's even worse when someone quotes an authority, especially when the person doesn't have any deep knowledge of the area.

One example is, "People only imagine they see ghosts because there can't be any such thing as ghosts." Telling us how things have to be really doesn't prove that they are that way. It uses the worst kind of evidence because it really isn't any evidence at all. Proofs using observations are always much better. I'll talk more about that later in the discussion on the Ring of Truth.

Many people use proof by authority even though it isn't very meaningful. I suggested that you remember the tone of voice the servant-girl used when she said, "Ah, 'twas no quality at all. 'Twas only a pack of fairies." When someone gives you a proof by authority, it might be satisfying to say, "Ah, 'twas no quality proof at all. 'Twas only proof by authority."

Personal Experience

We always start with personal experiences. We need to notice something before we can know there is a question. If we think there is only physical reality and we meet an angel, we wonder what is going on. The same is true for anything else that requires soul reality to exist.

It's rare for someone who has seen an angel to say angels don't exist. Most soul-related experiences are like that. We believe in them when they happen to us. We usually continue to believe even when people tell us it isn't possible, although sometimes we forget. The usual change is that we stop talking about it.

Is personal experience of some part of soul reality evidence that souls exist? Yes. Is it proof? Maybe to the person who had the experience. We live in a world with other people. We are affected by what those around us believe. Sometimes we can be convinced that what happened to us didn't really happen after all. We can certainly begin to doubt our experience when no one agrees with us.

Granted, we can be mistaken about what we experience. We can imagine something that didn't happen. Some of what we experience as soul reality may be just a reflection of ourselves. Or it may be something we wish to see. Personal experience is important, but we need to verify it, too. Other kinds of proof are ways to do that.

Observers' Reports

We don't have to have every kind of experience to accept that souls are possible. It usually starts with something that happens to us personally, and then we look at the rest of the world. We can talk with other people or read about what happened to them.

When we find out about other people, we get the idea that what we experienced is more than our imagination. The more reports there are, the more we think that they are true. When we have personal contact with other people who had the same experiences, we can compare what happened and learn from each other.

Reading reports or working with others who share the same experiences can be a kind of proof. Some people think that if there are enough reports by credible observers, beliefs will change. Sometime that is true.

Consensus Belief

When enough people share what happened to them, it can change what the world believes. We can reach a new consensus about how things really work.

As an example, let's look at near-death experiences (NDEs). In the 1970s very few people thought NDEs were real. They pointed out that brains can't have experiences when they are shut down by a near-death state. Over the last 40 years there have been thousands of reports of NDEs. Because of all the reports almost everyone now accepts that NDEs happen.

Whether souls have anything to do with them is still a question for many people. Those who doubt souls exist now say NDEs are a possible function of the brain. That shift in belief about what the brain can do is part of the reason NDEs are accepted. Another reason is the overwhelming number of reports by believable people.

As a culture, we have formed a consensus that NDEs are real. Those who do not accept souls have been pushed into the position of trying to find out how the brain can do something they were once sure it couldn't do. Of course, I think they were right about the brain before and that the soul has the experience.

We haven't reached an NDE type of consensus for other evidence we looked at. Maybe we have a consensus on angels because 55% of us believe they exist, but this is a special case. The people saying there are no angels are usually scientists who are tied completely to physical reality. In the case of angels there is another authority, the Bible. For many people that's enough by itself to prove there are angels. As you know, I'm not a fan of proof by authority, even if the authority is the Bible. So I don't think we can say we have a consensus yet. The voices speaking out against the possibility of angels are loud. The voices for angels are often afraid to speak up. I think we need more people speaking up before we can say angels are accepted by society as a whole.

The Sense of Connection is the other possible exception. Most people say they have observed it. The problem is that it is not a strong effect and not very important in most people's lives. So they let it go and accept the idea that it's just coincidence.

For the rest, we have many observations. But skeptics look at them one at a time and dismiss them as a mistake or a lie. Skeptics don't find the observers credible. One reason skeptics who deny soul reality work so hard to discredit these observers is that the explanations based on only physical reality aren't very credible themselves. If the observations are accurate, then soul reality exists.

Consensus does not have to be shared by our whole society. There are often smaller groups that accept a part of soul reality. They study their part without thinking about how it ties in with the rest of the observations.

I've seen this in martial arts where the concept of ki or chi is part of the teaching. Few people think about what that means as part of physical reality. When I was practicing karate at Caltech and later at the University of Colorado with my Caltech friends, we were a rare group. We knew that the physics we learned at Caltech did not allow for life force. One of my best friends in Colorado who was working on her PhD in microbiology knew that there was nothing in what she learned that allowed for acupuncture points. It was an interesting time trying to figure out what was going on. At the time we just did what most people do — we accepted life force for our practice and didn't look at the broader implications.

After more experiences, things have changed for me. Those discussions are one of the reasons I'm sure we have souls with regions.

Other groups are similar to our karate group. Here are some examples: In energy healing practice the group of healers knows they are using life force. Military and law enforcement people want to learn how to sense threats because their focus is on staying alive. People who work with spirits in soul reality think about contact with the spirits, but not about the larger picture of soul reality. People who are interested in using life force to change things, as in magic, study how their magic can improve without thinking about other aspects.

Each of these groups studies to learn more within the group. But it doesn't carry over to other groups working on other aspects of soul reality. In most of these groups, people focus on one thing without looking at how it connects to the larger picture.

I think we need to look at how all of these practices point to the same conclusion. We all have souls. Working together we can take the consensus we have in each group and make it part of our whole society. That understanding will enhance what all of the groups do.

Ring of Truth

I'm borrowing the term ring of truth from a 1987 PBS television show, with an accompanying book.[74] They, in turn, borrowed the term from the sound gold makes when it is dropped on a hard table. It rings true, which helps to show that it is really gold.

The show was about science and how discoveries in science need to have a ring of truth before they are accepted. It's another way of saying the ideas make sense. They fit together. They make things simpler instead of more complex. I think that's happened with this book. We took a wide range of evidence and put it together in a simple package.

You might ask, "Is this really simple?" Let's look at the other choice.

The heart of the other choice is that there is only a physical reality. That's simple. But then we have to explain why all of these observations of soul reality are wrong: Billions of people know when someone is staring at them. Billions of people believe angels exist and millions have seen them. Billions use chi in martial arts and energy healing. Millions have seen ghosts. Millions know what happened to someone who was far away. And millions (perhaps billions) travel shamanicly to the upper and lower regions of the world. Each of those billions of cases needs its own unique explanation for why each person was wrong.

Saying we all have souls connected by a life force is pretty simple compared to that.

That brings us to the thud of denial. That's the sound you hear when the ring of truth is muffled by a denial landing on it. It's some authority saying it can't be true, the person who thinks there are souls is mistaken or a liar. It's true that many of the reports are about one-time events. But many believable people — millions or billions of them — make those reports. When we do things that can be checked more than once and by other people, the event becomes even more believable and the thud of denial seems more worthless.

The thud of denial goes against what we know. It is proof by authority. It means we need to believe what the authority believes. We aren't allowed to look at anything that questions the authority.

That's the value of the ring of truth. You ask yourself which rings truer — the description of what happened or the denial by someone who wasn't even there? Reports aren't always accurate, but most of the time I'll go with the experience. We check. We question. We look for more evidence. But we don't deny or accept something without thinking just because someone says so.

Reasoning

Reasoning is how we come up with ideas that might have a ring of truth. Another way to say it is that we figure out what is going on. This is especially important when what we have to figure out can't be seen. It's what Isaac Newton did when he developed the laws of gravity. James Maxwell and others did that with electromagnetism. Albert Einstein figured out relativity. Many psychologists, including Abraham Maslow, Carl Rogers, and Carl Jung, have figured out parts of how humans act. All of these people were proposing ways to explain something that caused an effect without being visible. Be it photons of light or the way we decide want we need, all of these people had insights into hidden processes.

We can use the same kinds of reasoning processes to figure out what is going on with life force and souls.

Before we see how reasoning helps to prove we have souls, we need to look at the three types of reasoning: deductive, inductive, and hypothesis. This is useful information if you plan to get in deep discussions with skeptics. You can also skip most of it and still get the important points about using reasoning. To do that, read the heading and the short first paragraph for each type of reasoning. Start reading again at the heading Applying Reasoning.

For this discussion I'm borrowing ideas from a book by Phillip Weibe.[75] He looked at proofs that are available for the Christian God and other spirits using the three types of reasoning. Each type has a different purpose and is used for a different kind of evidence. As we will see, we need to use the right kind of reasoning for each piece of evidence when we are trying to prove souls exist.

Deductive Reasoning

Deductive reasoning takes general statements and combines them together to conclude something about a specific case.

Let's look at an example. We can start with the general statement, "All physical bodies die." Now let's look at what we can deduce about a specific case. Here's one: "Tom has a physical body." Using deductive reasoning we can conclude, "Tom's body will die." We can't conclude, though, that Tom will die. That would require a starting statement like, "All beings die," which I don't believe is true.

This is an important aspect of deductive reasoning. If the general statement is not true, then what we deduce from the statement may or may not be true. Let's look at a different example: "All bald men are grandfathers." "Andy is a bald man." "George is a bald man." It turns out that Andy is a grandfather, but George is not. What we deduce may be right or wrong. When we find a deduction that is right, it supports, but does not prove, the general statement, in this case, "All bald men are grandfathers." When we find a deduction that is wrong, we know that the general statement is wrong, too.

Many people say that deductive reasoning is how science is done. Let's look at that right after I change to a more scientific way of talking. When we are testing something, science calls the general statement a hypothesis. This is something that may or may not be true.

When we consider deductive reasoning, we find that it's possible to prove something is wrong. "All bald men are grandfathers" is not true. But it's almost impossible to prove that something meaningful is true. We might say, "All physical bodies die." We can't prove that is true unless we look at every physical body that ever existed and ever will exist. There might be one that doesn't die. We'll talk more about this in the section on inductive reasoning.

When they want to test a hypothesis, scientists usually state it in a way that lets them look for one case to disprove it. For example, one statement is, "We all have souls that continue after death." That means we have to look at all souls, past, present, and future. This can't be done.

However, if we want to prove that souls exist, we can hypothesize, "We have nothing that continues after death." Then all we have to do is find one example of something that continues after death and we have disproved the hypothesis. Reincarnation studies have shown something that continues. If we accept even one of the reincarnation studies, we can say, "Sometimes there is something that continues after death." We can't say, "There is always something that continues after death." That would require checking every death, which we can't do.

If you choose to call that something a soul, as I do, that's just assigning a name. What matters is that there is something, not what it is called.

So there are uses for deductive reasoning in science and in proving we have souls. However, figuring out how things work isn't one of them.

That's what hypothesis reasoning is all about. We'll look at that after we look at inductive reasoning.

Inductive Reasoning

Inductive reasoning takes a set of single observations and turns them into a general rule.

Let's look at examples. At the shopping mall we run into Andy. He's bald and he's a grandfather. We talk with Cal and he's a bald grandfather, too. Maybe we're onto something. So we start asking all the bald men we see if they are grandfathers. After 20 or so say yes, we might use inductive reasoning to decide, "All bald men are grandfathers."

Here's where things get difficult. We know that to be sure, we have to ask every bald man. Not possible. So the question is how sure can we be with the sample we have. Even that has no easy answer.

Think about these two cases: (1) Everyone seated on the bus is moving northward. (2) Everyone seated on the bus was born on Tuesday. Checking one person lets us prove that case (1) is true. One person is enough because we know, through inductive reasoning, that every seat on a bus moves in the same direction. For case (2), we would usually have to ask everybody. Days of birth are not restricted in the same way as bus seats.

The need to make guesses from incomplete samples doesn't mean that inductive reasoning has no value. Most of the time we use it successfully in our daily lives — but sometimes not so successfully. Here's an example of that. Let's say we observed that Mary was friendly to me every time I saw her. We can use inductive reasoning to decide, "Mary is always friendly." That's our hypothesis.

We would use deductive reasoning to figure out that the next time we see Mary she will be friendly. So, Mary is having a bad day and she isn't friendly. Our hypothesis is wrong. Mary isn't always friendly. But we might have a next hypothesis, "Mary is a friend." Now friends are usually friendly, but they may have bad days when they are not.

This is where inductive reasoning gets really complicated. We have to ask how much of the time does Mary need to be friendly to be called a friend? Are there other actions, such as being cruel, that stop her from being a friend? We continue to add the experiences to our store of information and may use inductive reasoning to revise our hypothesis after any interaction. It's an ongoing process.

It's actually far more complicated than this example. If you want to look at the incredible level of detail related to inductive reasoning, I suggest the article called "The Problem of Induction" in the Stanford Encyclopedia of Philosophy.[76]

I used inductive reasoning when I was thinking about whether there was something besides physical reality. Each of those instances I included in the evidence was another point in favor. Some were more important than others, but they all added to the general hypothesis that physical reality is not enough to explain everything that happens.

Remember in the discussion of deductive reasoning, I pointed out that reincarnation disproved the hypothesis that there was nothing that continued after death. The other parts of the evidence disproved the idea that physical reality is enough to explain everything that happens. By disproving the case that there is only the physical, we show that there really is something else. In the next section on hypothesis reasoning we'll look at the even bolder statement, "We all have souls."

Hypothesis Reasoning

Hypothesis reasoning (often called abductive reasoning) is different for two major reasons. First, it doesn't start with first principles or a set of assumptions. Second, unlike the other two types of reasoning, it can handle objects that we can't see. It starts with observations, just as we did with our evidence. Then it proposes something — a hypothesis — that explains the evidence. It pulls all the observations together and explains them with a simple principle. It has worked very well in physical reality.

This type of reasoning was used to explain electromagnetism. A set of formulas was developed to calculate what happens when we are working with electricity and magnetism.

The same type of reasoning was used to explain physical matter. The levels of current understanding started with the idea of atoms. Then researchers described parts of atoms — protons, electrons, and neutrons. More evidence led to other sub-atomic particles and later on to quarks. It wasn't that people observed these things. They just thought of something that made sense of what they could see. Then they tested what they proposed.

Success of a proposed model has two parts. The first is whether the hypothesis explains a large set of the evidence. The second is whether we can predict what will happen in different situations. The second part is where deductive reasoning can be used. We take the hypothesis and deduce things we could see if the hypothesis is true. Then we test to see if the predictions are true. Hypothesis reasoning works in soul reality, too.

Applying Reasoning

In this book I used all three kinds of reasoning to come up with a theory for soul reality. My work with soul reality started with inductive reasoning. One by one I found things that didn't fit with physical reality. Ghosts seemed to say something continues after death. Karate kept giving me examples of life force. Eventually I decided that there was something to study.

I used hypothesis reasoning to simplify what I was seeing into souls using life force. As it was supposed to, hypothesis reasoning eventually led me to the model that is in this book. It's not complete yet, but it meets the first test of success by explaining many observations. Let's look at some examples.

The hypothesis that humans have souls that continue after our death explains reincarnation, ghosts, human spirits, and near-death experiences. We don't need more to explain them.

The hypothesis that other beings also have souls explains angels, nature spirits, Sidhe, and other beings we encounter. Non-human contacts described by shamans, witches, and other magic workers are covered, too. Having souls allows these beings to exist outside physical reality. It also means that they don't have to follow the same laws of physics that our bodies usually follow.

The hypothesis of life force gives us a way to talk about the non-physical parts of martial arts and energy healing.

When we combine souls and life force, we can explain the Sense of Connection and the many kinds of ESP.

All of these seem straightforward. Just hypothesizing that we have souls that use life force will let us deduce most of this set of evidence.

Where we need more is in understanding the connection between the physical and the soul. In energy healing we need to explain how giving life force to a person's soul helps heal the physical body. There is a similar question about life force and martial arts. The place where we really need to do more work is in the superpowers. My favorite question is how do we explain St. Teresa floating in the air?

Not knowing how life force and physical reality interact does not say our current hypothesis about souls and life force is wrong. But it does point out that there is more work to do. Proposing life force and souls in humans is like proposing protons, electrons, and neutrons in atoms. It's a model that helps explain a lot of things, but there are deeper levels to discover. Interactions between physical reality and soul reality is one of those levels.

The second test of success asks if we can deduce predictions that we can test. My earlier book, *Calculating Soul Connections*, has a large set of predictions for soul connections. So, the answer is yes, we can find predictions.

Let's look at a simple one. The Sense of Connection looks at the connection between two souls. Our concept of souls allows them to learn. We can deduce that souls can learn to sense connection better. That's testable. If we just go out and ask a set of people to do the Sense of Connection experiment, we might expect that people will get better at sensing as they do the experiment more times.

There are statistical techniques to analyze this kind of data. That's beyond the scope of this book. But it's important to understand that there are never absolutely clear answers. It's a bit like the problem with inductive reasoning. We can't test everyone. Problems also show up because the Sense of Connection effect is very small. We have to use a large group to be sure of the effects of practice. We'll talk more about some of those issues in the next section on accuracy of predictions.

A similar experiment could be made from Caylor Adkins' practice of stalking sentries. The people in that practice did get better. What we would search for are the effects of different types of training.

Another study might look at when people remember previous lives. It's rare. The current hypothesis is that people remember when they wish to finish something from the life before or feel a deep commitment to stay with the ones they love. Some questions include: How strong does the wish need to be? Does sudden death make a difference? Is love or anger a stronger reason?

To sum up, my belief is that our hypotheses have been successful. They account for what we have seen. And they give us ideas about more things we can study. They aren't the end of the road, but they lead us in a promising direction.

Lessons

I'll be the first to agree that there are some deep concepts when we talk about reasoning. We barely touched the surface. So here is a short exercise to see if you have learned to pick apart the kinds of reasoning. It will help you when you are listening to other people try to explain why their views are correct.

One-Minute Exercise

Let's take a look at the specific hypothesis, "We all have souls." Did we actually prove that? Take a minute to think about the kinds of reasoning that you might use to prove souls exist.

If you've followed the discussion, you might say no, we didn't prove we *all* have souls. And you would be right.

Hypothesis reasoning was successful in explaining and predicting. Deductive reasoning let us know that we have evidence to disprove "Nothing exists after death." That leads to the conclusion that something does continue.

But then we run into a problem. We would need to check all of us and also have a way to tell if a soul is present. We can never check all of us and we don't have a reliable check for souls right now.

I'm not feeling bad about that, though. I think we have proven that souls exist. It's okay that we only have inductive reasoning to suggest that we *all* have them.

Accuracy of Predictions

Now we look at the official scientific style of proof. You run an experiment to see if you get the expected results. If you get the right results, you prove your hypothesis.

If only it were that simple.

In our world, whether it's soul reality or physical reality, there are two complications. One is that it's hard to measure something accurately. The second is that what we're looking for doesn't have to show up every time. It just has to show up more than we would expect by chance.

Measurement problems may mean that we can't be sure what we have found. We can never measure something exactly. When the effect we hope to see is less than the measurement uncertainty, we can't tell if we are really seeing an effect. The scientific standard for saying there is an effect is that there is about a 95% chance that the effect is bigger than the measurement uncertainty.

Comparing our results to chance is done with numbers. We use statistical calculations to figure out how likely our results are. The standard for most scientific research is that you would get the result less than one time in twenty.

I'm going to talk more about each of these issues. As with the reasoning discussion, you don't need to read this unless you want to talk to someone using a lot of scientific detail. The most important conclusion we get from the discussion is that it's really, really likely Sheldrake's Sense of Being Stared At experiment proves we have some ability to know when someone is staring at us. But we can only sense the stare a little bit, so we can't be sure we will be right every time. If you want to, you can now skip down to the section on Physical Evidence.

Measurement Error

In physical reality we can never measure something exactly. In a simple case, we know that using a ruler will tell us if something is about 12 inches long. If we have a good ruler and are really careful, we can probably get the measurement to about 1/32 of an inch. But what if we need to measure a difference of one thousandth of an inch? We just can't measure that well with a ruler.

So we find a better measuring tool. But there are always limits, and experiments are always pushing them. In the end, we can't make the tools good enough for the tiniest of differences. The Heisenberg uncertainty principle, which tells us the limit to how well we can measure something, makes that clear. And that's a topic for a completely different book.

Most of the things we want to measure aren't that small. But there are still uncertainties in measuring them. When I use a ruler, I expect to measure to an eighth of an inch. So if I predict exactly 10 inches, any measurement between 9 7/8 and 10 1/8 inches would agree with my prediction. If I got 11 inches, though, I would have to say my prediction was wrong.

There are detailed ways to combine measurement errors. Those aren't important here. The bottom line is that our hypothesis is wrong if the prediction it gives is outside the error limits. If it's inside the error limits, we can keep on using the hypothesis. And inductive reasoning gives us another case to help show the hypothesis is correct.

Measurement error is used when we are looking at physical things like weight, distance, and time. Since soul reality doesn't seem to have any of those, we only care when we are measuring how soul reality changes physical reality. The only evidence we have that soul reality might cause changes to something physical is from the special powers.

Let's imagine we can put St. Teresa on a scale and she weighs 100 pounds. We measure her a few more times and she ranges from 98 to 102. If we weigh her in a state of ecstasy and she weighs 98 pounds, we haven't shown anything. If she weighs 50 pounds in ecstasy, I'd say we were outside the measurement error. Even without actually floating, we have real evidence of a special power. The less she weighs, the more certain the proof is.

Probability

Probability talks about how often we expect something to happen. Let's say we have a coin that has an equal chance of coming up heads or tails. If we flip the coin 10 times, the most likely outcome is five heads and five tails. That will happen about 25% of the time. But it is almost as likely that there will be four heads and six tails. That happens about 21% of the time. There is even a chance that the 10 flips will all be tails. That will happen about one time in one thousand.

But no one ever promised that all coins are fair. In this case fair means that the coin has an equal chance of coming up heads or tails. We can check how fair coins are by flipping them. Let's say we flip another coin 100 times and there are 60 heads. For a fair coin this would happen about 1% of the time. Based on our result, we could use inductive reasoning to say that this unfair coin is more likely to come up heads in the future.

It doesn't matter how many times in a row a fair coin has come up heads. The chances are still 50-50 that it will come up heads on the next flip. With this particular unfair coin, the odds on every flip are 60-40 in favor of heads.

So how does this apply to proving we all have souls? Let's take a look at the Sense of Connection experiment. In that experiment the starer acts and the person being stared at reacts. Much like the coin can come up heads or tails, the person being stared at has two choices. If there is no soul connection, we expect the person to be right half the time and wrong half the time. If there is a positive effect from a soul connection, the person will be right more than half the time.

We compare the results of the experiment with the possibility in which there is no effect. The no-effect case (called the null case) is that the receiver will be right half the time.

What we are looking for is how likely it is that the scores in the experiment could happen by chance. There's a scientific standard for this. It's considered statistically significant when the probability that the results happened by chance is less than 5%. That's shown in research papers as "p < .05" ("p is less than point oh five"). Results like that will get you published in a scientific journal. It's highly statistically significant when the probability is less than 1%. That's even better. If your results mean something, you can be published in an *important* scientific journal.

Here's an overview of what researchers look for in the Sense of Connection experiment.

To show we have souls we want to know how often people get six, seven, eight, nine, or ten out of ten. It is much easier to find the average than look at all of the cases, especially when there are a large number of results. An average greater than five out of ten shows we have souls.

When the average score increases, there is more evidence that we have souls. If people are usually right seven times out of ten, it's more likely that we have souls than if they are averaging six times out of ten.

When we give more tests and find the same higher average, it is more likely we have souls. That's an inductive reasoning idea that can be calculated in this kind of experiment — the more times we find something, the more likely it is to be true.

The details of the calculations are too difficult for this book, but we can look at some results. These are from Rupert Sheldrake's "Online Staring Experiment from October 14, 2003 to December 4, 2014."[77]

> Altogether 1751 pairs of people have taken part, giving a total of 35,020 trials. By chance people would be right 50% of the time. In fact the overall score was 56.4% correct. The statistical significance of this result is astronomical, with odds against chance of quadrillions to one.
>
> There was a difference in the results in looking and not-looking trials. People were more successful at guessing correctly when they were being looked at than when they were not being looked at. In the looking trials the average hit rate was 60.1%, and in the not looking trials 52.7%.

Just in case it's not clear, "odds against chance of quadrillions to one" is way better than the scientific standard of $p < .01$. At least some of the people in Sheldrake's experiment seemed to have souls.

This kind of proof using probabilities can be used in other places. It helps if we are dealing with numbers. We also need to know what a random score would be. Many ESP experiments use this kind of proof.

Reincarnation might be another place for this kind of proof. A girl might be asked how many brothers and sisters she had in her previous life. Finding the p-value is not as simple as the yes-no of the staring experiment, but it can be done.

Probability is the gold standard for science. There are many pieces of evidence for souls that can't be proven this way. It takes tests that can be repeated many times with clear numerical answers. The good news is that some of our evidence can be proven this way using one of the most important kinds of proof.

Physical Evidence

Let's end with the standard of proof that is almost impossible for us to meet: physical evidence of a soul. We don't know how to extract a soul to look at it with physical instruments. Yes, there are Kirlian photographs that show an aura around a body or a leaf or whatever. They are done using electrical discharges.

We don't claim to know how souls and electricity interact. It's even harder to predict what they will look like on a photograph. If we had a prediction for how to change the aura, and the results were what we expected, then we'd have some proof. We're not there yet, so we haven't proven souls exist by using this kind of physical proof.

There is, however, another kind of physical proof that we should look at. We know that when a person dies, something changes. Cells in the body that were acting together before death start to act separately. Since we say that everything has a soul, each of these cells would have their own souls, too. Let's look at the hypothesis that our soul coordinates all of the souls in our cells and in the other cells living on and in our body. We would predict that the parts of the body will start to act on their own when our soul leaves.

This is pretty much what happens. But sometimes the body carries on with medical support. I suggest that the soul is hanging around to meet the wishes of loved ones or doctors who want it to stay there.

Sometimes the body comes back to life even when the vital signs have stopped for long enough that the medical team says the person has died. I suggest that the soul has returned for whatever reason and is in charge of the body again.

The moment of death has always been a puzzle for those who believe in just physical reality. They usually say it's handled by the brain. There is some truth in that, especially with breathing. But they really can't tie death to any physical part of the body. I think that a close look at the moment of death might provide indirect physical evidence that we have souls.

But we can't put a soul on a dissecting table and do an autopsy.

Evidence and Proof

Let's take a look at the evidence we have and how it proves that souls and life force exist. We described evidence in four areas: connections in physical reality, use of life force in martial arts and healing, souls that continue after the body dies, and ways we interact with soul reality. Let's go through them the same way here.

Connections in Physical Reality

Rupert Sheldrake's Sense of Being Stared At experiment satisfies six of the eight types of proof for most people. Eighty percent of the people Sheldrake surveyed have had the personal experience. In addition, many people report that they know when someone is looking at them. At 80%, it is a consensus belief. For me it has a ring of truth. It makes sense that we will survive better with the sense. We can use hypothesis reasoning to propose souls and life force to make the connection. Other hypotheses are possible, too. But they all need soul reality. Experiments show that people can sense when they are being stared at, agreeing with our predictions. For me it is clear proof that something like life force connects us. We also need to have something like souls to feel the life force connection.

The same proofs work for Sheldrake's telephone experiment. The consensus may be weaker. The prediction proof may be a bit stronger.

Caylor Adkins' description of his work with sentries includes personal experience and observer's reports. I find the same ring of truth there as I do for the Sense of Connection. I especially like how people improve with practice. Souls and life force work as a hypothesis to explain what Adkins observed. If we have souls, my deductive reasoning says we would use them to protect ourselves. We don't have numbers to test the accuracy of predictions. I think this is solid proof, partly because I've felt it. It certainly provides good support.

All of this evidence can be tested by you. Sheldrake's phone test is online at http://www.sheldrake.org/participate/telephone-telepathy-test. If you want to spend more time and money, you can go to a class on military training.

ESP proof is based on personal experiences, observer's reports, and predictions. For me it has a ring of truth, but it does not have consensus belief. Most of the experiments do not come from deductions about soul reality. They often have mixed results. Even so, they seem to provide support for soul reality. With different designs, these experiments could provide better proof.

The evidence for perception at a distance is based on personal experience and observer's reports. It has a ring of truth for me, but there is not a consensus that it can be done. Having souls explains the evidence. I would deduce perception at a distance from the hypothesis that we have souls. But I don't know of a good way to test it well enough to prove a prediction. It supports the proof of souls and life force, but it's not enough by itself to prove they exist.

The evidence for knowing the future is also based on personal experience and observer's reports. I don't think there is a consensus that it can be done. By itself, having souls and life force does not explain the evidence. We also need a hypothesis for space and time. I haven't seen convincing experiments yet. Robert Moss's work with synchronicity and dreams[78] might head in that direction, if he chooses to go there. I don't think predicting the future helps prove we have souls. It does prove that our view of physical reality is missing something. Soul reality might be part of it.

Life after Life

Reincarnation has proof by authority in many of the world's religions. People have personal experiences, although Ian Stevenson's work makes experiences as adults less certain. We have observer's reports. In some cultures there is consensus belief. In the West there is not. It has a ring of truth for me because most people seem to wish to go on living. Coming back makes sense as an alternative. The hypothesis of souls matches the evidence. We can also deduce reincarnation if we start with the idea of having souls. I think Stevenson's work has a lot of the data needed to check the accuracy of predictions. There are two things that haven't been done yet. One is to figure out what random answers look like. The other is to find a good way to decide how much difference there is between the answers the children give and the random case. I think this work provides proof for souls that continue after death.

Ghosts and other human spirits have been experienced by many people. A lot of them made reports. Some cultures have a consensus belief in ghosts. Western culture is close to a majority, and we might also define consensus by looking at the acceptance of movies with ghost-related themes. I hear the ring of truth for people being stuck here after death. The hypothesis of souls matches the evidence. Some parts of the hypothesis of life force are shaped by the ways we see ghosts act. Making predictions that we can test seems unlikely. It seems unethical, too. It's much better to send ghosts on to a better place than to subject them to a series of boring tests here on earth. Ghosts provide supporting proof for souls.

Places with memories and residual hauntings have been experienced by many people. You can have a personal experience by visiting a major battlefield and checking your mood before and after. We have observer's reports with battlefields and other places. I do not think there is consensus belief. I used to have trouble with the ring of truth on places with memories. I thought it was the souls that remained that caused the residual haunting. Now I feel that places as well as living beings have souls. Places with memories and souls staying in places both explain the evidence. I think it is possible to measure a change in mood to prove the accuracy of a prediction. I don't know of anyone who has done it yet. These places provide supporting proof for life force. They also provide supporting proof for some kind of soul, either human or in the land. If someone ran careful experiments that found a significant change in mood, I would say that these places provided solid proof.

Human spirits was the next set of evidence. These are beings who choose to stay on earth, as opposed to ghosts who are stuck here because they don't know any better. The proofs are pretty much the same as for ghosts. The proof of souls is as strong or stronger. We predict that spirits are stronger than ghosts because they are aware of what they are doing. Being able to correctly predict the contrast helps prove life force exists.

Near-death experiences have proof by authority, personal experience, and observer's reports. There is a consensus belief and a ring of truth. Souls explain the evidence well. (Memories when the brain isn't active do not.) NDEs can be deduced from souls. I don't know of any ethical way to conduct clean experiments to test accuracy. Memories of events during an NDE might be compared to a random set of memories, but that would be hard to define. NDEs provide supporting evidence for souls.

Using Life Force

Martial arts have proof by authority, personal experiences, and observer's reports. Many martial arts groups have a consensus belief that life force exists. Perhaps there is consensus belief in the outside world, too. As with ghosts, we certainly see it shown and accepted in a lot of movies. It has a ring of truth for me. Life force explains the evidence. Souls are not necessarily required. There have been experiments to show that predictions of the effect of life force are accurate. We might even say this is one of the few places where we have a hint of physical evidence. Martial arts, especially the experiments, provide useful proof for life force, but almost no proof for souls.

Energy healing has personal experience and observer's reports. It does not have a consensus belief in the larger community right now. That seems to be changing, though. It has a ring of truth for me and for those who have worked with it. Life force may explain part of the evidence. We would predict that souls use life force to heal other souls. Predicting that life force can heal physical bodies is not as clear. We are missing a hypothesis for how souls and bodies are connected. People have done standard tests to see if energy healing works. Most have been poorly done. The techniques that have been well tested, such as EFT, do not have a clear soul reality component. Better tests can be done. For now, I think energy healing gives supportive evidence for life force and souls.

There are personal experience and observers' reports for special powers. People are not shocked by stories of mothers who lift cars off children, so there may be consensus belief and a ring of truth. There probably isn't a consensus belief that life force is involved. What we usually hear is what amazing things bodies can do under stress. People floating in the air is a whole different story. Very few people think that is possible. Life force explains special powers. Special powers in emergencies can't be tested. If we could find someone who could float in the air at will, we would have something to test. Testing someone who floated actually was done in the late 1800s with D. D. Home. It was done badly and provides no useful evidence. At this time I think special powers provide no proof of souls. Being able to lift a lot of weight might provide a little bit of proof for life force.

Interactions with Soul Reality

Inspiration is a really exciting concept. The experiences and the reports of people who have experienced it are often profound. Too bad it can't be tested to see whether it comes from within a person or from outside. Souls explain the evidence, but I don't think inspiration provides any real proof for souls or life force.

We have much better proof with interactions with other beings. It has proof by authority, personal experiences, and observer's reports. There is a consensus belief, especially for angels. In many cultures, including some in the West, there is also a consensus on other beings, such as fairies. I get a loud ring of truth from the idea that souls come in all sizes and shapes. Souls and life force explain the evidence. There are a few kinds of experiments that can be done to test the accuracy of predictions. Most involve comparing contacts by two different people with the same being. There is supporting proof for souls. Some of the things these beings do give supporting proof for the concept of life force, too.

Human magic workers have personal experiences and provide observer's reports. Within their groups, there is a consensus that what they are doing is real. There is less consensus outside of the group. Often one group will say that what another group is doing isn't real. It makes for some interesting, but not productive, controversies. I do magic and have felt it work, so it has a ring of truth for me. Souls and life force explain the evidence. Testing predictions is almost impossible. Sometimes we can test them when the goal is healing a particular physical or emotional problem. Even then, good tests are difficult to figure out. Magic workers provide some support for souls and life force.

Continuing Research

We aren't through finding out about souls. In fact, I believe we are still very near the beginning. So how do we go on from here? Jeremy Berg, a teacher in the Lorian Association, sent me the following thoughts about research[79], saying, "I was just tapped on the shoulder with the following idea." Let's include it in our examples of inspiration.

> The power of science resides not in its accumulation of facts — as useful as they may be. Rather the power of science lies in the simple proposition that every fact and conclusion is offered to the world in as transparent a way as possible: the hypothesis is straightforward, the experiment is well described, and the conclusions are narrowly drawn without undue speculation. All of this is done clearly and concisely so that anyone *sufficiently trained and well versed in the field* is free to test the hypothesis for themselves and draw their own conclusions. In other worlds the experiment is replicable.

> This is also true of investigations into non-physical domains. Take for example your citations of Chi in the book as evidence of soul. The hypothesis is that there is a non-physical energy of Chi which has demonstrable effects. The method of investigation is for someone to become *sufficiently trained and well versed in the field* so that they can see for themselves and experience Chi first hand. The investigator can then draw their

own conclusions. If sufficient number of *trained* investigators came to the same or similar conclusions about Chi it could be said to have a high probability of being fact. This would be a properly run investigation into Chi.

Obviously one would not expect a person not *sufficiently trained and well versed in the field* to run an experiment in particle physics or to be able to interpret the result without sufficient math and physics competency. Yet people routinely pass judgment on shamanic, spiritual, martial art, psychic, NDEs, angelic encounters, and other subtle world assertions without any training at all. A materialist who does not take the time to run a honest experiment into subtle phenomena or comments about it based on presumptions that it cannot exist is not much different than someone who doesn't believe in atoms because they have never seen one.

The problem, it seems to me, is that assertions made about soul are generally made in terms of revelation and not as a working hypothesis which could be shown to be wrong or only partial truths. And, it is also true that in realms of spirit one's attitude toward the experiment gains greater weight than in a purely physical experiment — although it may also play a role in material science as well. Soul investigations may require a more robust (albeit temporary) suspension of tightly held beliefs to do justice to the experiment.

Jeremy is saying several useful things. The one that means the most to me is that Proof by Authority is even more worthless when the authority has no training in what he or she is talking about. Perhaps to them we say, "'Twas only proof by authority. But 'twas no authority at all."

Conclusions

We are looking for phenomena that are rare. The exciting ones mostly happen in special places and at special times. There are many careful observations that need to be done, by you and others.

Luckily, the less exciting cases give us two strong pieces of proof. Sheldrake's connection tests show that there is life force. Stevenson's reincarnation work shows that there are souls. Some energy healing, including EFT and EMDR, has been experimentally proven. But it may not require soul reality.

But there is more to proof than the individual pieces. All of the other evidence comes out of the same basic hypothesis. It all helps prove souls and life force exist. Being able to tie many pieces of evidence together with just these two concepts makes the hypothesis much, much stronger.

There is a lot of skepticism to overcome. Doing that will be very difficult. But here's the interesting part, all of us who have felt soul reality have to ask ourselves, "Is that real?" If we decide it is, then we have a reason to work together to show that there is more to life than physical reality. If we are honest, if we are careful, we can put together a case as compelling as many others in science. And we're working for something that can really help us find more positive connections and caring in our world.

9. PURPOSE

> People say that what we are all seeking is
> the meaning of life I don't think that's what
> we're really seeking. I think what we're seeking
> is an experience of being alive.
>
> — *Joseph Campbell*

Our purpose here is to create glorious, awe-inspiring, soul-expanding moments. We are here to be alive, to be part of our world's ongoing creation. We are here to do things that fill us with joy and wonder. We are here to create more beauty and deeper expressions of love.

In a reality filled with souls, each mess we clean up and each good work we devise exists for all time. What we do makes a difference for ourselves and for every soul we connect with. And we get to share our triumphs in making positive changes.

Is there evil in the world? Yes, there is a lot of it. We're here to deal with that, too.

Light is present when things are created. These are the parts of our world that have positive life force. But there is also shadow. That's the dark side that doesn't work in the best interests of the beings who run into it. We can see both of them all around us all the time. I don't think we ever get rid of all the shadow.

The purpose of being is to understand our shadow and create more light. Those of us who have been blessed with bodies in physical reality have specific ways we can do that. We'll be looking at those ways in this chapter.

If you are looking for a personal purpose, start with being happy because you can make some of your deepest wishes happen. You can clean up some of the problems that are making you unhappy in this lifetime and others. Find love and share it with others. You can end up better than when you started.

Knowing that you have a soul makes it clear that combining some work with your fun is worthwhile. Knowledge of souls shows how you can choose a happier life.

At the heart of choice is the idea of free will. Having a soul explains why we can choose. There is something outside of physical reality that interacts with it, mostly through the way our bodies and souls connect.

In the rest of the chapter we will look at six ways having a body to go with our soul is a good idea. One is separateness. It's hard to learn about ourselves when we are closely tied to everyone else. Another is change. Physical reality may be the only way to look at the idea of cause and effect. The third is thought. I think our brains let us think more clearly and about more complicated ideas. The fourth is connecting by choice. The lesson is that we can be sovereign in ourselves and also connect with others in friendship and love. The fifth is experiencing and thanking. Our bodies give us good things in our lives and some less good experiences that we can learn from. The mix of blessings and sorrows is what gives life meaning. We need to be part of what happens and give thanks for who we are. The sixth is explaining and understanding our reality. Having a body lets us look at a completely different reality that souls otherwise can never know.

Separateness

To be separate from all that is around us is rare. We may talk about feeling separate, but it isn't what is really going on. Most of us connect daily at school or work. We also have texts, social media, music, and video. Sometimes we even spend time in person with friends. Sometimes the contact is even physical.

Even with all that connection, we often feel alone. Let's look at how having bodies affects our feeling of being separate.

When we are not in our bodies, things are different. We interact with other souls very freely. We may be so tightly connected that we can't tell which soul is which. Our thoughts and feelings are more open to everyone else.

In bodies the distinction between souls is much clearer. In physical reality it is always clear where one body ends and another one begins.

Even from a soul point of view, having a body helps the I-Am draw a line between two souls. Most of the time our thoughts and feelings are shared using something physical like talking, writing, or touching. It is very hard to use life force to share thoughts or feelings while we are in bodies. And touch is possible only for bodies.

Having an I-Am also lets us study our soul more carefully. For example, I can study my Heart and not confuse it with your Heart. The problem is a little harder for empaths, who often can sense what is going on in someone else's Heart. But, even for them, having a body makes the connection and the separation clearer.

Separateness may be even deeper than that. Many practices talk about three regions of the world: upper, middle, and lower. I don't think the middle region was always here. I think it happened when some beings decided to separate the other regions. Some people like to speak of the creator of the middle region. Based on the fact that we are the ones who are here, I think there is a chance that the creators of the middle region include us.

It's hard for some to think that humans have that kind of power. But I don't think humans are a lesser form, still in the early stages of learning about both physical and soul realities. What I believe and what I hear from some other people is that we humans are partners in creating this physical reality. We may not remember creating our world, but I think there are other reasons for that. We won't look at those in this book.

The creation of a middle region didn't happen without the concept of separateness. The middle region lets us study separateness more deeply. When we come right down to it, the middle region and the separateness of beings depend on one another to exist.

This leads to the idea that it may be easier to reach to the upper region and make connections there when we are in bodies. It may be easier to tap into the deep levels of energy that we have automatically when we are without bodies. It is certainly easier to explore those connections with a body. When we have edges, how we get through them to the upper, middle, and lower regions is clearer. And so are the properties of those regions.

Albert Einstein speaks about separateness and connection:

> A human being is a part of a whole, called by us *universe*, a part limited in time and space. He experiences himself, his thoughts and feelings as something separated from the rest … a kind of optical delusion of his consciousness. This delusion is a kind of prison for us, restricting us to our personal desires and to affection for a few persons nearest to us. Our task must be to free ourselves from this prison by widening our circle of compassion to embrace all living creatures and the whole of nature in its beauty.

I agree that we must learn to connect. But let's look a little more at the benefits of separateness.

We must not get caught in the belief that physical reality is something to be disdained and that soul reality is more important. If we do that, we lose two things. The first is that we are caught up in the glamour of spirit beings and lose our ability to stand in our own sovereignty, as equal to them. And we are equal to them in our right to be sovereign. The second is that we lose sight of the miracle we have created in physical reality. To be here, to be solid, and to still be able to reach soul reality is a very powerful achievement.

Lessons

It's hard to design a separation exercise that doesn't run into problems by causing too much separation. We're already so separate. I think it's safer to go the other direction. So we will look at what happens when we are much more closely connected. We'll imagine what it's like between lives to see how being in a body gives us more freedom to learn.

One-Minute Exercise

Start by bringing your thoughts and feelings together in a safe place.

Imagine yourself turning into a raindrop in a cloud. Breathe yourself into the shape of a drop. You are separate from the other raindrops. If you were a magic raindrop, you could go anywhere.

Now fall out of the cloud and land in the ocean. Suddenly you are part of a much larger mass of water. You are connected with all the other drops of water and that limits what you can do. You can flow with the current of the ocean. You can rise and fall in waves. But you are doing that with all the other drops that are connected to you. There are no individual choices.

Now imagine a storm with whitecaps. At the top of waves, individual droplets break away from the ocean. You are one of them.

Before you fall back into the ocean again, come back to your body and experience being separate from the billions of other humans around you, just like the drop is separate from the ocean.

Humans have the choice of working or playing alone. We can also work or play with a team for a group goal, but the group is not all the people on the planet. We're more like the ocean when we are voting for a president. It's a group decision. Each person adds a little to the choice, but the final result is a decision shared by all of us. For earth to work the way I think it was intended, we need to retain our freedom to choose while also being part of our culture.

Change

We sign up for some hard lessons when we decide to be human. Just getting into a body seems to be pretty traumatic. I think most of us lose a portion of our souls when we enter the physical realm. We almost always lose our memories of past lives. Rionagh na Ard's experience as a Sidhe taking over a human body is an example of this.

Then this physical body keeps on changing. And so does everything else in the world around us.

Understanding and accepting that things are not always going to be the same is one of the important lessons of physical reality. It's all part of the plan. As Brian Andreas whimsically describes it:

> Most people don't know there are angels whose only job is to make sure you don't get too comfortable and fall asleep and miss your life.

Another aspect of change is that it happens even if we don't want it to. In soul reality all the souls may agree to a change, but on earth change happens even when we have no say in the decision. In fact, it's that way a lot of the time.

We have time here so we can make decisions and see the results. It's part of our training. We learn that sometimes we can cause things to be different all by ourselves. In small decisions, we can make choices that make a difference hundreds of times a day.

Time helps us another way by giving us a past, present, and future. When we are hurt, we remember being hurt in similar ways in the past. We don't want to be hurt again in the future. That motivates us to make changes now that will reduce the pain in the future.

Deborah Bryon works with people who want to change what they are doing because they are hurting. She puts it this way:

> I have noticed working as a psychologist, that people are the most accessible when they are in pain. [The pain] is bringing them in to my office for the first time. I have learned that with some people, if I am not able to connect with them

right then and there in some capacity, and work with them to help them shift into an energetic experience that they can feel and that registers with them, then once they start to feel better — I cannot, it's gone.[80]

We all face this kind of situation whether we ask someone else for help or not. We're hurting because of something we did. We say we're going to change. Then when we feel better, we forget that we wanted to change and do the same dumb thing again. In a healthy life we get better at keeping track of who we want to be little by little. The changes stick.

Living in a place with change reminds us that we can change, too. Healing and growing because of those changes is another reason for souls to come into bodies.

Lessons

As we get more skilled at living in soul reality, one thing that may happen is that we can see a little way into the future. If we know the future, we can change it. This is a big advantage for living in soul reality. If we don't like what we see in the future, we can look for ways to make things different.

One of the important lessons we get from change is that we can make changes. Here's a lesson that can help you learn about changes you can make. The first part should take 20 seconds when you do it now. The second part will take 40 seconds when you do it a month from now. You can take longer if you want to.

One-Minute Exercise

Think about things you want to change. Write down the first one that you can easily change all by yourself in one month. Date it. Put the change in a place where you will see it again either every day or a month from now.

At the end of a month, look at your change. Write down if you made the change. Write down how you succeeded or failed.

You may have made the change. You may have forgotten. You may have decided the change didn't need to happen. You may have been unable to make the change. It's a good idea to figure out why things happened the way they did.

If you want to, write down the same change or another change and continue the exercise for another month. You can also add what you see in the future if you make the change. Then check to see if you were right.

The more you see yourself as able to make changes, the easier it gets to change things.

Thought

All living things have the ability to process what is in their world and decide what actions to take. For simpler creatures, the action might look like a reflex. But it still is what happens instead of many other possible actions.

Some living beings are able to consider a large number of factors when they choose what to do. They may remember the past as a guide. They may even have models or visions of possible futures to help them decide.

At a more complex level, humans and a few other physical beings look at the rest of the environment for tools that will help them. Let's say being able to find tools means there is thought. Other things that I include in thought are coordinating complex actions with others and creating something new. The new thing could be a song or an airplane. It can be simple or complex. The test is whether it is new.

I believe thought is one of the purposes for joining bodies and souls.

Whoever created this world put a lot of work into giving us brains. Our job is to use our brains and the Minds in our soul. It may be for solving problems. It may be for painting pictures. The most important use may be the ongoing creation of physical reality, working on the smaller and smaller structure of matter or the larger connections of the whole universe. As Isaac Asimov said,

The most exciting phrase to hear in science, the one that heralds new discoveries, is not "Eureka (I found it!)" but rather "Hmm, that's funny…."

One huge thing that we have done to expand what our brains can do is to create computers. Brains process some things well. Computers process other problems much faster and more accurately.

We live in a time when thought is not always appreciated. We may be told that feelings are more important. One of the good points about looking at a soul with regions is that we see the need to have balance among all of them.

We can't get so tied up in thought that we lose all realities. We can't lose our Heart to thought and cause harm to others. But in the same way we can't get stuck in just feelings because that stops us from thinking about how to change them. We can't get tied up in thoughts and feelings and lose our wishes. And with all that we experience, we need to use our Will to get things done and our Voice to tell others what is happening.

Thought is special because we created a brain to help the Mind. Then separateness and change and thought can all work together to teach us about possibilities. We can keep what is good, change what is not, and invent even better ways of being. As Galileo Galilei said in the 1600s,

> I do not feel obliged to believe that the same God who has endowed us with sense, reason, and intellect has intended us to forgo their use.

It's still true today.

Lessons

Let's take a look at how separateness, change, and thought can work together to solve a problem. You'll just read through this to make one simple choice at the end.

One-Minute Exercise

Go to a safe place. And don't take this exercise too seriously.

- Imagine you are a special raindrop soul that can form tiny wings to control where you will fall.
- You come into a raindrop life. And here you are falling out of a cloud. You think. "Falling, falling, falling. Ooh, getting close to a rock." Splat. Ouch, that really hurt. I can do better.
- You come into a new raindrop life. And you're falling out of the cloud again. You think. "Falling, falling, falling. Ooh, getting close to a rock. Move right. Dry ground." Splat. Ouch. Better than the rock. Let's try again.
- You come into a new raindrop life. And you're falling out of the cloud again. You think. "Falling, falling. Ooh, rock down there. Dry ground, too. Gotta get to those leaves. Yes!" Falling more. Splash. Well, that wasn't so bad. But what about the lake instead?
- You come into a new raindrop life. And you're falling out of the cloud again. You think. "Falling. Rock, ground, leaves. To the water this time!" Heading toward the lake. Falling, falling. Splash. [HUGE, DEEP LAKE THOUGHT.]

Pick your favorite ending. You might like the lake, but notice that without separateness, change, and thought we never see what is possible. With those three things we can make or do something that was never done before. We can unfold reality to find even more mysterious beauty inside.

Connecting

It may seem strange to say that connecting is one of the purposes of having a body when separateness is also a purpose. We are more connected when we are not in bodies. What we learn from being in a body is that we can choose our connections. Let's look at some of the connections we can make. They include connections within our body, connections with physical reality, including other people, and connections with soul reality.

Ten trillion individual cells work together in our bodies to keep us alive. Let's see what happens when we take the viewpoint that each of these cells is an independent being with its own soul. It may seem like a stretch for the cells that share our DNA, but that's only a third of the cells we are considering. The other two thirds are cells that come from the environment. Some live on our skin and others live in our gut.

Each of those cells, whether we share DNA or not, can be an ally of ours as we move through physical reality. We don't bind them to our Will. They are independent, but connected. We connect because it is good for both us and them.

Some body parts, such as bones and muscles and livers, work as a unit with a united purpose. This is a good thing because it frees us from having to keep track of each cell. Our soul is an ally of the unit. The body part has a soul of its own that coordinates all the cells in it.

We also make connections outside the body with the rest of physical reality. These can be physical connections like wearing clothes. But I think we also need to learn to make connections with the souls of other things in our world.

David Spangler talks a lot about these connections in his Incarnational Spirituality. He senses that everything in our lives can connect with us. Even things like our tables and chairs or our cars. Tables and chairs may seem strange, but I know lots of people who think of their cars as alive.

Other connections we make in our world are with humans and other things we call living, like our pets. We learn the idea of intentional connection from these, too. The most important point is that we have an I-Am. Each of us can learn to say, "I am sovereign in myself."

The other thing we learn in our connections with other people is how to work together. One of the best feelings I know of is reaching a difficult goal while working with others. It might be a sports team winning a championship. It might be getting to the top of a mountain. It could be something in the world of business, like launching a product, or in the arts, like putting on a play. Learning to work as a team with those we choose to work with is a powerful lesson of separateness combined with connection. We may find even more intense connections when we are in a healthy, loving relationship.

Beyond the physical, another purpose for being in bodies is to learn how to reconnect to soul reality. This may be the most important lesson. Moving into a physical body seems to tear us apart from soul reality, at least in Western culture. Finding our way back to our soul is a hard task. When we do that, we have accomplished something important.

Reconnecting with other beings in soul reality might actually be easier. It is important to learn to do that, too. I think this is the real lesson: We can be ourselves in our bodies, contained in our I-Am, and connected with other beings. When we can do that, we might be able to hold our self after we lose our bodies. Instead of being a raindrop falling into an ocean of souls, each of us might learn to be our own self and have a choice who we connect with in soul reality, too. I'd like that.

I think that true peace comes only when our souls know soul reality. Speaking in the early 1900s, the Native American seer Black Elk said it this way:

> The first peace, which is the most important, is that which comes from within the souls of men when they realize their relationship, their oneness, with the universe and all its powers, and when they realize that at the center of the universe dwells Wakan-Tanka, and that this center is really everywhere, it is within each of us. This is the real peace, and the others are but reflections of this. The second peace is that which is made between two individuals, and the third is that which is made between two nations. But above all you should understand that there can never be peace between nations until there is first known that true peace which is within the souls of men.

Lessons

There are other lessons about connection in this book. Here, let's try one where we connect with the objects in our home. This one is a quick version of something I learned from David Spangler. It can make the home a much nicer place to be.

This exercise works best if you are reading this in a comfortable place in your home. If you aren't, the best way to do the exercise in a minute is to imagine you are in your favorite place at home.

One-Minute Exercise

In reality or in your mind, take a look at your favorite place.

- Close your eyes and gather yourself together so you reduce your connections to things outside your I-Am.
- Pick your favorite thing to sit on in your favorite place. We'll call it a chair to keep the discussion simpler. Look at it if you can or imagine it deeply.
- Feel how you and your chair interact. Experience its shape and support. Notice the comfort. Thank it for being there.
- It's hard to think of a chair as having a soul because we usually think something needs to be alive to have a soul. But ask yourself this. If you replaced this chair with exactly the same physical chair owned by someone you totally hate, would you still feel as comfortable? I think you'll find you and the chair connect with something beyond its physical parts.
- Thank the chair again for being what it is and its connection with you.

You can expand this to any or all of the other things in your favorite room, including the floor, walls, and ceiling. Then you can do the same sensing and thanking in the rest of your home.

If some part is messy or dirty, it's a good time to clean it up. If some part feels bad, it may be time to look into some kind of soul healing for the part of your home that makes you feel uncomfortable. Also heal or cut the connections to any people who might have created the bad feeling there. There are many practices that can help with this healing. I would start with a shamanic practitioner. I plan to discuss more of these practices in another book.

What you want from the expanded exercise is a home that feels safe and friendly for you and the ones you love. Then it can be a place where you can do your own healing and growing.

Experiencing and Thanking

Let me start with my ideas about experiencing our personal physical reality and all of the world we are a part of. Then I'll try to explain why we give thanks.

There is majesty in the overall immenseness of a forest, but there is, perhaps, more beauty in the dew glistening on a spider web where a branch reaches out from the trunk of a young tree. Or beauty is in the dogwood flowers on the tiny tree under mammoth Douglas firs.

The ocean is vast. But the sound of this wave breaking in this moment on this shore is where the beauty is. Or it's the fingers of a green sea anemone waving in the moving water of a tide pool. Or a tiny crab hiding under a rock.

The city is, well, a city with people and noise and probably grime and pollution. But there is a corner café that serves the best coffee. A restaurant with the food we want at this moment. Music that lifts our hearts may be playing in the club down the street, or in the park, or in the concert hall. The art museum holds the beautiful and the strange — ancient, merely old, and modern. And in cities we can meet to talk with people who share the most exciting ideas from all around the world.

Then there is the touch of the hand of a friend.

From where we are now in physical reality, we may think that when we die we'll get to a much better place and understand everything. I don't think so. And I'm certainly not counting on it. We might see the big picture, like we see a forest in pictures on Google Earth. But it's not really all that wonderful. I think we see the details — where the real beauty is — only while we are right here on earth.

We experience this life, touching the other beings in it with our senses and our souls. We preserve the good things and work to create more of them. We give thanks for what we have here.

That's my opinion about this purpose of being here. Let's look at ideas from other people, too.

Albert Einstein says:

> The most beautiful thing we can experience is the mysterious. It is the source of all true art and all science. He to whom this emotion is a stranger, who can no longer pause to wonder and stand rapt in awe, is as good as dead: his eyes are closed.

Here's what José Luis Herrera, a teacher of Incan medicine, says about the Q'ero, a native people descended from the Incas:

> I think in the case of the Q'ero, what I love about them is, [they think] why not live life to the fullest? We do not need to save anything. Water the land, feed the land, and walk in *ayni* [right relationship] with the land. It is not that your goal is to save the land or to save yourself. Your goal is to live life to the fullest.

One of the first Western environmentalists, John Muir, says:

> I used to envy the father of our race, dwelling as he did in contact with the new-made fields and plants of Eden; but I do so no more, because I have discovered that I also live in creation's dawn.

I love the way James Stephens describes experiencing the world in *The Crock of Gold.* The nature god Pan is explaining the purpose of humans. For the word "brute" think about a being that does all the things beings with bodies do.

[Pan said,] "Man is a god and a brute. He aspires to the stars but his feet are contented in the grasses of the field, and when he forsakes the brute upon which he stands then there will be no more men and no more women and the immortal gods will blow this world away like smoke."[81]

So from Pan's point of view, we need to find joy in our bodies and in the good physical things in the world — at least if we want our world to stay around.

The other part of this purpose for being in bodies is to be thankful. Sometimes we forget that giving thanks is important. We are part of something more than ourselves. There are others around, both in physical reality and in soul reality, who help make the good parts of our lives possible. We have so many blessings here. We need to remember them to keep getting joy from them. Giving thanks is a way to remember.

In the previous section we thanked our favorite chair. We also need to thank our friends and family. Most traditions say there are great spirits who guide parts of the world. We should thank them, too.

Lessons

Two of the beings I thank every day, and sometimes several times a day, are Pachamama and Inti Tayta. Pachamama is in charge of the earth and all the things on it, such as rocks and water, plants and animals. Inti Tayta is in charge of the sun that provides the energy for Pachamama and the earth.

There always seems to be at least one time in the day when I walk outside and realize that this earth is beautiful — sometimes beautiful beyond words. So I stop and say thank you. I'm sure that whatever you believe in will appreciate being thanked, too.

One-Minute Exercise

Stop right now and think of the most recent good thing that happened to you. Think about who or what helped it happen. Even people who think the world is meaningless can thank chaos.

Say thank you to who you thought of for the good thing that happened. Repeat as necessary for other good things and beings that brought them. It's a good idea to do this at least once a day.

If you can't think of anything good that happened to you, I hope you'll accept my ho'oponopono apology. I'm sorry. I wish my writing was doing you more good. I hope you will forgive me. I love you. The next book in this series will have more on the Huna practice of ho'oponopono.

Understanding and Creating

Experiencing our bodies and being thankful are powerful purposes, but I think we can do more. Two additional purposes are understanding the world we live in and creating something new in it. We can live better when we know more about who we are. We can make the world better by adding beauty and love to it. Both of these acts help the people around us, too.

Understanding requires us to spend time looking at ourselves, other humans, and all the other beings we share the world with. It doesn't have to be done formally the way a scientist would do it. It's enough to look at how we affect other people and to choose ways that increase positive life force. If they are ready to hear it, giving what you learn to others will help them understand how to live better, too.

Understanding is not easy when we are in our bodies in our physical-reality culture. Here's a quote from science and science fiction writer Arthur C. Clarke. I don't know if he thought souls exist, but that doesn't take away from the truth of his quote.

It is really quite amazing by what margins competent but conservative scientists and engineers can miss the mark, when they start with the preconceived idea that what they are investigating is impossible. When this happens, the most well-informed men become blinded by their prejudices and are unable to see what lies directly ahead of them.

In other words, you can't see what you aren't looking for. It can be souls or anything else you want to understand.

Creating might actually be easier than understanding. It certainly is more intuitive and more filled with inspiration. There are so many ways to create something that makes the world a better place. You might grow a flower in your window. You might write a song or a whole symphony. You could write a poem or a book. You could take a picture or make a feature-length movie or a dance or a piece of art or a new way to present delicious food. It doesn't matter what you create as long as your purpose is to increase positive life force and reduce hoocha.

Is everyone called to increase understanding or create something? I think the answer is usually yes. The problem I see is that we lose part of ourselves when we come into a body because being in a body is so difficult. One part we lose is the part that holds our wishes, which is where we hold what we want to learn about and create in this life. Getting that back is an important part of realizing who we really are.

Rionagh na Ard's story illustrates how hard it can be to remember why we came into a body. As you recall, she was a Sidhe who came into a human body and reincarnated in body after body for hundreds of years.

Rionagh's original wish was to help the Sidhe learn more about humans with the goal of bringing humans and Sidhe closer together again. She was supposed to hop into a human body for a short time and come back with a report. It didn't work out that way. You can find her book and read more about her on her website http://www.ravensidhe.com.

She wonders why she was stuck in human form for so many lifetimes. I suggest two ideas. I think both apply to Rionagh.

Wishes are powerful and, done properly, give us what we wish for. Rionagh's wish was to understand humans. She hoped it would happen quickly, but it didn't. She had to return many lifetimes before she fulfilled her wish. She and her companions wished well and now have what they wished for. It just took a long time.

The other is that the culture of our world is so strong that it can cut off our connections to souls outside physical reality. It may even rip our soul apart and take parts of the Wish region away from us. In that case we need rituals to remake the connections. Unfortunately our culture lost those rituals a long time ago. Rionagh, working with her Sidhe companions, had to set up a series of rituals for this lifetime. These worked, so now she can go back.

We can understand and create in both soul reality and physical reality. Creating rituals to bring back lost parts of our souls is one of the best examples. We can still find some rituals in non-Western cultures. Recovering them for our culture is a good purpose for a life here on earth.

Lessons

Let's try a simple creation as a lesson for this section. The important point is that creating something positive doesn't have to take a long time and each positive creation adds something to the world. This exercise can be done in a few seconds. Of course you can repeat it as often as you like.

One-Minute Exercise

Find your Heart. In your Heart find some joy. Sing a note or a few notes to express what you feel.

If you are alone — well you're not really alone because everything around you is alive, too. All those things will hear your joyous creation.

If you are in a public place where singing would be too weird, make your song in your Voice and Mind, but not out loud. Beings that are sensitive to soul reality will still hear you.

Singing your song aloud with other beings, human or not, might be the best.

10. NEXT STEPS

You can blow out a candle,
But you can't blow out a fire.
Once the flames begin to catch,
The wind will blow it higher.

— Peter Gabriel

We've looked at the proofs that we all have souls. We've talked about some of the purposes for coming to earth in human bodies. Those purposes included making our lives better and making the world better, too. Now let's look at things we can do to make our souls healthier, more skilled, and better able to connect with the ones we love.

These are ideas that can make your life happier, healthier, and more fulfilling. Pick the ones that resonate with what you are feeling today. As you change, you will want to come back here to see if other ideas become meaningful.

It's important to be careful about what you choose to work on. It has to make sense to you. You have to see that it is a solution to one of your problems or a way to grow in a direction that feels good to you.

The reason you need to see the possible benefit before you start is that anything you do related to your soul will be at least a little bit of work. It might be very difficult. Seeing that it will make your life better gives you strength to continue.

I've been on this path for a long time. It can be discouraging, so let me offer a bit of advice. Start with the easy ones. What is easy will be different for everybody, but you should be able to tell which ones will be easiest for you. Every positive thing you do to heal and enhance your soul is a step forward. They all count. When you've done a few easy ones, the more difficult ones will seem possible.

The other thing to remember is that this process never ends. There is always a new and exciting discovery waiting for you when you're ready to do the work. Deeper meaning and deeper love. For the sake of yourself and the world, I hope you will decide to try.

You will discover that this work is a lot easier when you are working with other people. From time to time, most people who travel in soul reality ask themselves, "Is this real?" It's especially true for those just starting to have soul-reality encounters. Our larger culture does not support soul reality. So we need to be part of a group that offers support and, yes, soul reality is real. You just read the proof.

This chapter is divided into six stages. They are my stages for increasing information about soul reality. It's great if you think about the process differently. That means you are already on your way. Sort the suggestions so they make sense to you.

The first stage, being safe, creates a foundation for all the rest of the work. If you aren't in a safe place, working on changes in your soul will be much harder. The next stage is to know more about your soul. That's followed by work to heal it.

Then we will look at ways to use your soul, expand its abilities, and teach soul reality to others. I believe that when the number of people who are doing soul work gets to be about one billion, soul reality will be accepted in the world as a whole.

For the good of the planet and the human race we need to get the message to a lot more people. As Bruce Chatwin[82] writes, "In Aboriginal belief, an unsung land is a dead land ... if the songs are forgotten, the land itself will die." The same is true for our souls.

Lessons

Here's how you can sing to the land and keep it alive. Here's how you can remember that you have a soul and that you care about it. Here's how you can create better connections with the other good beings in the worlds. All in one minute.

One-Minute Exercise

Think of something positive in your life. Say thank you to yourself, to the world, and to all the beings who help make that positive thing possible.

That's why this exercise takes a minute instead of five seconds. You thank as many beings, human and nonhuman, as you can. Listen closely and you'll hear them thank you back for appreciating them.

Say thank you every time you notice something that makes you feel good. Make sure you look for something at least once a day.

Staying Safe

In the world, there is both being and doing. We need to *be* safe while we *do* our practice to heal and grow. In this section we'll look at both kinds of safety.

As we will see, there is no way to be completely safe in the physical world. The best guideline is to do the best you can.

Safety in Being

The first rule for working with soul reality is that it needs to be done where we feel safe. Sandra Ingerman, one of the leaders of American shamanism, thinks being secure is an important part of the work she does. Here is how she describes the feeling of safety in being:

Most of us are looking for a strong sense of self. We find that the only feelings of wholeness come from within. We find that outer security is false and that we must feel secure inside ourselves. When we are all here, or home, it's much easier to feel peaceful and secure and in harmony with the greater whole — the universe.[83]

Let's look at some of the things we need to do to find this wholeness. Some involves our connections with physical reality and other humans. We'll start by looking at basic wishes that need to be met.

We can't be afraid about having enough food or drink. We can be fasting, which is a good spiritual practice, but we can't be afraid. Having access to clean water seems to be a requirement for good soul work.

We can't fear the physical place we are in. Native Americans have rituals for becoming a man that include walking into the wilderness in search of a spirit guide. The wilderness isn't safe. Some boys die. But the spirit journey truly begins when we have made peace with out fears.

We can't be afraid of being attacked, physically or emotionally. If we are in an abusive relationship, it's very hard to do effective soul work. If we have no positive connections with others, it's almost impossible. Where can we get the energy we need for the work? It often isn't there.

We can't let that stop us from working with our souls, though. Staying stuck in the same bad place for lifetime after lifetime is not the best option.

So the first task if you are in an abusive place is to find a tiny place that is safe. Do your healing in the best place you can find now, and then find a better place to be. Make positive connections with others when you can. Increase your positive connections and move to the safer place. Use life force from others to help you move. If the abuse has gone on for a long time, you probably don't have enough life force to move on your own.

When you have more safety, your soul can make real progress to heal and grow. You're ready to take the next steps.

If you're not in a safe place now, you can still work on getting better. It's part of our reality that there are no completely safe places in physical reality. Even the safest place can be wiped out by a large meteor, for example. We need to be in a place that is safe enough for us to do our practice.

Another aspect is that when we are stronger, we can do our work in less safe places. There is a Zen saying related to where we do our work: The truly enlightened person is not the one sitting alone on the mountaintop. The truly enlightened is the one who gets down in the mud to help others get out. We learn to keep ourselves safe.

The good news is that as our souls heal, we get better about knowing whether a place is safe. Healing and growing are ongoing processes. When we heal, we find better places and ways to live. Better places let us do more extensive healing and growing. Then the place we live in improves, too. In this case positive feedback is a good thing.

Worrying about safety in physical reality is frustrating for us. It can also be incredibly frustrating for the beings we work with in soul reality. They see us flicker in and out of their reality whenever something in physical reality distracts us. We get pulled back and forth. They can't tell why. The best we can do is to accept that this is part of being in a human body. Apologize to the beings you are working with, and then share a laugh about the difficulty of being human.

We stay as present as we can in soul reality. If we get pulled back by our body, we need to try to return to the same interaction and the same state of being. It takes practice. The same problem happens when our brain (or maybe Mind) brings up memories. We need to wave them on and get back to what we are doing in soul reality.

Bouncing between realities is one of the reasons shamans use drums or rattles when they journey. The sound covers a lot of the distractions in physical reality. It helps, too, that the beat moves the brain into less distractible theta waves.

The long-term goal is to be able to move into and out of soul reality at will, whenever and wherever we wish. It doesn't happen right away.

So use whatever works best for you to be in a physical, mental, and emotional place that lets you do your best soul work. That lets you have safety in being.

Safety in Doing

Safety in doing looks at being safe while we are doing something in soul reality. There is a myth, told by some influential people who do shamanistic practice, that soul reality is safe. It just isn't true. Some parts are safe. You can do things that help you stay safe. But you can also do a lot of things on purpose or by being careless that will hurt you a lot.

Not doing anything because you are afraid isn't the best option either. Well, maybe if you are totally satisfied with your life, it's all right to stay away from soul reality. I think most of us have the feeling that some things are worth a risk. For me, soul work is one of those things. It just pays to be careful.

In this section we'll talk about some of the general rules for staying safe. It won't be complete. There are many things out there that I don't know about, so how can I warn you about them? As you will see later in this chapter, I'll be suggesting several other practices that can help you heal and grow. Each of them has its own set of protections. Learn those protections before you try any of the practices.

There are some guidelines that work for anything you do. They fall into two categories: knowing your allies and knowing yourself. We'll look at those now.

Knowing Your Allies

The most important thing I know for being safe is to ask the question, "Are you here for my highest and best good?" You ask that of every being you might want to work with.

You can say the question a different way if you want to, but what you want to know is whether the being you are interacting with is there to truly help you. The answer should be a quick and unqualified yes. If it's anything else, walk away and look for another being to work with. There are lots of them.

You should also ask humans you are working with the same question. The general belief of people working in soul reality is that beings that don't have bodies tell the truth. Beings that have bodies can lie. I know beings that have bodies can lie. I'm not as sure that all beings without bodies always tell the truth. I also allow for the possibility that the being might be wrong.

So when I ask the question, anything that isn't a clear yes means I should walk away. I leave my truth detectors on for a while with a spirit being. With a human I leave them on longer. It's always all right to ask about anything the being suggests, "Is what you are suggesting now for my highest and best good?"

And remember that the spirit or the person has the right to ask the same question of you. When you work with anyone in soul reality, it's a partnership. Getting help is not something you can get by just requesting it.

You can also ask, "What are the risks?" and make your own decision about whether this is something you want to do. You are sovereign. Don't do anything just because someone tells you to. Ask yourself the question, "Is this for my highest and best good?"

If the answer is no, and it might be, you have a great place to start your soul work. You can ask yourself why you are doing something that isn't all that good for you.

This leads into the next idea for staying safe. Make sure you work with humans you trust. As part of your journeys into soul reality, find a set of reliable spirit guides who will go along with you. Make some plans for what you want to do before your go into soul reality — at least as many as you need to go into a physical place you don't know. Talk over your plans with your guides, human and not. If you're not sure you and your protectors can handle what may happen, find more protection before you go. Don't go into unsafe places unless you have a lot of backup and understand the risks.

Here's a place lots of people start to work with souls — an Ouija board. My friend Sydney on alt.folklore.ghoststories[84] describes why she thinks most Ouija board experiences turn out badly.

> Just imagine you are a spirit. Not good or bad. Just there. And you hear this:
> "Like, am I *ever* going to get a boyfriend?"
> "Oh just shut up, this stuff NEVER works."
> "You are pushing it!"
> "I am not!"
> "OH, MY GOD, IT SAID DIE!!"
> "NOW, like, why won't this stupid thing answer me? Am I going to get that BMW?"
> "Oh, AS IF."
> Now I don't know about you, but bad spirit or not, I would possess the hell out of them just to get them to SHUT UP!

Makes sense to me. I don't like Ouija boards at all. I think they attract all sorts of bad spirits. But if you decide to use one anyway, ask the spirit if it is there for your highest and best good. And be careful even if it says yes.

I am not saying you shouldn't do anything that is risky. That doesn't work either. We need to take on challenges to grow. We just need to make sure they are worthwhile challenges. If we are climbing a mountain — and a lot of soul work is described that way — we rope up for the climb. The goal is to challenge ourselves with the climb. But the rope keeps us from dying if we slip and start to fall. Soul reality is like that, too. Do the hard work for yourself, unless your allies tell you to let them do the work — and have allies there every time to protect you if something goes wrong.

And that's the first part of safety when you are doing soul work. Know who you are working with and be sure you are doing what is best for each other.

Lessons

Many people with a little bit of experience in soul reality have a spirit animal. It's often one of the first things people find. If you have one or any other kind of ally in soul reality, here's an exercise you can try.

One-Minute Exercise

Take a moment right now to visit your spirit animal or other spirit ally. Ask it the crucial question: "Are you here for my highest and best good?"

If the answer is yes, thank your spirit ally and let it know you are there for its highest and best good, too.

If the answer is no, it's time to say goodbye and find another contact in soul reality.

You can also ask any other allies you have in soul reality.

Knowing Yourself

In all the work we do with souls, knowing ourselves is the hardest thing of all. To truly be safe we need to learn who we are and where we come from.

When we do soul work in any of the traditions, we bring ourselves and all of our history to the work. As we reincarnate, we bring echoes of all our past lives into the present. Most traditions say we bring parts that are handed down to us from our bloodlines, too. We carry good and bad things that affect what we do. The good things bring light. It's important to remember that we can't ignore the shadows.

Who we find to work with in soul reality depends on who we are. If you are filled with fear and anger, you will find allies that feed on that and cause you even more fear and anger. They will control you and lead you into darker places. Know yourself so you don't go there. As José Luis Herrera, a teacher of Incan medicine, says[85], "In the West we live in a culture of such fear that our souls are very fragile." We need to learn to make our souls strong and full of positive life force if we want to lead more connected lives and make the world better.

What we need to do is look clearly and carefully at ourselves whenever we are making a decision. We ask, what is fueling my desire? What is behind my wish? Am I doing this because of fear, or pain, or feelings of abandonment? If it is any of these, the work we do will only make things worse.

If we see a wish to help or cure — to reduce fear, pain, and abandonment — to increase love and connection — we can move forward. When we bless the worlds and beings in those worlds with our work, the worlds will bless us in return. As Orion Foxwood, a teacher of conjure and witchery, says,[86] "Powerful witchery makes us seize the reins of responsibility for our lives. We never say, 'The devil made me do it,' because we never give ourselves away to the devil."

Every tradition has ways for you to know yourself better. We all start with a lot of shadow — the parts of ourselves that we can't see clearly. Learning about our soul seems to be part of any positive work that we do. We do our best when we know ourselves well.

It can be challenging to find out about yourself. No one really likes looking at weak points, but it can be done. The best ways I know have a lot of support from teachers who have done the same kind of work for themselves. Whatever path you decide to follow, make sure that those ahead of you know themselves well.

Later in this chapter I'll talk more about specific ways some of the traditions help us know ourselves. But the path to knowing yourself belongs mostly in another book. It's a huge topic. For now it's enough to know you have a soul and there are important things you can do with it. In the beginning, just make sure you pay enough attention to why you want to do something so that you know it's not intended to cause harm to others or yourself. And be sure you are as safe as possible.

Lessons

It can be hard to sort out the reasons for your wishes. Let's do an exercise that looks at the difference between trying to harm someone else and protecting your sovereignty. We'll look at an argument you have had. An argument is a way to bring about a change in a relationship. It's an action that comes out of your wishes. So this exercise will help you see the kind of wishes you have.

One-Minute Exercise

Think of an argument you had with someone. The first one you come up with will be the right one to use. The topic of the argument is not all that important. The wishes behind the argument are, so answer these two questions.

- What was your role in the argument?
- What was the other person's role in the argument?

In the simple case, there are four possibilities to consider. You might have more than one role.

- I was trying to help the other person in the argument or someone else.
- I was trying to harm (or make fun or say bad things about) the other person or someone else.
- I was defending myself when I thought I was right.
- I was defending myself when I knew I was wrong.

Helping someone else or defending yourself when you think you are right are usually positive reasons to act. Looking at why you argue with someone else is one way to know yourself better. The fact that arguments are stressful means that you are looking at yourself below the surface. Knowing who we are when we are under pressure is an important key for doing positive work with souls.

You can ask the same questions about other arguments, if you want to understand more.

Knowing We Have Souls

Once we are sure we are safe, the next step is knowing we have a soul. But that can be a problem because one of the things that happens to most of us when we come into a physical body is that we forget about our soul reality.

I think that is part of the plan. We forget because the wish of everything that comes into physical reality is to learn how to be separate. What we are missing is the second half of the plan — learning to connect again while still in our bodies. Western culture has lost the ways to relearn our connections while we also have our separation. Let's look at some of the reasons we want to have both.

In soul reality everything is much more connected. When we're there, I don't think we can say that a wish belongs to just one soul. Wishes and every other part of what the soul does are shared freely with all the other beings that are there. There may be some limit to the sharing based on connections, but every being is connected to lots of others.

When we are so connected with others, we can't learn about the aspects of our own soul (wishes, feelings, thoughts, etc.). So we decided to run an experiment. We created physical reality where we can be separate from everyone else.

Many people say that only a part of our soul comes to earth to be in our body. I don't agree, but if you believe that, we can still work together. It's a tiny detail in the larger picture of soul reality. It's going to take about a page to explain my point of view. Then you can decide which idea you like best. We're all allowed to change as we learn more. I won't be surprised if I change my view about this point.

I think this body thing is so hard that we can't do it with anything less than every bit of soul we have. Beyond that, leaving a part of the soul behind is the exact opposite of what I think the goal is. If we want to learn to be separate, we can't leave most of ourselves connected.

Still the people who say that most of our soul stays in soul reality are making an observation we need to explain. We don't throw away observations, but we are allowed to question interpretations.

Let me propose this. In soul reality we are closely connected with many, many souls around us. The connections are so close that a single soul really can't be sure which is me and which is you. So we separate. One complete soul becomes one body.

When we start to reestablish our connections to soul reality, we find the group we were part of. Because we were so closely connected to the group in soul reality, it feels like the group is another part of us. But I think the soul group leaves most of itself in soul reality when one soul comes to earth. The single soul is complete in itself and all of it is on earth, alone, separate, and following its individual wishes. Those things that feel like part of us are really just the group we used to belong to.

Does it matter? I think so. Sovereignty is a vital part of the lesson. We aren't sovereign in the way I understand it if part of us is in physical reality and another part is in soul reality. I don't think we learn the lessons of physical reality unless all of us is here, fully responsible and fully at risk for everything that we do. Otherwise, it's just a game that we don't need to take seriously and we really don't learn anything.

The plan for taking on bodies seems to be starting with no connections. The I-Am cuts us apart from others. Then we establish connections as we wish. The connections might be to others in physical reality or to beings in soul reality. We are supposed to learn both. Unfortunately we've lost the ways to do that.

Somewhere along the way, some human cultures made a bad choice. They decided that only their priests or gurus could connect to soul reality. When the priests turned out to be corrupt, those cultures decided that there was no soul reality to connect to. People in those cultures are seeking the connection their souls need. But they have no faith in people who say they can help. It leaves a wound that is very hard to heal.

Our Western culture is one of those cultures. In the West we've thrown out most of our rituals or made them ineffective. Here are some examples. We've kept marriage, sort of, which should be a deep and lasting connection between two people. We've thrown out the idea of a vision quest or dismemberment in a shamanic ritual. The Christian rituals, such as baptism, have a hint of soul. But they have been turned into more of a connection with a particular sect in physical reality and less with the greater soul reality behind religion.

The good news is that the rituals aren't completely lost. By recovering them we can learn about our souls while we experience our separateness in physical bodies. Realizing we have souls that wish to be connected as well as separate is a good place to start. There are many soul practices that will let us continue, if we are willing to do the work.

The first step is to explore the possibilities of having a soul through personal experiences. Those include shamanic journeying, connecting with nature spirits, and conscious dreaming. These can be profoundly convincing, but not always.

We have a problem with believing the people who can teach us how to do these things. We may forget what we have done when everyone around us tells us the experiences aren't real.

It's good that we have reproducible experiences like the Sense of Connection or Rupert Sheldrake's Telephone Telepathy Test to help us hold our belief in something outside of physical reality. But even the best healers, Sandra Ingerman,[87] for example, sometimes have doubts. Here's what she says:

> When we start to use our soul to heal other people, we can remember the successes. Sometimes in the middle of a shamanic healing, my mind will intrude and ask, "Sandy, what are you doing? Have you totally lost your mind?" I quiet my mind by repeating, "This really works." Doing this allows me to enter a deeper state of consciousness where my connection with Spirit is strong. Trust comes through experience. In over eleven years of doing shamanic journeying, I have never been let down by the spirits.

The bottom line is that we can only know we all have souls when we do something often that reminds us. It gets easier to remember, when you work hard every day to heal your soul, use it, and learn more about what souls can do.

And we can't worry too much about what others think. As the comedian philosopher George Carlin says, "Those who dance are considered insane by those who cannot hear the music."

Healing Our Souls

There are many, many reasons why our souls may need healing. We carry problems from previous incarnations. Problems are passed down to us from our family bloodlines. There can be problems related to our physical bodies. Things happen to us in our current lives. All of these, and more, affect the current health of our souls.

It can seem overwhelming. This world is not the easiest place to receive healing, but that's part of the point of being here. If we can learn to be healthy souls here, we can be healthy and strong almost anywhere.

Always remember that the most important person in healing your soul is you. It's your energy, wish, will, heart, voice, thoughtfulness, and inspiration that lead you on your quest. I may never come close to living up to this, but it is my goal: "With each step, with each breath, I choose a path toward deeper understanding, connections, and love."

If that goal sounds like it's too much, you might try saying this at appropriate times, "That's a really stupid idea. I'm not going to do it." Given what this life can be like, even that decision can be hard to carry out. But I suggest you try.

Here are some reasons why. Positive life force counteracts negative life force. (And negative life force counteracts positive.) If we want to heal ourselves and the world, we need to gather and share as much positive information and energy as we can. We need to avoid negative life force whenever possible. When we are in the presence of negative life force, we need to have our protective shields up and our souls full of as much positive life force as we can gather. It's best in the beginning to avoid places that are full of negative life force.

When you look at healing yourself, the first part is staying safe. Keep yourself out of situations where your soul may be hurt. Share positive life force with people who are also looking for it.

Always avoid people who clearly intend to do you harm. Standing up to them needs to wait until you are clearly stronger because it will be a battle.

Some people and places can harm you without really intending to. Learn to avoid or deflect harm from them. As recovering addicts know, being with slippery people is a slippery slope back to drugs. The negatives keep growing until the positives are gone and then there is no way to stay clean. We need to take care of ourselves first. We always leave an opening for people to change, and sometimes we can help them when they ask. But we can't force it on them.

So find people and places that are healthy for you. If you look, you will find more than enough love, excitement, and challenges there.

Of course, this is a huge topic. I plan to put together at least one additional book on healing and using our souls. I'll talk a little about it here, with some suggestions to get you started. The theme of all these ideas is to increase your positive life force and decrease the negative life force in you and around you.

Removing Hoocha

To find healthy places, start by removing hoocha. That's the black gunky stuff that stays around when we act with less than the best intentions. It gets in the way and keeps us from seeing what we can do to get healthier. Here's a quick exercise you might try to get rid of some of it.

Lessons

I've talked about ways to remove hoocha by calling on hoocha stars and hoocha earthworms. These ways include saying to the hoocha eaters, "Please get this hoocha out of my way." They often work, but only for hoocha. They don't help with negative life force, which is much more powerful and dangerous.

Here are two hoocha-removing techniques that use water.

The first technique is more powerful, but it takes longer than one minute and you need to travel to a suitable place. You can try it to remove anything inside your soul that is causing you harm, including negative life force, and replace it with blessings.

Before you decide if you want to do the first technique, sit quietly and find the hoocha or other thing inside your soul that you wish to remove. You need to have a clear image of what you want to remove before you do the exercise.

The second exercise is set up so you can do it right now. Removing hoocha is probably what it does best. I don't recommend it for negative life force.

Twenty-Minute Exercise

Find a clean stream, creek, or other moving water that you can safely walk across. Some people can do this with a stream in soul reality, but a stream working for you highest and best good in physical reality will usually be more helpful. Breathe in and out until you have a sense of the spirit of the stream.

Explain to the stream that you wish to walk across it so the stream can wash away something that is harming you. Ask the stream if it will help you and work for your highest and best good. If the stream says no, you can ask why, but you need to honor the answer.

Stand or sit quietly on the bank of the stream and form a clear image of the thing in your soul that is harming you.

Walk into the stream until you are half way across. You can stand, sit, or lie in the stream with your face pointed downstream so the water washes away what you want to be free from. If you are sitting or lying in the stream, your feet will be downstream from your head.

When you feel like you are through, or the stream has done as much as it can, walk the rest of the way across the stream.

Thank the stream.

Stand or sit quietly on the bank of the stream and form a clear image of the blessings you would like to receive.

Walk back across the stream until you are half way across. You can stand, sit, or lie in the stream facing the opposite way from the first crossing so the water can wash blessings into you.

When you feel like you have enough, or the stream has given you as many blessings as it can, walk the rest of the way back across the stream.

Thank the stream again.

One-Minute Exercise

Take about 30 seconds to notice a bit of hoocha either in your soul or somewhere nearby. It might feel like sticky stuff that is keeping you from doing your best or dust that is stopping you from seeing clearly. If you are confused about a situation, there is probably hoocha involved.

Watch the hoocha and ask the earth if it is willing to absorb it.

If the earth agrees, stand up or sit tall and imagine an incredible downpour of rain roaring through your soul and washing everything from the air around you.

Keep the rain going and even getting harder, if you need to, until the hoocha you are watching is washed down onto the ground and then absorbed into the earth.

Thank the rain and the earth.

Healing in Physical Reality

We need to remember that there are ways of healing that deal with physical reality and ways that deal with soul reality. It's important that we use both. I respect Mary Shutan for her no-nonsense attitude toward shamanic practice. As she points out, there is a difference between psychological help and spiritual help. She says,

> While many people could use spiritual work, and are receiving psychotherapeutic-style work instead, there are also many people who need psychological help, and are not

receiving it. Until someone is mentally healthy enough, and balanced enough, to accept changes in their lives, spiritual work does not have as large of an impact as it could, and can lead to someone spending a lot of money (and time) seeking out shamans when a counselor down the street might have helped them to get to the point where they felt ready for significant, life-changing spiritual work.[88]

Get medical help and psychological help when you need it. Our physical bodies and brains need to be as healthy as possible as part of healing our souls. Our souls need to be as healthy as possible to heal our bodies, too. As we get healthier, there will be a change in the areas we need to work on. So keep working on everything and notice which parts are doing you the most good.

Connecting with Others

There are many ways to connect with others for better health. The basic idea is to connect with good beings in all of the realities. While we can do some healing for ourselves, we can't heal ourselves completely without help. It's like asking a doctor to remove an infected appendix instead of doing it ourselves. Other people often have skills and perspectives we don't have. There are parts of ourselves that we just can't see. This is especially true in the beginning of the healing process, but there are always shadow parts of us that stay hidden.

One of the worst things that can happen to us is that we think we are healthy when we are not. It's easy to go a long way down that path when we are on our own. Even when we are working with others in physical reality, we can go in directions that are not good for us. Mutual delusions happen. The quest for power over others is a powerful addiction. This causes damage to our souls that is very hard to heal.

Having many connections in soul reality gives us more hope that one of them will let us know we're headed the wrong way. Physical beings can lie, but beings in soul reality are usually honest. Ask if what you are choosing is for the highest and best good of the beings who will be affected — including yourself.

I need to point out here that the question of highest and best good can be tricky in complex situations. And everything in physical reality tends to be complex. For example, slugs are invading my garden as I write this. When I ask the question of highest and best good for the system, what do I include? There's me, of course. I want to include the plants and the food I'll get from them. There are all the other animals and insects that are part of the garden ecology. And then there are the slugs.

Getting rid of the slugs is best for my garden and me, but probably not best for the slugs. For those of you who don't know, slugs are migratory. In other words, if I move them away from the garden, there's a good chance they will come back. They also hide really well so there's no way I could find all of them to move them.

What I decided was to put out pellets that are toxic only to slugs and snails. It's true that this is probably not the highest good for the slugs. However, it is the slugs' choice to come into the garden. And it is their choice to eat the pellets. There are plenty of other places on my property where they could live and eat well. There is no danger that protecting the garden in this way will seriously harm the slug population here. To do anything different would not be the highest good for my garden or me.

My spirit advisors agreed. Their thought was that in physical reality the balance of nature is important. Some beings (plants, animals, insects, or whatever) die so that others can live. It's what physical life is all about. And it gives us the responsibility to look carefully at the choices we make. We may never find a perfect choice in physical reality, so we need to find the one that leads to the highest and best good for the world we are in. No one ever said life in physical reality would be easy.

Healing Techniques

There are many possibilities for soul healing. I'll list a few here that have worked for me. I'll be including more in the next book.

Emotional Freedom Techniques

We've already looked at healing in physical reality, but the first of these techniques is related to that. The idea of Emotional Freedom Techniques is that you can reduce or eliminate bad effects you feel from past trauma. It will reduce fear and anxiety related to specific events and can eliminate some addictions.

EFT studies have shown a measurable effect in reducing PTSD.[89] EFT is not usually considered part of the magic tradition. Practitioners usually give physical-reality explanations for why it works, but I think it is related to soul retrieval. It makes more sense in a soul model than in physical reality.

Some people use EFT to bring abundance into their lives. I think this is often a mistake in our complex physical reality. It also may violate the idea of highest and best good for everything. However, if you don't allow yourself to have any good things in your life, then it is useful and appropriate.

Most people will find EFT useful for some problems. Check out Gary Craig's website, http://www.emofree.com/. Start with the Gold Standard to solve an issue that is blocking you from doing what you want to do.

Huna

The Hawaiian practice of Huna is based on their concept of right relationships. It says we have three parts: an unconscious, a conscious, and a higher self. The higher self is like a trustworthy, parental spirit. It is balanced between male and female, connects to the higher realms, knows the future, and does not make mistakes.

The trick is to use our conscious and unconscious parts to connect with the higher self. If we do that, we can remove negatives and old trauma from our lives. There are several Huna techniques that I have found helpful. Using the usual precautions, find a Huna teacher for more information.

One technique lets you change how you connect with others. Some methods are good at breaking away from relationships that are harming you. Others improve relationships that you want to keep.

Another technique helps you make decisions that are for the highest and best good for you and for all. It invokes the higher self and uses the body's reactions as a compass to judge which choice is best.

A third technique is called ho'oponopono. It lets you clear up problems without even talking to the other person. We did a ho'oponopono exercise in the evidence chapter. You might find it useful to do the exercise again now.

Shamanic Practice

There are many aspects of shamanic practice that are appropriate for soul healing. All of them involve working in one of the three shamanic regions: the upper region, the middle region, and the lower region. Remember that in my model the top region of the soul connects with the upper region of the world. The bottom region of the soul connects with the lower region of the world. The rest of the regions are part of the middle region. The I-Am holds the middle regions of the soul and may be able to expand into the upper and lower regions of the world.

Our souls are hurt by many things during our lives. Shamanic healing works whether the wounds occurred in the present life, in past soul lives, or as part of our ancestry. All of these have an effect on us now, but the details are beyond the scope of this book.

What I want to talk about here are four shamanic practices that can help you heal your soul.

The first is regaining your connection with soul reality. This is usually done by learning how to journey into the lower region and upper region. The journeys almost always include finding a spirit guide. The spirit is a connection and a guide in further journeys into soul reality.

When you understand the process, you can continue to journey and work with a spirit guide by yourself. The rest of the techniques, at least in the beginning, should be done for you.

The next step is usually soul retrieval. When we are hurt physically or emotionally, part of our soul can be lost. A shamanic practitioner can journey to retrieve the pieces for you. If the journey succeeds, you will feel more whole.

Somewhere in the first two steps we need to deal with our feelings of separateness. If we don't, we'll fall into one of two patterns. In the first we will go from one teacher to the next like an infant looking for a mother to take care of us. In the other pattern, we reject all teachers because none have helped our separated selves. Neither pattern helps us feel less alone or more loved. We need to accept our longing for nurturing connections. If we do, we can reshape our connections with the world so that we receive the life force we need. We do it as our adult selves, which then take care of the younger soul parts inside us as we integrate them back into our souls.

A further step in healing is curse removal. When we think of curses, we often think of elaborate rituals. Usually it's not like that. It can be as simple as someone who is angry with you saying, "I hope you get what you deserve." If enough life force goes into it, you might have problems. We can also curse ourselves.

You should consider that you may have been cursed if things suddenly change for the worse. Curses may also cause bad luck that affects a whole family for several generations. Old curses can be passed down through families. A good shamanic practitioner can find the origin of the curse and unravel it. One typical reaction to a curse removal is that a weight has been lifted from you.

The final practice I want to consider here is depossession. Possession means that some other being has attached itself to you and is taking some of your life force. Sometimes the being tries to make decisions for you. Most of the time a shamanic practitioner can help the being find a better place to live. Done well, it's not a battle. Everyone ends up feeling better, and you may feel more like yourself again.

You need to find a skilled person to perform all of these practices. The best list of practitioners I know of comes from Sandra Ingerman, one of the pioneers of shamanic work in North America. Her list is at http://www.shamanicteachers.com/.

Energy Healing

I have less experience with energy healing than the other techniques listed above. People I trust use them effectively, but they are not part of my tool kit. As such, I have less information about them than the other methods.

There are many types of practices that can be considered energy healing. The ones I think of first are usually Reiki, acupuncture, and therapeutic touch. Other types of energy healing include work with crystals or stones, radionics, and magnets.

None of these techniques make sense in physical reality. Unfortunately, the people who practice them often try to explain them in physical terms. For all of these techniques, I think finding a healer you trust is more important than the method they use. All involve using life force to heal your soul and body. The healer's ability to give you positive life force is what makes you better.

EFT is sometimes considered a type of energy healing. I also think the deep massage technique known as Rolfing has energy-healing aspects. Both of these have helped me.

Doing the Healing

I know what used to happen when I read about healing techniques. That's all I would do — read about them.

These days it's different. I try the technique. You should, too.

The most important message for this book is that we all have souls. But a close second is that we need to take care of that soul and heal it from the trauma of living in this physical reality. And that means doing the healing we need. Now!

A healthy soul can do much more than one that is damaged, so we need to continue to heal ourselves for our whole lives.

Here's the truth as I see it:

There will never be a magic moment when we are healed. No one will ever step up to take care of us, although, thankfully, there are beings who will help if we ask.

If we don't heal during this lifetime, we carry most, if not all, of our hurts into the next lifetime. Between-lives healing is not all that useful.

When we heal ourselves, we also heal our ancestors. That's pretty cool. If we don't heal ourselves, we pass our damage on to our children. That's not cool at all.

I was told by a karate instructor that he didn't want to consider reincarnation because it meant we would put our hard practices off. It would lead to thinking that there was always time to get better. He had it backwards. Knowing that we have more than one life means we should heal now. If we don't we'll keep on hurting for a very long time.

The best news might be from José Luis Herrera, a teacher of Incan medicine. He says,

> As human beings, our bodies have memory of our healed state, so it is accessing that healed state and … making that memory active. That is what healing is about.[90]

Lessons

This exercise gives you a chance to try something now. It makes sense in both physical and soul reality.

Twenty-Minute Exercise

Expressive Writing is really simple. Think of something that is bothering you. Get out a piece of paper and a pen. You can also use an electronic writing device. Start writing about what is bothering you and don't stop writing for 20 minutes. If you can't think of something to say, just write, "still writing, still writing…."

What happens when you keep writing is that the deep parts of your soul have a chance to express themselves. The Mind and Voice region show up first. The other regions start to say what is going on for them after the Mind and Voice have said all they have to say.

Do this four days in a row and you will be healthier. If the writing doesn't take care of the whole problem, *Expressive Writing: Words That Heal* by James Pennebaker and John Evans has ideas on how to do it better. *Expressive Writing* also describes the proof that the technique works using accuracy of predictions.

Healing Other Souls

If we are really aware of having a soul, the connections the soul gives us can be there all the time. Sometimes we may need to quiet the soul information, like when we are driving on crowded city streets. Other times, though, soul reality warns us of dangers we can't see yet. For example, there was the night this bear came charging down a hill and ran in front of my car. I sensed it before I saw it, so I slowed down just enough to keep from hitting it when I had to slam on the brakes.

Beyond being open to our souls in everyday life, we can try to improve them. We start by healing ourselves, and we always need to keep looking for how we can be healthier. That's what we looked at in the previous section.

When people have a good start on healing themselves, they might learn how to heal others. Some move beyond that to try to heal the worlds. Let's look at some of the ways we can do both kinds of healing.

Background for Healing

There are so many practices from all over the world that I will never be able to name them all. I will put in a few that I know about, just as examples.

The important thing is that the path increases positive life force. Many people say that it should be a path with a heart. I agree and add that you need to make sure the Heart part is positive. And don't forget to use your Mind and Info to do it the best way you possible can. Use your

Will to make it work. Do what fits with the positive aspect of your Wish. And use all that you can find in your Energy region to power the healing.

It may seem difficult to know what to do, but there are three observations that make things easier.

The first is from José Luis Herrera. We saw what he said about people earlier. Here's where he says that applies to everything in the worlds:

> Everything in the universe has a healed state…. Once the [being] recognizes the healed state, aligns itself with it, that is it. The healing is done. [91]

The second is that all humans are sovereign. That means that each of us who are adults have the right to decide what happens to us. No one has the right to harm us or help us or make decisions for us without our permission. And we are not allowed to harm or help or make decisions for anyone else when we don't have their permission. The exceptions I know are parents who have some rights and responsibilities to protect and guide their children and people who make decisions for those who are not able to make decisions for themselves.

Other beings in the worlds seem to have different amounts of sovereignty. Smaller things like raindrops seem to have less sovereignty than large beings like sequoia trees. Do the best you can to respect every being's sovereignty.

The third observation is that you should always ask if this is in the highest and best good of the beings involved. In physical reality the answer may be mixed, but do the best you can. Deciding between garden slugs and lettuce plants might give you a way to think about the problems we have in physical reality.

With that, let's look at a few of the ways we can heal others and the world.

Healing People

There are many ways to heal people. You can choose anything from physically based Western medicine to soul-based shamanic practices.

Applied with good Mind and Heart all of them can help. My experience is that all of them help the most when the person doing the healing knows which type of healing is best for the current problem.

For example, I'll go to a Western doctor for a broken bone. I'll go to someone who knows Eastern medicine to balance the energy flow in my body and soul. I'll go to a shaman to remove a curse. All healers have things they know how to do. The most effective healers know their skills well. They also know when some other kind of healing will help more. Mary Shutan, a shamanic practitioner, is quite clear that shamanic healing works best when psychological issues are taken care of.[92] On the other hand, removing a curse will make counseling more effective.

So, if you are interested in healing people, pick a path that matches who you are. Just remember that you can't learn to be a healer in a weekend. To be a good healer takes years of learning, being healthy yourself, working with a good practitioner, and enough humility to know when you are trying to do something that you can't do.

As you know from reading this book, I like karate. I think teaching any martial art that considers life force is a way to heal people. Students learn to move better and have stronger bodies. They learn about how energy flows. They learn how to make their Will more powerful. And they learn about how to handle powerful connections with others.

There are other mind-body practices that I think can help. EFT and similar work knocks hoocha off connections so that energy can flow. The hoocha needs to be carried out of the system, but EFT doesn't talk about that. The energy flow through the opened pathways helps heal the physical body. Other techniques, such as Reiki, deliver the healing to the damaged area. But they may not improve flow for longer-term healing. Chiropractic, Rolfing, and acupuncture improve life force flow by working with both the soul and the body. They all help us heal.

Then there are the many practices that are soul-based. Some are shamanism, Wicca, sorcery, and conjure and other magic. Some heal. Some harm.

I hope you will choose the ones that increase positive life force. Here's one reason why. Any time you cause harm to other people, you are chained to them, through all lifetimes, until the harm is released. That means, among other things, that in lifetimes where the other beings are more powerful, they *will* find you and harm you. It's just not a good plan.

On the other hand, if you heal some of these past hurts, both of you are healthier. It's good when your best interest and the best interests of others can be met at the same time.

Two practices that are shared by many of the soul-based practices are healing past lives and healing ancestors. When they have been done for me, both practices made my life better. I am also grateful for the chance to help others in this way. The healing can be profound beyond words.

A practice I really hope you will avoid is working with evil beings. They will harm you when you ask for their help. The conjurer Orion Foxwood has seen what working with evil forces has done to people he knows. It's not good.

So work with the spirits that are good. They have more power than you will ever need to do your healing work in this world. If you run into evil spirits, find allies who will help you. And remember that you are sovereign. You have the right to not be harmed. Evil beings in soul reality seem to respect sovereignty when you state it clearly and have plenty of allies to back you up.

There is a lot more to be said about healing other people, but that will have to wait for another book. I'll leave you with one last thought on healing other people: We are not all called to heal other people. But if you are, follow your wishes. Find the path that you love. And work hard to understand how to bring the most positive life force to the people you help.

Lessons

Tonglen is a Tibetan Buddhist breathing meditation practice that helps us compassionately open our hearts to care for and reduce our own and others' suffering.

The exercise opens our heart to the pain of those around us and helps us and others heal. It is especially powerful because it breaks down the walls we put up to keep from feeling another person's pain. These walls also keep us from feeling our own pain.

To do this exercise effectively, we accept the pain before we send out the healing. In simple terms, it removes our selfishness, so we can offer help to others. It also lets us know that our problems aren't really as bad as we thought they were. You can find more details in Pema Chödrön's "Transforming the Heart of Suffering."[93]

Ten-Minute Exercise

To perform this exercise, sit or lie in a comfortable position in a quiet and safe place. Think of someone you know who is hurting. While breathing normally, notice your breath. As you inhale, breathe in the person's hurt with the wish to take it all away. As you exhale, gently send the person happiness and freedom from pain and fear. Continue for at least 10 minutes.

At another time you may want to try this exercise for something you and others are feeling stuck with or miserable about. For example, you might work on poverty or oppression anywhere in the world. It could be as simple as working on how disrespectful and mean people can be to each other. As you inhale, breathe in the pain for all the people, including yourself, who have the feeling. As you exhale, send out relief and whatever else helps you and all the others.

You are likely to find that doing this practice regularly lightens your own load.

Healing the Worlds

There are many ways to heal the worlds. David Spangler has one path with Incarnational Spirituality. Ana Larramendi uses shamanic practices to teach Earthtenders who heal damaged places in the land. There are several online communities that gather for specific efforts to heal problems with humans and our interactions with the world.

I think our world has big problems and I'm not sure we understand how they can be solved. This is not to say that we shouldn't try. We should. But we need to search for effective solutions that reach the heart of the problems.

For example, I don't think it's enough to send wishes of peace to war-torn areas. I think we need to go back into the history of the region and remove the original hurt. Then we need to remove each additional act of revenge, curses, and whatever else has gone into creating the present situation. The poison needs to be removed as it was added, one act at a time. That's not easy when millions of people are involved in creating the problem.

Healing can be done for people who are currently being hurt by the situation. They, in turn, can work to heal their families and their ancestors. If enough people join in the work, we can eventually heal our world.

Where do we start? I believe the first task is healing ourselves. Then I think we need to learn how to heal others. We need to study the ideas of sovereignty and always working for the highest and best good. When we have those skills, we can think about working on places where many people are being hurt all at once.

None of this will be easy. And it's not for everyone who is reading this book. But I ask you to consider healing the worlds and learning to love them again because it really needs to be done. The past hurts affect all of us. This is good because we will benefit if we are successful. It is bad because it is very hard to heal a problem we are part of.

I'm doing the work of writing this series of books to heal the worlds because that's where my heart takes me. If you decide on a similar journey, welcome to this important path.

Lessons

This exercise is a start to learning how to make yourself and the worlds better. It's simple enough that I'm sure you can do it. And it's remarkable that such a simple practice can make so much difference in your life. David Spangler was the one who taught this to me, along with many other ways to interact well with other worlds.

This exercise builds a loving connection between our souls and objects in physical reality. David and I believe that these objects have a soul. After you do the exercise a few times, you can see if you agree.

One-Minute Exercise

Touch of Love Exercise.[94] This is very simple but powerful. You start in a room that you like to be in. Go inwardly and center in your heart center and recall something or someone that you love very deeply and get in touch with that love and then build it up in you until you are ready to burst. Then allow that to flow down into your hands.

Now move around the room allowing the love to flow to various things in the room. Note that you are allowing it to flow, not sending it or forcing it. And be aware of any back flow from what you are engaging with. When you are through, release any residual love as a blessing to the room.

I think you'll find that your room feels more welcoming or comfortable after you send it your love. Check to see if that's true.

Teaching

To make the world healthy, we need to increase the number of people who know about their souls. The only way this will happen is if those of us who have experience with soul reality spread the word.

This book is a start. It introduces a way of looking at souls, evidence that they exist, and some of the things we can do with them to make the worlds better. But that is just the start.

My current intention is to write another book with more ideas about how you can heal your soul. I'll be working with several others on this project. The working title is *User's Guide for Your Sovereign Soul*.

I'm planning more books after that. Many of the practices mentioned in this book need to be discussed in more detail. The **We All Have Souls** series is intended to do just that. Books in the series will look at single topic areas, such as martial arts or Incan medicine healers.

Some books will focus mainly on how that topic helps prove that souls exist and how readers can verify the proofs for themselves. Other books will primarily discuss ways our souls can heal, grow, and make our world a better place. Most of the books will look at life paths that have proof and improvement mixed together. I hope you will join me and all the expert coauthors in learning how taking care of our souls leads to a healthy, enlightened life.

In the meantime, you will be walking your own path. If you and your friends want support for your explorations of soul reality, you can help all of us by signing up for the newsletter on the We All Have Souls website (weallhavesouls.com). Let us know what you are doing and we will put it in the newsletter and on the website. By working together, we can teach the world.

Exploring Soul Reality

If you are an explorer, there are many ways you can discover more about soul realities and bring that knowledge into our world. That's one of the ways we can use the knowledge that we all have souls. There's not much reason to know we have souls if we don't try to learn more about them.

We can't be complacent and think we ever know enough or are strong enough. This is an extension of the need to practice. As we practice we improve. There is so much that has been lost that we need to relearn. There is even more to find out beyond what humans used to know.

Remember that real learning comes from picking one path and following it deeply. The surface understanding you get from an introduction to a path isn't enough to change your soul. It takes practice and study — sometimes a lot of effort — to actually get somewhere. We have this glorious chance to experience life. We should put the effort into living well, helping others, and learning the most we can.

Michael Landon, an actor and philosopher who died too young, put it this way,

> Somebody ought to tell us, right at the start of our lives, that we are dying. Then we might live life to the limit every minute of every day. Do it, I say, whatever you want to do, do it now.

I agree. Also thank the world for giving you this opportunity. I hope what we want to do will make the world better.

We're humans. And one thing humans are good at is figuring things out. Knowing we have souls opens up whole new areas to investigate.

In this section we'll take a look at some of the paths we can follow to explore soul reality, including how to heal ourselves and others better. What you decide to explore is up to you.

First I will take a quick look at the kinds of worlds we might study and then look at magic workers and shamans in more depth. At the end of this section we'll talk about choosing a path.

Many Worlds

For most of this book, I've talked a lot about the three regions of soul reality: upper, middle, and lower. I haven't said as much about the different kinds of worlds. This seems like a good place to do that.

The beings who live in these worlds, including us, have created a lot. If you choose to be an explorer, there are many places to go. Let's look at brief descriptions of a few of the worlds I walk in and a few others that I have heard about. I'll limit the discussion to the middle region of each world because that's where I have explored the most.

The first is the physical reality of our world. I'm not sure I need to say much more about that, since we all share it. I do want to point out that we see echoes of the other worlds here. And things happen here that go beyond the physical forces that are currently accepted. The Sense of Connection and dowsing are two. If you want to study in this world, I also recommend Tom Brown, Jr.'s work on tracking. All of these areas are tied directly to the physical with strong connections to soul reality.

My second world is martial arts. In that world I sense the energy and movement of people. Sometimes I study how to fight them. Other times I look at how they stand and move as I teach them. It's a dynamic world of connections between people with at least part of the connections in physical reality.

The psychological study of humans is part of another kind of world. So much of what we think we know is based on models without souls. It's time to go back and look at the models again to see what happens when soul is added. Some of the ideas were nonsense, but some were not. Psychology as a whole makes more sense when souls are added. If this is what you are interested in, it's worth taking another look.

David Spangler talks about the world of Subtle Realms as part of his Incarnational Spirituality. That world celebrates the life in all that is around us. We have animals and plants and objects in physical reality. In the Subtle Realms each of these has a soul of its own that we can connect with. We've lost the loving connection with these physical beings and places. It's time to get them back. This path is also known as animism. Beyond animism, there are other beings we work together with to change both worlds. Some are powerful beings with the job of coordinating groups. Walking in that world, I feel the connection between all things and the ways humans can expand to reach other types of beings. I believe followers of Shinto live in a similar world.

One more world where we find mostly humans is the world of dreams. Robert Moss's describes his research there. It is closely tied to his study of synchronicity.

For me, the closest world without humans is the world of the Sidhe. The parts I can see are similar to our human world. There are buildings, but they are made of "light." People live and love and work there, just like here. The Sidhe feel like brothers and sisters to me.

There is a related world I call Fairy. This is a bit like the world of the Sidhe and a bit like the Subtle Realms. But it's wilder and less human. I see it as including djinns, elementals, nature spirits, and other beings that work with or against humans, as they wish. Bigfoot and the Loch Ness Monster are also part of this world.

There is a world where it is easy to work with angels, devas, and other powerful spirits. And there is another world where we feel the gentle acceptance of Pachamama or Mother Earth. Mother Earth does not seem as gentle as she once did, so it may be a good idea to work more thoughtfully with her in the future. The World Tree, Yggdrasil, is a symbol for a world with several regions that is related to these two. There are great powers in these worlds who are often willing to be our allies and teachers.

I have walked in the world of stone circles in Scotland, but so far I haven't been to the most famous one, Stonehenge, which is in England. For me, these are places of power where the worlds can be reshaped. They are also places where many types of beings can meet to work with one another. Some are places of teaching.

Other places of power include Uluru in Australia, which I haven't seen. This is in a world that lives in the Dreamtime of the Aboriginal culture of Australia. But they also include the place in Albuquerque I talked about in Chapter 3. Michael Dunning introduced me to a similar world where yew trees are the beings who watch over the place and heal or teach those who ask. In those places we can see the world from the point of view of totally different beings.

Then there is the world of humans when they are not alive. This can be closely tied to the physical world with ghosts and poltergeists. Mediums and others who speak with the dead are part of that world. There are other worlds for humans who have moved away from the physical, where we find what we call the afterlife. Heaven and hell are part of these worlds. Some people say the place we go between lives is like a school where we are taught by wise mentors. We find hints about these worlds in studies of reincarnation, past lives, and near-death experiences.

There may be a world of strange events. This world includes ghost lights and ball lightning and falls of fish from the sky. There are great disagreements about whether such things are possible and how they can be explained by physical reality. We see crop circles and ask if they are outside of physical reality or just made by humans. If you want a long list of these kinds of things, look for books by Charles Fort.[95] I don't think studying these things is the best use of your time. They mostly left me saying that the life force can do some strange things. They really don't help me understand myself or the worlds better.

One important set of worlds where I have spent almost no time belongs to star beings and other ETs with their UFOs and other ways of contacting humans here. There are some beings who are reported as helpers of humans and others who are not kind. They are divided into Grays, Reptiloids, Pleiadians, Cetians, and many other types. This can be a dark world to walk in with many of these beings seen as plotting to dominate humans. Most people who walk in this world see it as a physical place filled with mechanical devices. I suggest the possibility that these beings are closer to the Fairy and the mechanical parts are just how humans translate soul reality into something they can talk about.

Some of the worlds are even less pleasant. There are worlds where negative life force is preferred. Demons who want to harm us live there. My experience is that beings who act in evil ways will choose to work with positive life force when they are reminded that they can. Even so, I stay out of these worlds as much as I can.

The first book I read that talked about many worlds and how they interact with one another was *Daimonic Reality: A Field Guide to the Otherworld* by Patrick Harpur. I think anyone who wants to explore all of the other worlds should read his book. It provides a map, of sorts, that is far better than the list of worlds I describe here. I guess that shouldn't be too much of a surprise since Patrick used a whole book to do what I tried to do here in a couple of pages.

What I love best about Patrick's book is his advice on exploring the other worlds, whether we are visiting in Fairy, on an ET's starship, or in the Oregon home of Bigfoot. He says, with his tongue somewhere in the region of his cheek:

> Travel light. Don't believe everything you have been told, either for good or ill. Don't stay in hotels which replicate your own culture (you may as well have stayed at home). By all means drink the water, but sparingly at first, until you have built up immunity to its foreign properties. Don't expect the inhabitants to speak your language; rather, try and speak theirs (even stumbling attempts will be appreciated). Observe local customs; respect local gods. Talk less than you listen. Try to see as well as sightsee. Be polite but firm; take advice but do not be gullible. If in doubt, smile. Do not laugh at the natives, but don't be afraid to laugh. Avoid the black market — you are always liable to be taken for a ride, especially if you think you know better or best, or if you think you can get something for nothing. Barter but don't haggle. Do not be superior or aloof, but don't try to dress like a native (it's embarrassing). Don't join in the dancing unless you really have learnt the steps. (Remember: you can never become one of them — you can only rejoice in their otherness. Against the odds, there can be fruitful exchange on the basis of mutual strangeness.)

Lessons

This exercise is an extension of the Touch of Love Exercise in the last section. In that exercise we built a loving connection between our souls and objects in physical reality. In this exercise we try to experience the connections as it is felt by the objects. This exercise is harder to do because it requires stepping into another world.

One-Minute Exercise

As before, go inwardly and center in your heart center and recall something or someone that you love very deeply, Get in touch with that love and then build it up in you until you are ready to burst.

Now pick a favorite object and let your love flow into it. Breathing deeply may help the flow, but remember you are not sending or forcing the love.

Feel what comes back to you. Then feel what goes out from this object to other objects in your room. Maybe you can trace your love being shared. Also try to feel the connections between the objects that the objects create on their own. Move with the connections from one object to another and try to be part of the web of connections between everything in the room.

If the exercise goes well, you might even sense places that can be changed for the better. For example, on the floor to my left I have this grumpy pile of tasks that should have been done long ago. The pile is better off there than on my desk where it would distract me even more, but it will be best for all when I find the time to take care of it. Harmony in your room or your whole home is a world you can step into and change.

Magic Workers

The world of magic workers is filled with connections. It reaches into other worlds and brings pieces back into physical reality, sort of. It's a world of blessings and curses, with power from soul tied to physical objects. These are kept on the body or driven deep into the soul. Good and evil may be closely intertwined.

The traditions of magic workers seem to go back to the first humans. But most of the traditions have breaks where a lot of knowledge was lost. The biggest influence in the last 2000 years was Christianity's sweep through the world. The second biggest was Western science. While some of the magic was kept, it often had to be hidden inside Christian rituals or folk tales. Explorers in this world are currently sorting out the pieces.

Some of the traditions include Wicca, witchcraft, conjure, Voodoo, Huna, and ritual magic. They find power in words or symbols, magic ingredients, soil from the graveyard, animal sacrifice, music and dance, rituals, sex, and many other places. Some traditions seem to focus on good works, but others seek to harm and bind. To me, most seem lost between good and bad without a clear intent. It's not a world where souls and long-term consequences are often considered.

The good parts include the idea of cleaning up bloodlines. I talked about this earlier when we looked at healing. Some magic workers have found ways to heal their ancestors. That is an area that is worth studying. Huna practices, such as ho'oponopono, can also be used as part of this cleaning.

I also like meeting the Rider at the Crossroads, sometimes known as the Dark Rider. But here's a hint for how to do that. Bury the coins as the ritual usually goes. But don't ask the rider to do something for you. Instead ask him what would be best for you. He's seen a lot of misery coming from the wrong kinds of requests and will probably be able to offer some good advice. Or ask him simply to do what's best for you. I'd trust him to know that.

Many people find the world of magic fascinating. They try simple spells to get a lover or curse someone they envy. Magic seems like such an easy way to get what you want or get even with someone. So here's my warning. Pay attention to the work on bloodlines and bindings between souls. Look at what happens to you when you do something to someone else. You are tied to that person until the spell is broken, perhaps through lifetimes. Harm you do to others bounces back and harms you, too. Even blessings, if they bind someone else, bind you, too. And be careful — one person's blessing may be someone else's curse.

If you want to work magic, there are two things to do first. Clean your bloodlines so that you are free of any harmful influences from the past. Clean your own soul right down to the root so you are entirely clear that what you do matches exactly with what you wish at the very deepest level. "I want to get even," is only a reaction to anger in the Heart. We need to find a deeper place than that before we act. If we wish to make the world better, we need to ask if what we are doing makes the fire of the creator stronger and the water of creation cleaner.

Shamans

I'm separating the shaman's world from the magic worker's world because I see the shaman's work as healing. The things shamans do can harm others, but that work is usually called sorcery. I put sorcerers in with magic workers. You are free to make your own divisions. But in this section I look at people whose intent is to heal the worlds or the beings in them.

There are many types of shamanism. The term comes from people in Siberia. But it has been applied to native practices in many parts of the world. Related terms, such as medicine workers or curanderos, which is Spanish for healers, show that the emphasis is on healing.

Most of these practices have a long tradition going back hundreds or thousands of years. There have been influences, but not large breaks in how the practice was taught. Sometimes skills are lost, but new ones are also being added.

The only exception I know to the long histories of shamanism is the Western version. There are a few varieties. Most were put together from several different practices found in other parts of the world. If Western shamans continue to do research, Western shamanism will add to our knowledge of the shaman's world.

Most shamans do their work on journeys. They go to a place where an answer can be found or a request can be made. They usually talk about both an upper region and a lower region in addition to our middle regions. The journeys may be made by using drugs. But they may also be made with the sound of a rattle or drum or singing. I usually journey without any of these. I suggest you avoid drugs because I don't think it's good to give your sovereignty to the spirit of the drug.

Shamans work with allies in the other regions. The allies range from plants to gods. Respect is shown to each of them because shamans know they all have souls.

One of the good points of the shaman world is that it is easy to find. There are probably several teachers nearby who can introduce you to the world. They may be glad to show you the basics of journeying. Perhaps they will even show you how to find a spirit guide. It's a place to start. But, if you are an explorer, you can't stop there.

The good news is that there are also many groups that meet to explore more of the shaman's world. This is a good time to explore the shaman's world and it is usually a healthy world to explore. As with everything you do, if you are not sure a particular group is helping you reach your highest and best good, it's time to move on.

I don't think you need to sample a lot of different types of shamanism. The real exploration is to go deeply into one type. Just make sure it's a deep tradition and you have a teacher who is skilled at showing you what is there. Also, be sure that you are safe.

My Vision

As beings living in physical reality, there are many things we can do. If we accept that we have souls along with our physical bodies, there are many more things we can do. My vision is that knowing we have souls will lead us to work on healing our souls and finding our spiritual power.

We can reach into the energy of the earth. We can reach into the information of the upper region, into its crystal clarity of vision and understanding. We can combine both in our Hearts and reach out with love to the ones we care most about and then to all of the life on our earth.

We can feel the energy of the life force bringing everything into being — the seeds waiting to sprout, the drive to reproduce, the competition of each thing holding its place in the universe. The energy is raw and powerful. It can be overwhelming, if we let it. But, it can also be used for healing, growth, and wonderment.

We can feel the music of the spheres, the information about how everything can fit together. We can see heaven's plan, or at least a direction for life to move, to be coordinated one part with another.

As humans, we have souls that can reach, at times, to both extremes. Our Hearts can combine these parts, our Minds can consider the best plans, and our Wills can bring the plans to fruition.

If the Heart is filled with positive energy, we can work with other lives on earth. We can connect with the Hearts of all the other beings. Together we can join in a joyful celebration of what life in our world can be.

We can touch the spirit. We can shout, "I am!" as loud as any being. We can be fully alive — creating good, positive energy for everything.

It may not be the easiest path, but it is a loving and joyful one. Little by little, we can move hoocha to the side, convert it to good energy, and use the wisdom we gain to light the next step on our way. We work with those who have stayed in the spirit because that's part of our path, too. We live between heaven and the depths of the earth, in physical reality and in soul reality.

That's also why I wrote this book — to describe why we need to follow a path. We can move toward the healing light. We can move toward the energy of the earth. We can move toward making ourselves able to live fully in this life we have chosen. I hope we can join together to help each other find our ways.

Choosing a Path

I want to start this section with an important warning. If you think anything you are doing or anything someone else asks you to do is wrong or dangerous, don't do it. Stop. Get help from people you trust. Find another way to reach your goal. You are the one who is responsible for taking care of you.

With that said, we can look at what you might do now. This whole chapter has been about what can be a next step. Let's look at how the ideas apply to you right now. When we get to something you haven't done yet, there's a good chance that it will be your next step.

The first step is to be in a safe place in any world you visit or live in. It will never be perfect, but you need to find a place where you can practice without being badly hurt. If you have that, you can move on.

The next step is to find safe people and other beings to work with. They should respect you, look out for your highest and best good, and challenge you to learn. At least one of the things you do should make your body stronger and healthier. If there is a soul aspect to the physical work, it's even better. I chose karate. You might also choose a martial art or yoga. You might dance. Or you could choose to get out in the woods as a tracker. Pick something where you can celebrate your body.

Moving your body is a way to know yourself. You need to look at why you want to work with your soul. If it's to heal, or learn about yourself, or help others, or improve connections with loved ones, you're in good shape. If it's to gain power over others, there will be problems. When you are looking for power, you can be sure other power seekers will be looking to trap you. You need to be safe from your own harmful wishes before you travel very far on a path. If you have good people as guides, they can help you find your way.

When you are in a safe place with safe people, you can work on knowing about souls. If your physical practice includes soul work, then just do it. To learn something you need to spend an hour or two a day on it. Most of it can be fun, but you need challenges, too. I think it works best when you are with others. This is normal for martial arts. In shamanic work you might be part of a drumming circle or a journeying group. When people share what they are learning, everyone learns faster — and enjoys it more.

In anything valuable there will be times when you will feel like it's too much. You need to find a balance. Working through the hard parts is how we grow. But you also need to like what you are doing enough to keep doing it. So sometimes you may need to try something else, at least for a while. The best advice I have is still to be with people you love. Your friends can help you through the rough times.

One of the rough times I'm sure you will have is healing yourself. You need to do that to move forward. When you are starting to find parts that need to be healed, it's no fun at all. The good news is that most healing feels glorious when it happens.

There are lots of ways to heal. I will remind you that you may need to heal your body and emotions before you heal your soul. Soul healing may help with your body and psychological issues, but Western medicine has a place, too. The best idea is to work with a team of healers who cover all of your needs. Find a team that will listen to your ideas. Expand the team if you need to.

Heal enough so you can do the next steps effectively. But don't try to heal everything before you move on. To have a healthy soul you need to give back as well as receive. And giving back is what practice in the world of soul-reality is all about.

If you have made it to the place where you are safe and know there are souls and you are healed enough to move on, congratulations. Now comes the best part.

As you can probably tell from this book, I love walking between the worlds. I love discovering new ideas and bringing them back to share. I love finding new ways to look at what others have studied before. And I'm learning to love an understanding that deep down we are all the same. It's time to stop trying to find out how we are different. We need to start noticing that we all have souls. We all have the spark of the Creator and live in the community of creation. We are all connected. At the deep levels we are all the same.

So follow your Wish and your Heart. I have enough trust in soul reality to be sure that if you are this far on your path, you already know what your next step will be. You probably know who you want to work with as you go along the path.

If you're not sure, take a look at the We All Have Souls website www.weallhavesouls.com. I expect to have a few good ideas up there for a while. I hope you will send ideas for me to add.

Whether it's healing others or teaching or exploring the worlds or something I haven't thought of yet. I hope you find a path you love to walk.

When they are deciding what to do, the Q'ero shamans ask, "Can you grow corn with it?" They are asking if their path is practical and useful. You can also ask if it is for the highest and best good. If the answer is yes, then the only thing you need to do is find the Will to keep going.

Find friends, love deeply, make your community strong, and you'll be and do just fine.

NOTES

[1] Sheldrake, 1995. pp. 107-108.

[2] Sheldrake, 2005.

[3] Adkins, 2009.

[4] The original description is on the Sheldrake website:
http://www.sheldrake.org/Onlineexp/offline/staring_experiment.html
There are alternative techniques, discussed on the site, that might lead to more reliable results.

[5] Sheldrake, 2005.

[6] In this experiment there is an equal chance of staring or not staring. There are two choices, so if the receiver guesses randomly, he or she will be right half of the time. In a set of 20 guesses, that would be 10 correct.

[7] Sheldrake, 2014.

[8] Sheldrake, 2014.

[9] Flammarion and Brooks, 1921.

[10] Flammarion and Brooks, 1921, pp 148-149.

[11] Flammarion and Brooks, 1921, p. 139.

[12] Flammarion and Brooks, 1921, pp 143-144.

[13] Green, 1960.

[14] McClenon, 1982.

[15] This is a deep subject. You might want to start looking at it here:
https://en.wikibooks.org/wiki/Special_Relativity/Faster_than_light_signals,_causality_and_Special_Relativity. You might also want to simple accept the statement that knowing something before it happened would damage the current state of physics.

[16] Murtha, 1999.

[17] Except where there is another endnote, the information about reincarnation comes from Tucker, 2005.

[18] Stevenson, 1987.

[19] Stevenson, 1997, pp. 43-44.
[20] Tucker, 2005, pp. 101-102.
[21] Newport & Strausberg, 2001.
[22] Peris, 1963.
[23] Head and Cranston, 1967, pp. 38-39.
[24] Harpur, 2003, p. 108.
[25] Teresa of Avila, 1957.
[26] Strieber, 1988.
[27] Spokane Daily Chronicle, 1979, p. 1.
[28] Elizabeth Gilbert, 2009. Her whole talk on nurturing creativity is fascinating. You can watch it at
    http://www.ted.com/index.php/talks/elizabeth_gilbert_on_genius.html
[29] Servants of the Elder Gods, et al., 1992.
[30] Luke 6:31. Bible.
[31] Harpur, Patrick, 2003.
[32] MacManus, 1997, p. 99.
[33] ibid, p. 100.
[34] Spangler, 2014.
[35] van Gelder, 1997, p. 64.
[36] Azathool CatDragon, 1999a.
[37] Azathool CatDragon, 2 Sep 1999b.
[38] Bryon, 2014.
[39] Foxwood, 2012.
[40] Bryon, 2014.
[41] Foxwood, 2012.
[42] Goswami, 1999, Veda, 2011.
[43] Head and Cranston, 1967.
[44] Maslow, 1954.
[45] "Defenses." www.psychpage.com. Retrieved 4 April 2011.
[46] Lennon, 1967.
[47] Fuller, 1981.
[48] Suicide, 2011.
[49] Shumsky, 2003, pp. 160-161.
[50] Home, 1864.
[51] Ekman & Wallace, 1975 and Ekman, 2003.
[52] Ouimet, 2002.
[53] Personal communication.
[54] Lawrence, 2011 from Blackiston et al., 2008.
[55] Ingerman & Wesselman, 2010
[56] See Judge, 1964, for more information.
[57] See for example Jung, 1970.
[58] Bouchard, et al., 1990.
[59] Foxwood, 2015.

[60] Mayer, E. L., 2007, p. 100.

[61] Wagner, 2011, p. 2.

[62] Mayer, E. L., 2007.

[63] See, for example: Radin, 2006, or Radin, 2009.

[64] Funakoshi, 1973, p. 248.

[65] Dubuc, 2011.

[66] From a set of quotes in the Guardian, 2011.

[67] See, for example, Children Who Remember Previous Lives: A Question of Reincarnation by Ian Stevenson, 1987.

[68] Pahl, et al., 2010.

[69] na Ard, 2014.

[70] Goswami, 1999, p. 15.

[71] See Moss, 1996 and Moss, 2012.

[72] Moore, 2005.

[73] Baylor University, 2008.

[74] Morrison & Morrison, 1987.

[75] Weibe, 2004.

[76] Vickers, 2014.

[77] You can look up the rest of the results here. Sheldrake, Rupert, 2014b. The Online Staring Experiment: Results up to December 2014. http://www.sheldrake.org/participate/online-staring-experiment-results

[78] Moss, 1996 and Moss, 2012.

[79] Berg, 2017, n.p.

[80] Bryon, 2014, pp. 264-265.

[81] Stephens, 1956, pp. 44-45.

[82] Chatwin, 1988.

[83] Ingerman, 2006.

[84] *sydney*, 1999.

[85] Bryon, 2014, p. 191.

[86] Foxwood, 2015, p. 97.

[87] Ingerman, 2006.

[88] Shutan, 2016.

[89] Newhouse, 2008.

[90] Bryon, 2014, p. 269.

[91] Bryon, 2014, p. 284.

[92] Shutan, 2015.

[93] Chödrön. 2016.

[94] David Spangler developed this exercise. Spangler, 2015.

[95] His books are collected in a set: Fort, Charles. 1941. The Books of Charles Fort.

REFERENCES

Adkins, Caylor. 2009. *Iron Ball, Wooden Staff, Empty Hand*. Enumclaw, WA: Pine Winds Press.

Azathool CatDragon. 2 Sep 1999a. "Ok, i'll bite... was Soooo". alt.folklore.ghoststories.

Azathool CatDragon. 2 Sep 1999b. "SV: Ok, i'll bite... was Soooo". alt.folklore.ghoststories.

Baylor University. 2008. Baylor Survey Finds New Perspectives On U.S. Religious Landscape. http://www.baylor.edu/mediacommunications/news.php?action=story&story=52815.

Berg, J. 2017. We All Have Souls. private communication, 12 January 17.

Blackiston, D. J., Silva Casey, E., Weiss, M. R. 2008. Retention of Memory through Metamorphosis: Can a Moth Remember What It Learned As a Caterpillar? *PLoS ONE 3*(3): e1736. doi:10.1371/journal.pone.0001736.

Bouchard, T. J. Jr, Lykken, D. T., McGue, M., Segal, N. L., Tellegen A. 1990. Sources of human psychological differences: the Minnesota Study of Twins Reared Apart. *Science 250*(4978): 223–228.

Brown Jr., Tom. 1999. *The Science and Art of Tracking: Nature's Path to Spiritual Discovery*. New York: Berkley.

Bryon, Deborah. 2014. *Lessons of the Inca Shamans, Part 2: Beyond the Veil*. Enumclaw, WA: Pine Winds Press.

Chatwin, B. 1988. *The Songlines,* Penguin, London.

Chödrön, Pema. 2016. Transforming the Heart of Suffering. www.lionsroar.com/transforming-the-heart-of-suffering. Accessed 8 November 2016.

Chomsky, Noam. 1968. *Language and Mind*, New York: Harcourt, Brace & World.

Dubuc, B. 2011. The brain from top to bottom. Canadian Institutes of
    Neuroscience, Mental Health, and Addiction.
    http://thebrain.mcgill.ca/flash/a/a_07/a_07_cr/a_07_cr_tra/a_07_cr_tra.html
    retrieved 8 Aug 2011.

Ekman, Paul & Friesen, Wallace V. 1975. *Unmasking the Face: A Guide to
    Recognizing Emotions From Facial Expressions*. Malor Books.

Ekman, Paul. 2003. *Recognizing Faces and Feelings to Improve Communication
    and Emotional Life*. Times Books: New York.

Flammarion, Camile and E. S. Brooks (trans.). 1921. *Death and its Mystery
    Before Death: Proof of the Existence of Souls*. New York: The Century Co.

Fort, Charles. 1941. *The Books of Charles Fort*. New York: Henry Holt and
    Company.

Foxwood, Orion. 2012. *The Candle and the Crossroads: A Book of Appalachian
    Conjure and Southern Root Work*. San Francisco: Weiser Books.

Foxwood, Orion. 2015. *The Flame in the Cauldron: A Book of Old-Style
    Witchery*. San Francisco: Weiser Books.

Fuller, R. Buckminster. 1981. *Critical Path*. New York, N.Y.: St. Martin's Press

Funakoshi, Gichin. 1973. *Karate-Do Kyohan: The Master Text*. (translated by
    Tsutomu Ohshima). New York: Kodansha International.

Gilbert, Elizabeth 2009. Elizabeth Gilbert on Genius. TED talk.
    shttp://www.ted.com/index.php/talks/elizabeth_gilbert_on_genius.html

Goswami, Shyam Sundar. 1999. Layayoga: The Definitive Guide to the Chakras
    and Kundalini. Rochester, VT: Inner Traditions.

Green, C. 1960. Analysis of spontaneous cases. *Proceedings of the Society of
    Psychical Research, 53*:97-161.

Guardian. 2011. The Body Beautiful: Is it possible to remember being born?
    http://www.guardian.co.uk/notesandqueries/query/0,5753,-2899,00.html.
    retrieved 8 Aug 11.

Harpur, Patrick. 2003. *Daimonic Reality: A Field Guide to the Otherworld*.
    Ravensdale, WA: Pine Winds Press.

Harpur, Patrick. 2003. *The Philosopher's Secret Fire: A History of the
    Imagination*. Chicago: Ivan R. Dee.

Head, J. and Cranston, S. L. (Eds.). 1976. *Reincarnation*. New York: Causeway
    Books.

Home, D. D. 1864. *Incidents in My Life, fifth edition*. New York: A. J. Davis.

Ingerman, S. 2006. *Soul Retrieval: Mending the Fragmented Self. New York:
    HarperCollins.*

Ingerman, S. & Wesselman, H. 2010. *Awakening to the Spirit World: The
    Shamanic Path of Direct Revelation*. Boulder, CO: Sounds True.

Judge, William Q. 1964. The Ocean of Theosophy. Pasadena, CA: Theosophical
    University Press.

Jung, Carl. 1970. *The Structure of the Psyche*, CW 8, par. 325. Princeton, NJ:
    Princeton University Press.

Lawrence, M. 2011. Market Newsletter. February 25, 2011. The particular experiment is in Blackiston, et al. (2008).

Lennon, John. 1997. All You Need Is Love.

MacManus, Dermot. 1997. *The Middle Kingdom: The Faerie World of Ireland.* Colin Smythe Ltd.

Maslow, Abraham. 1954. *Motivation and personality.* New York, NY: Harper.

Mayer, E. L. 2007. *Extraordinary Knowing: Science, Skepticism, and the Inexplicable Powers of the Human Mind.* New York: Bantam Books.

McClenon, J. 1982. A survey of elite scientists. *Journal of Parapsychology,* 46:127-152.

Moore, David W. 2005. Three in Four Americans Believe in Paranormal. http://www.gallup.com/poll/16915/Three-Four-Americans-Believe-Paranormal.aspx.

Morrison, P. & Morrison, P. 1987. *The Ring of Truth: An Inquiry into How We Know What We Know.* New York: Random House.

Moss, Robert. 1996. *Conscious Dreaming: A Spiritual Path for Everyday Life.* New York: Harmony.

Moss, Robert. 2012. *Dreaming the Soul Back Home: Shamanic Dreaming for Healing and Becoming Whole.* New York: New World Library.

Murtha, R. P. 1999. "I Should Have Known Better- a true account of a precognitive lucid dream." *Legends Magazine 89.*

na Ard, Rionagh. 2014. *Awakening: Life Lessons from the Sidhe.* RavenSidhe Press.

Newhouse, Eric. 2008. *Faces of Combat, PTSD & TBI.* Ravensdale, WA: Issues Press.

Newport, Frank & Strausberg, Maura. 2001. Americans' Belief in psychic and paranormal phenomena is up over last decade: Belief in psychic healing and extrasensory perception top the list. Gallup News Service. http://www.gallup.com/poll/releases/pr010608.asp.

Ouimet, Chantal. 31 December-2002. "The gut has a mind of its own." *The Globe and Mail,* p. R7.

Pahl, M., Tautz, J., & Zhang, S. 2010. Honeybee Cognition. In: *Animal Behaviour: Evolution and Mechanisms.* Kappeler P (Ed). New York: Springer Verlag.

Peris, M. 1963. Pythagoras, birth-remember. *University of Ceylon Review, 21:*186-212. Cited in Stevenson, Ian. 1987. *Children who remember previous lives: A question of reincarnation.* Charlottesville, VA: University Press of Virginia.

Radin, D. 2006. *Entangled Minds: Extrasensory Experiences in a Quantum Reality.* New York: Paraview Pocket Books.

Radin, D. 2009. *The Conscious Universe: The Scientific Truth of Psychic Phenomena.* New York: HarperOne.

Servants of the Elder Gods, Rocky Mountain Coven and James C. Taylor. 1992. With These Eight Words the Wiccan Rede Fulfill: "An It Harm None, Do What Ye Will." Internet Book of Shadows, Various Authors. 1999. sacred-texts.com.

Sheldrake, Rupert. 1995. *Seven Experiments That Could Change the World: A Do-It-Yourself Guide to Revolutionary Science.* New York: Riverhead Books.

Sheldrake, Rupert. 2005. The Sense of Being Stared At Part 1: Is it Real or Illusory? *Journal of Consciousness Studies, 12,* 10-31.

Sheldrake, Rupert. 2014. Telepathy in Connection with Telephone Calls, Text Messages and Emails. Journal of International Society of Life Information Science, 32(1), 7-15.

Sheldrake, Rupert. 2014b. The Online Staring Experiment: Results up to December 2014. http://www.sheldrake.org/participate/online-staring-experiment-results.

Shumsky, Susan. 2003. *Exploring Chakras: Awaken Your Untapped Energy.* Franklin Lakes, NJ: Career Press.

Shutan, Mary. 2016. Some Musings on Spirit Release. http://maryshutan.com/some-musings-on-spirit-release/ accessed 15 Jun 16

Spangler, David. 2014. *Conversations with the Sidhe.* Camano Island, WA: Lorian Press.

Spangler, David. 2015. World Work, Part 1. https://lorian.org/94-world-work-part-1/

Spokane Daily Chronicle. December 6, 1979. 5-Foot-3 Woman Lifts Car off Child.

Stephens, James. 1956. *The Crock of Gold.* New York: MacMillan.

Stevenson, Ian. 1987. *Children Who Remember Previous Lives: A Question of Reincarnation.* Charlottesville, VA: University Press of Virginia.

Stevenson, Ian. 1997. *Where Reincarnation and Biology Intersect.* Westport, CT: Praeger.

Strieber, Whitley. 1988. *Communion: A True Story.* New York: Avon.

Suicide. 2011. http://www.medicinenet.com/suicide/article.htm. Accessed 2 April 2011).

sydney <chibimoon@home.com>. 1999. Why I believe most Ouija experiences are bad ones. Accessed 22 Oct 1999.

Teresa of Avila 1957. *The Life of Saint Teresa of Avila by Herself.* trans. J. M. Cohen. London: Penguin.

Tucker, J. B. 2005. *Life before Life: Children's Memories of Previous Lives.* New York: St. Martin's Press.

Tyler, Royall (Trans & Ed.). 1987. *Japanese Tales.* New York: Pantheon.

van Gelder, Dora. 1977. *The Real World of Fairies.* Wheaton, IL: Theosophical Publishing House, Quest Books.

Veda. 2011. The Chakras. http://veda.wikidot.com/the-chakras retrieved 28 June 2011

Vickers, John. 2014. The Problem of Induction. *Stanford Encyclopedia of Philosophy*. http://plato.stanford.edu/entries/induction-problem/#ConNotInd. accessed 14-Jul-16.

Wagner, S. 2011. Twin Telepathy: Best Evidence. http://paranormal.about.com/od/espandtelepathy/a/Twin-Telepathy-Best-Evidence_2.htm. retrieved 12 Sep 2011.

Wang, L. J., Kuzmich A., & Dogariu, A. 2000. "Gain-assisted superluminal light propagation." *Nature 406*:277.

Weibe, Phillip H. 2004. *God and Other Spirits: Intimations of Transcendence in Christian Experience.* New York: Oxford University Press.

INDEX

Voodoo, 84, 85, 305
Wakan-Tanka, 258
Wallace, William, 107
want, 144
Warburton, Acton, 39
Warburton, Canon, 39, 42
water cleansing, 283
We All Have Souls
    book series, 32, 84, 298
    website, 299, 311
Weibe, Phillip, 226
welcome, **1–7**
West Africans, 56
Western culture, 279
Western science, 3, 32, 305
Western world, 2, 14, 172
whale songs, 205
whales, 205
*Where Reincarnation and Biology
    Intersect*, 52
whirlpool
    life force, 63
white ladies, 59
Wicca, 1, 172, 294, 305
Will region, 17, 104–9
    and Energy, 100, 108
    and Heart, 111, 144
    and Mind, 162
    and Voice, 119, 175
    and Wish, 100, 107, 144
    belly, 106, 140
    commands, 107
    control, 103
    cooperation, 105
    decisions, 104
    decisiveness, 90, 101
    domination, 105
    energy, 17
    gut reaction, 107
    guts, 106
    healing, 293
    healthcare, 106
    Incan medicine, 140

intention, 183
karate, 150, 211
lessons, 108
life force processing, 107
limits, 115
martial arts, 173, 294
memory, 206
parents, 106
power, 106
solutions, 168
sovereignty, 29
sports, 175
superhuman strength, 107
superpowers, 107
touch, 194
win friends and influence people,
    175
wish
    changing, 101
    true, 102
Wish region, 17, 98–103, 162
    and Energy, 93, 101, 144
    and Heart, 100
    and Mind, 100, 162
    and Voice, 119
    and Will, 100, 107, 144
    beginnings, 98
    connections, 185
    decisions, 98
    desire, 99, 110
    domination, 105
    energy, 17, 93
    harm, 102
    healing, 293
    hopes, 90
    lessons, 102
    life force, 101
    life force processing, 100
    lost wishes, 265
    overpowering, 175
    plans, 99
    processes, 153
    shadow, 99, 168

About the Author

Tom Blaschko earned a Bachelor's degree in astronomy from the California Institute of Technology, where he learned something about science. He earned a Master's degree in developmental psychology from the State University of New York at Buffalo, where he learned several seemingly contradictory things about the inner workings of people. He has practiced Shotokan Karate since 1970, where he continues to learn about the martial arts aspects of the life force called ki of chi.

He has been interested in paranormal phenomena since grade school and went on his first (unsuccessful) ghost hunt in the 1970s. Scientific influences include research by Rupert Sheldrake on morphic fields, Ian Stevenson's studies of people who remember past lives, analysis of the effects of Emotional Freedom Techniques and other energy healing, and research on ki by Kuo Kanshin and Shigeru Egami's group.

He has also studied with the Incan shaman Adolfo Ttito Condori, American shamans Betsy Bergstrom and Ana Larramendi, Incarnational Spirituality teacher David Spangler, and others who live and work in soul reality as part of their daily lives.

Beyond the research and soul-based practices there are thousands of stories from seemingly credible people who have talked with angels or fairy folk or apus or djinn, seen ghosts, and lived in Dreamtime. Rather than discredit these reports, Tom asked the question: What needs to be added to Western science to make these stories possible? It was a two-item list: souls and the life force. Both of these are accepted in many cultures, so nothing new was needed.